The Christian Religious Tradition

THE RELIGIOUS LIFE OF MAN
Frederick J. Streng, Series Editor

Texts

Understanding Religious Man, 2nd edition
Frederick J. Streng

The House of Islam, 2nd edition
Kenneth Cragg

Japanese Religion: Unity and Diversity, 2nd edition
H. Byron Earhart

Chinese Religion: An Introduction, 2nd edition
Laurence G. Thompson

The Christian Religious Tradition
Stephen Reynolds

The Buddhist Religion, 2nd edition
Richard H. Robinson and William L. Johnson

The Way of Torah: An Introduction to Judaism, 2nd edition
Jacob Neusner

The Hindu Religious Tradition
Thomas J. Hopkins

Anthologies

The Chinese Way in Religion
Laurence G. Thompson

Religion in the Japanese Experience: Sources and Interpretations
H. Byron Earhart

The Buddhist Experience: Sources and Interpretations
Stephan Beyer

The Life of Torah: Readings in the Jewish Religious Experience
Jacob Neusner

The Christian Religious Tradition

Stephen Reynolds
University of Oregon

DICKENSON PUBLISHING COMPANY, INC.
Encino, California and Belmont, California

ISBN-0-8221-0204-8
Library of Congress Catalog Card Number: 76-52746

Printed in the United States of America
Printing (last digit): 9 8 7 6 5 4 3 2 1

Interior art by Merilyn Britt
Cover by Preston Mitchell

Priekš Krišjāna un Annas:
patiesība darīs jūs brīvus.

Contents

Part V: THE MODERN WORLD

Foreword

THE RELIGIOUS LIFE OF MAN series is intended as an introduction to a large, complex field of inquiry—human religious experience. It seeks to present the depth and richness of religious concepts, forms of worship, spiritual practices, and social institutions found in the major religious traditions throughout the world.

As a specialist in the languages and cultures in which a religion is found, each author is able to illuminate the meanings of a religious perspective and practice as other human beings have experienced it. To communicate this meaning to readers who have had no special training in these cultures and religions, the authors have attempted to provide clear, nontechnical descriptions and interpretations of religious life.

Different interpretive approaches have been used, depending upon the nature of the religious data; some religious expressions, for instance, lend themselves more to the developmental, others more to topical studies. But this lack of a single interpretation may itself be instructive, for the experiences and practices regarded as religious in one culture may not be the most important in another.

THE RELIGIOUS LIFE OF MAN is concerned with, on the one hand, the variety of religious expressions found in different traditions and, on the other, the similarities in the structures of religious life. The various forms are interpreted in terms of their cultural context and historical continuity, demonstrating both the diverse expressions and commonalities of religious traditions. Besides the single volumes on different religions, the series offers a core book on the study of religious meaning, which describes different study approaches and examines several modes and structures of religious awareness. In addition, each book presents a list of materials for further reading, including translations of religious texts and detailed examinations of specific topics.

We hope the readers will find these volumes "introductory" in the most significant sense: an introduction to a new perspective for understanding themselves and others.

Frederick J. Streng
Series Editor

Preface

It is now easier to find short introductions to many other religions than to find such works dealing with Christianity, although the bibliography on Christianity is immense. So I think that there is room enough for a book of the sort I have attempted here. The Introduction will explain its scope and particular emphases, so I will use this page mostly to express thanks to the various people who have read and commented on drafts of the book or on chapters from it; to Richard J. Trudgen of Dickenson Publishing Company; to Frederick J. Streng, the editor of THE RELIGIOUS LIFE OF MAN series, and to all those who have given criticism, support, or encouragement during the writing of this book. I would be remiss if I did not mention specifically my own revered teacher, Georges Florovsky; although he bears no responsibility for any of the interpretations ventured here, anyone who has studied under him will doubtless find his influence easy enough to detect.

Stephen Reynolds

Introduction

An introductory book dealing with a particular religious tradition will always encounter a certain difficulty in relating the culture or cultures of that tradition to the culture of the majority of the book's readers. A book on Hinduism, for example, must overcome the "culture gap" that differentiates the assumptions of most Hindus from those of most Western readers. A book on Christianity has equally great problems, but not the same ones. Many, perhaps most, of its readers will come to the book with some image of the Christian religion and with some emotional relation to Christianity as they perceive it, either a commitment to it, or a reaction against it. In either case, the picture of Christianity is likely to be either inaccurate and misleading, or, at best, valid for one of the several more prominent varieties of Christianity in the reader's own society. So the author must try to overcome some of the more common erroneous assumptions and to expand the vision of Christianity beyond the limits of its more familiar manifestations.

Although *The Christian Religious Tradition* is not a formal history of Christianity, it does deal with Christian religious experience in a historical context. In this way, it differs from those books—some of them excellent—that explore the dynamics of Christianity from the perspective of a particular historical manifestation. This book is not intended either to promote or to discourage faith, and it does not presuppose any particular religious orientation in its readers. It is the author's hope that it will assist both Christian and non-Christian readers to gain an understanding of Christianity in its context in history, as a major factor in religious life.

Many contemporary church historians believe that at present it is impossible to find unifying themes for interpreting the entire range of the history of Christianity; the universal patterns set forth by historians in past generations no longer work, and no new ones are yet in sight. The point is perhaps overstated, but it contains a good deal of truth. My own judgments about which factors are most significant is utterly at variance with the commonly received opinions, particularly among academically trained "spokesmen" for Christianity, so that a certain diffidence seems necessary in attempting to steer a course between cowardice and arrogance.

A major focus of the book is on the intimate linkage that connects doctrine, worship, and spirituality. This entails a concentration on developments internal to the Christian tradition, at the expense of other factors. Often enough, important developments have had to be omitted or at most briefly sketched. Interaction with other religions, for example, is not thoroughly treated, although it is both important and interesting. In particular, the emphases of *The Christian Religious Tradition* run somewhat contrary to both the familiar "history of Christian thought" approach and the sociological orientation (sometimes even sociological determinism) of a number of contemporary writers. Methodologically, I agree with P. Berger that a dialectical view of these factors is necessary; this book does not represent a formal history based on such a dialectic, which would require much more extensive discussion.

Another emphasis is on the variety of forms in which the Christian religious tradition has been expressed. Introductory books in the past have been woefully inadequate in their treatment of Eastern Christian traditions; I aim to take a step toward more balanced presentation. This seems all the more necessary since the recent publication of several books on Eastern theological traditions. Surely the time is coming when introductory books will deal with, say, Maximus the Confessor as predictably as they always have dealt with Augustine, Aquinas, or Luther.

An introductory book has failed if the reader does not go on to more detailed writings. The list of suggested readings is as important as any other part of this book. Its contents range from devotional works written by and for Christians to critical rejections of Christianity. The student should expect to encounter variety in the intellectual perspective and emotional tone of the works listed. Since dependence on other writers is so pervasive in a work of this sort that only a few outstanding cases can be acknowledged in footnotes, the recommended readings will serve to some extent in this capacity as well. Only English-language works are included, a regrettable but realistic restriction.

The student may well find that understanding Christianity in the diversity of its expressions, in many parts of the world and over two millennia of history, is more difficult than he or she anticipated; it may contain surprises, both pleasant and unpleasant; it is a study with many rewards, and I hope that this book will help its readers to discover some of them.

I

THE FOUNDATIONS
OF CHRISTIANITY

1

The Setting in Judaism and Roman Hellenism

"Salvation comes from the Jews" (John 4.22). In its first decades, Christianity seemed to be hardly more than one of many Jewish sectarian movements. It cannot be understood without some grasp of its Jewish matrix, the Judaism of the transitional period between the biblical (Old Testament, in Christian terms) period and the period between ca. A.D. 100–500, during which the Talmud (a library of lore that forms the classical expression of post-biblical Judaism) was compiled.

In 586 B.C. the Babylonian Empire had conquered Jerusalem, the Holy City of the Jews, destroyed the Temple, and carried off many Judeans to Babylon. Yet this catastrophe did not mark the end of the people or their religion, as might have been expected. A well-known Jewish historian has written:

> The destruction of Jerusalem in 586 B.C. produced a crisis of faith, because ordinary folk supposed that the god of the conquerors had conquered the God of Israel. Israelite prophets saw matters otherwise. Israel had been punished for her sins, and it was God who had carried out the punishment. God was not conquered but vindicated. The pagans were merely his instruments. God could, moreover, be served anywhere, not only in the holy and promised land of Israel. Israel in Babylonian exile continued the cult of the Lord through worship, psalms, and festivals; the synagogue, a place where God was worshipped without sacrifice, took shape. The Sabbath became Israel's sanctuary, the seventh day of rest and sanctification for God. When, for political reasons, the Persians [who overthrew the Babylonians in 539 B.C.] chose to restore Jewry to Palestine, and many returned (ca. 500 B.C.), the Jews were not surprised, for they had been led by prophecy to expect that with the expiation of sin through suffering and atonement, God would once

1

more show mercy and bring them homeward. The prophets' message was authenticated by historical events.

In the early years of the Second Temple (ca. 450 B.C.), Ezra, the priest-scribe, came from Babylonia to Palestine and brought with him the Torah-book, the collection of ancient scrolls of law, prophecy, and narrative. Jews resolved to make the Torah the basis of national life. The Torah was publicly read on New Year's Day in 444 B.C., and those assembled pledged to keep it. Along with the canonical Scriptures, oral traditions, explanations, instructions on how to keep the law, and exegeses of Scripture were needed to apply the law to changing conditions of everyday life. A period of creative interpretation of the written Torah began, one which has yet to come to conclusion in the history of Judaism. From that time forward the history of Judaism became the history of interpretation of Torah and its message for each successive age.*

The reformers who led the reconstruction in Palestine were pledged to Torah as a comprehensive way of life. They had to emphasize the distinctiveness and uniqueness of the Jews among the nations of the world; exclusivism and a degree of xenophobia appeared. But a countervailing tendency expected the "gentile" (non-Jewish) nations to be joined to Israel at the end of history and recognized among them both true righteousness and cultural elements compatible with Torah. All the reformers—although not all of the Jewish populace—agreed on the necessity of the exclusive worship of the God of Israel and loyalty to Israel's covenant with God; no personification of the natural forces of order and fertility, this God was the sovereign creator of all, the Lord of history, utterly independent of the cult offered him, with no cult image and no cult myth (or at least a very odd one: the story was that of God's dealing with humankind in history, rather than of his dealings with other gods in a sacred time beyond history).

Babylon remained a Jewish center for many centuries; there the Jews encountered the "Chaldean" doctrine that identified the inexorable movement of the heavenly bodies with Fate, which no one can escape or alter; all the reformers, of course, rejected this astral determinism as incompatible with the way of Torah. But they also encountered followers of the Iranian prophet Zarathustra (ca. 600 B.C.), according to whom God is one and transcendent, the good creator of a world in which human beings and spiritual beings are free and responsible; the world, basically good, is divided between spiritual powers of good and evil; human beings choose to follow one or the other, and will ultimately be judged; they experience a good or an evil existence at the end of the world age; the body is in itself good and integral to human nature, and will be resurrected at the end of the age. So like Torah was this that it stimulated within Jewish reforming circles the development of the doctrine of the Last Judgment, of a limited dualism of good and evil in the present world

*Jacob Neusner, *The Way of Torah: An Introduction to Judaism* (Belmont, Calif., and Encino, Calif.: Dickenson Publishing Company, Inc., 1974), p. 5.

age, and perhaps of other beliefs that became more explicit in Judaism at this time, such as the expectation of the resurrection of the dead.

The Rise of Hellenism

The Persian Empire had overthrown the Babylonians and permitted Jews to return to Palestine; it in turn was overthrown by Alexander the Great, who in the years 334–323 B.C. united the eastern Mediterranean basin and Mesopotamia into a huge empire. At his death it broke up into several smaller (but still very large) dynastic states, which continued his policy of disseminating Greek language and culture everywhere, giving rise to an international "Hellenistic" culture that incorporated cultural and religious elements from Asia Minor, Mesopotamia, Syria, and Egypt. In all these areas, schools called "Gymnasia" appeared to train boys and young men in athletics and Greek literary arts; their graduates formed the upper classes of the towns. The library came into being in connection with gymnasia. The theatre, another Greek institution, likewise spread in the Hellenistic states, but declined in character and came to be associated with vulgarity and immorality.

Civic Religion.   Religious cult and culture were inseparable. Throughout the ancient world, all members of a community took part in its civic religion. Local civic cults were easily assimilated into Greek culture ("Hellenized") by identifying the local gods with Greek gods. (For example, the Syrian god Hadad was regarded as a manifestation of the Greek god Zeus.) Participation in these cults might be either a mere formality or an expression of a very real religious (and patriotic) fervor. To them, Hellenism added the cults of the rulers of great kingdoms; Rome inherited this system in the form of the cult of Caesar, which flourished in the East even while it was excluded from Italy.

Private Religion and the Mysteries.   As the appearance of the great Hellenistic kingdoms and an international Hellenistic culture weakened the city-state politically and socially and made for individualism, the civic cults also became for many incapable of providing symbolic forms by which experience could be seen as ultimately meaningful. To meet this need there arose cults, membership of which was voluntary. Small, private religious associations flourished. The most important aspect of this development was the appearance of the "mystery religion," a typically Hellenistic syncretistic institution. The non-Greek "Orient" contributed the cult deity: Mithras from Persia, Isis from Egypt, Attis and Cybele from Phrygia, and so on, civic deities of order and fertility in their homelands who now spread (usually under their original, non-Greek names) throughout the Hellenistic world.

The Greek element (of non-Greek origin, but absorbed into Hellenic culture many centuries before in the Eleusinian and other rites) was the "mystery," the secret rite of initiation, employing symbolic acts and elements and believed to establish communion of some kind with the god, and to produce a better condition for the devotee both in the present life and after death. Myth and symbol dramatized the accessibility of divine purifying and life-enhancing power in a way that many found psychologically satisfying. Rules of ritual and moral purity for the initiate provided at least some moral guidance, which the civic cults had ceased to do effectively.

Processions on the deity's feast days gave the mysteries some public expression. They had not much in the way of doctrine; initiates continued to participate in the civic cult, and could become initiates of as many other mysteries as they pleased, or undergo the same initiation more than once in a lifetime. Neither the particular cults nor the movement as a whole had a theology or a creed. Nor was there any formal relation among mystery temples dedicated to the same deity; initiates who moved to another city might be reinitiated into the mysteries of the same god in their new place of residence.

Hellenistic Philosophies. Well-defined doctrines concerning the nature and meaning of the world and of human life, and the relation of the gods or of God to humanity, were taught not by religious cults but by the several schools of philosophy. In spite of much mutual influence and syncretism, membership in one school excluded membership in any other, and controversies continued among them. In the period 100 B.C. to A.D. 200, the main issue was the question of providence: the strict Aristotelians and Epicureans denied that the gods or God were concerned with people, and the Stoics (who believed in an all-pervading, immanent God), and the Platonists (who at this time believed in a transcendent God) asserted that God did care for humankind. The "providentialists"—Stoics and Platonists—were thus mostly monotheists, who were tolerant of popular cultic polytheism as a presentation of various aspects of divine power to the less reflective masses.

Among these masses, a sort of popular philosophy with many variations was formed by combining ethical, psychological, and metaphysical views from the schools (especially Stoicism) with popular science, folk morality, religious imagery, and so on. Interest in magic and wonderworking was high. Chaldean astrological fatalism was combined by some with the stoic virtue of resignation; others sought to placate the forces that ruled their lives.

Greek-speaking Judaism and the Septuagint. The coming of Hellenism found Jews not only in Palestine but also in the "Diaspora" or "Dispersion." They lived throughout the Mediterranean basin and Mesopotamia, with centers in Babylon and in Egypt, where the Hellenistic capital, Alexandria, came to have a huge Jewish population. In the third century B.C., Egypt and Palestine were ruled by the fairly tolerant Ptolemaic dynasty, a family of Hellenistic monarchs; Mesopotamia (including Babylon) and northern Syria were under domination of the rival Seleucid dynasty, also Hellenistic but less tolerant. Jewish communities in the Dispersion in Mediterranean countries, and some Palestinian Jews, adopted the Greek language for everyday use and for worship. The Torah and eventually almost the entire Hebrew Bible were translated into Greek in Alexandria; this translation, called the Septuagint (abbreviated "LXX"), was widely believed to be of miraculous origin and of equal authority with the original, and became a powerful missionary tool in the Hellenistic world.

Proselytes and God-fearers. Although Judaism was widely unpopular among most Romans, it was not without appeal to some gentile circles: transcendental monotheism and a lofty ethical standard commended themselves to many in the Roman Empire, and these Judaism did offer. A few (the "proselytes") became full converts, probably already, as in following centuries, with a baptismal washing; but conversion involved circumcision, and therefore men especially were more inclined to become "God-fearers," associated with a Jewish congregation but not bound by Torah and not given full membership. They were required to follow what were probably already known as the Commandments of Noah, which Jewish theology regarded as binding on all people and usually reckoned as seven: prohibitions of injustice, blaspheming God's name, idolatry, murder, robbery, and incest; and a dietary regulation understood minimally as forbidding the cutting of meat from a living animal, or more strictly as requiring the thorough draining of blood, as in kosher butchering.

Conflict and Tension in Palestine. Jews in Palestine, eastern Syria, and Mesopotamia continued during the Hellenistic period to speak Aramaic and worship in Hebrew. In any case, the tension between Hellenism and the way of Torah was too deep to allow of solution by linguistic accommodation. "In the ancient world everyone knew at least three things about the Jews: they would not be associated either directly or indirectly with any pagan cult (which seemed antisocial), they refused to eat not only meat that had been offered in sacrifice to the gods but also all pork (which seemed ridiculous), and they circumcised their male infants (which seemed repulsive)" (Henry Chadwick, *The Early Church*, pp. 18 f.). Jews who abandoned Torah for Hellenism or tried to compromise on crucial issues were regarded as traitors by Torah loyalists.

In the second century B.C., Seleucid rule replaced the Ptolemaic dynasty in Palestine and the government began to enforce Hellenization. Angered by Jewish resistance, the Seleucid King Antiochus IV Epiphanes tried to suppress the way of Torah by force, thus provoking the Maccabean Revolt, which drove the Seleucid forces from Jerusalem (165 B.C.) and led to a period of independence for Palestine (142–63 B.C.). This was followed by Roman domination, with either a client king or a Roman official as governor of Palestine. Hellenization continued, taxation was harsh, and offenses to Jewish religion and patriotism were frequent.

Wisdom and Wisdom Literature. During these difficult times, many Jews resorted to the ancient Wisdom tradition of the Near East in its Hebrew form. This consisted, on one level, of practical rules for success and happiness combined with prudential ethics (God rewards the good and punishes the evil in this life). But it also became a forum for discussing the failure of prudential ethics to correspond to experience, and for presenting various religious ideas. In the Hellenistic period, Jewish Wisdom literature was influenced by the Platonic notion of the preexistent and immortal soul. It hypostasized, or personified, Wisdom, apparently drawing on both the Greek philosophical notion of an intermediary between the transcendent God and the world, and the Jewish literary personification of God's powers, strengthened by the post-exilic preference not to speak of God directly. But is Wisdom then a mere literary device, a power of God himself, or a created being then active in the creation of other beings? Not surprisingly, Jews tended to equate Wisdom, created before the world, by and for whom the world was created, with Torah.

The Future Hope and Eschatology.   Wisdom literature is largely about time-less truths. The Hebrew prophets had concentrated, however, on history as the arena of God's activity, made meaningful by his covenant with his people. From this tradition came the conviction that history is moving toward a goal, the Reign of God, in which God's enemies would be overthrown and righteousness, peace, and prosperity would be established. The future hope was not uniform, however. In some circles, it was a hope for the restoration of the kingdom and dynasty of David under a Davidic King, the Son of David, the Messiah. For some, it was hope for a final victory of God, a cataclysmic, dramatic divine intervention and judgment of all people, the end of history, and the establish-ment of a new world age. The national and transcendental forms of future hope influenced one another, and from the time of the Maccabean Revolt the latter especially generated its own literary form, Apocalyptic literature.

Apocalyptic Literature.   "Apocalypse" means the *revelation* of a "mystery" or *secret,* in this case the secret of the end of history, contained in tablets, or a scroll, or a book in heaven and revealed to the hero and purported author of the apocalypse. The hero is usually an Old Testament figure presented as visiting heaven (either bodily or in a vision) and learning the secrets of the beginning and end of the world there. This literature was distinctively Jewish and dependent upon the Old Testament; in its view of the unity of history and the final victory of God, it was a development of prophecy, and in its idea of a final judgment it dealt with the failure of prudential ethics that had agitated the Wisdom tradition. But it also drew on Iranian and Hellenistic and perhaps other mythical and religious ideas for its images; dramatic imagery, often of a bizarre kind, is its main means of expression. Commentaries on and develop-ments of the book of Genesis, and testaments ascribed to Old Testament figures, were also produced by apocalyptic circles. Some apocalyptic books present a heavenly, preexistent, divine redeemer, often referred to in modern literature as "the Son of Man" (although it is doubtful whether the term was used in this sense by apocalyptic writers), who will inaugurate the Age to Come.

The "Four Parties" of Palestinian Judaism

The Jewish historian Josephus (ca. A.D. 37–ca. 100) provides the familiar list of parties in Palestine:

The Pharisees, a vigorous reform movement dedicated to keeping all the commandments of God faithfully; they held that this was possible on the basis of an oral Torah, which interpreted the written Torah and was of equal authority. The name may mean "Persians," a reference to their agreement with the Zoroastrians in "eschatological" doctrines (teachings about the end of the present world age); in any case, they had some affinities with the Apocalyptic movement.

The Sadducees, representing mainly the upper class of Jerusalem, rejected the Pharisaic oral Torah and concentrated on the sacrificial rites prescribed in Scripture. Finding no clear evidence of the resurrection of the dead and other eschatological doctrines in the Hebrew Bible, they rejected them. They were eager to maintain good relations with the Romans and were open to obvious and, to many, offensive Hellenistic influences, but kept Torah as they understood it.

The Essenes, a loyalist, Torah-centered movement, more withdrawn from the rest of society than the Pharisees and having a different interpretation of Torah and a celibate central group. Most scholars identify as Essene the Qumran community known from the Dead Sea Scrolls, who had a strongly eschatological orientation, identifying themselves as the faithful remnant of Israel at the end of the age dominated by the Evil Spirit. Essenes accepted the temple cult in principle, but refused to participate in it as long as Sadducean priests, whom they regarded as corrupt, controlled it. They also looked forward to participating in the eschatological battle in a realistic sense, and some scholars have preferred to identify them as representatives of the fourth group discussed by Josephus.

The Zealots (a party designation probably only after A.D. 70, the term is often used in place of Josephus' vague "Fourth Philosophy"), an active anti-Roman guerilla movement motivated by Torah loyalty and messianic expectation, and naturally regarded by the Romans as bandits.

All these "sects" were loyal to their interpretation of Torah. All but the Sadducees were opposed to foreign rule and to influences contrary to Torah, hoped for a new age, and were influenced by Apocalyptic.

The discussion by Josephus is now recognized as a simplification of a quite complex situation involving many local sectarian movements, which emphasized such features as baptism, asceticism, and special interpretations of Torah. The Samaritans, who rejected the Jerusalem Temple and had a rival center on Mt. Gerezim, were rival claimants to the Mosaic Torah tradition. Although they were widely hated among the Jews, there is evidence of affinities between the Samaritans and the Jewish sects. Among the Hellenistic Jews, the philosopher Philo, probably representing a whole movement, attempted to employ certain forms of Greek philosophy to express biblical religion. An attempt has been made to associate him with an alleged Jewish mystery religion existing apart from Pharisaic and later Rabbinic orthodoxy. Some sects apparently rejected animal sacrifice totally as a spurious later addition to the authentic Torah. In any case, the Judaism of the first centuries B.C. and A.D. included many diverse tendencies that later disappeared; it was a time of religious, cultural, and political ferment.

2
Jesus of Nazareth

Sources for the Life of Jesus

Jesus of Nazareth was born into the stormy world of Judaism in the period of Roman Hellenism. How much can we really know about his life? This question has become the center of a vast and interminable discussion, in which almost every conceivable hypothesis finds its defenders. In what appears an utter chaos of conflicting views, it is well to recall that very little independently valuable information about Jesus has been transmitted outside of the Gospels of the New Testament, and that after all they are closer to the original events than are the primary sources for most figures about whom a great religious tradition has grown up. Modern scholarship has concentrated on the formative role of the oral transmission of small units of traditions about the life and teachings of Jesus (form-criticism or form-history), and more recently on the intentions of the editors who shaped these traditions into books (redaction criticism); it is certainly not credulous about its sources. Yet it appears to permit at least a sketch of the life of Jesus to emerge as probable and defensible even from a quite critical viewpoint, and such a picture is adequate to our present needs.

Jesus and John the Baptist. The public career of Jesus lasted only a few years. It began with his baptism at the hand of John the Baptist, an ascetic apocalyptic prophet best understood against the background of sectarian Judaism. John's message of the imminent end of the Present Age and impending divine judgment reminds one strongly of the doctrines of the Qumran community, located only a few miles from where he was baptizing. He sharply attacked the Pharisees and Sadducees, as a Qumran sectarian might well have done. But instead of withdrawing from "sinners" whose lifestyle was not organized around Torah, as the Qumran sectarians did, he addressed to them an urgent call to "repent" in the specific sense of reording their lives toward the coming Reign of God, the new age that would result from God's final victory. His baptism "for the putting-off of sins" was an eschatological sacrament for those who accepted this message, not a repeated ritual bathing like the "baptisms" of Qumran. Jesus accepted John's baptism—Christian tradition sees in this a sign of Jesus' "taking on the sins of the world," not of course as a "putting off" of sins of his own—and took up the proclamation of the Kingdom of God (the word means the reign, kingship, or ruling power of God, not a territorial kingdom). Jesus did not act as a mere follower of John; he gathered his own disciples, and did not make baptism central to his work.

Jesus' Ministry. The northern province of Palestine, Galilee (which contained Nazareth, where according to all accounts Jesus was raised and where his family lived), was separated from the southern province, Judea (which contained Jerusalem) by Samaria. All three provinces were bounded to the west by the Mediterranean and to the east by the Jordan River. Across the Jordan was another Jewish province, Perea. Jewish travellers between Galilee and Judea either had to go through Samaria, which many held an accursed land and where pilgrims to Jerusalem were often ill treated, or detour through Perea. John baptized in southern Perea just above the Dead Sea. In spite of a symbolic value seen by some scholars in the geography, the tradition that locates Jesus' activity (his "ministry," as it is called) primarily in Galilee seems reliable; this does not exclude activity in the other provinces as well; the Gospel of John recounts activity of both Jesus and John the Baptist in Samaria. But primarily he addressed his message to the Jews of Galilee, where he lived as an itinerant teacher with a group of followers.

In the Gospels, Jesus is addressed as "Rabbi." In the first century, the formally trained interpreter and teacher of Torah was usually known as a Scribe (*Sopher*); "rabbi," literally "my master," was a title of respect used in speaking to a teacher whose authority might be charismatic rather than formal, as may well have been the case with Jesus. Both he and John the Baptist were hailed as prophets. This is striking, since prophecy was commonly held to have ceased with Daniel, (traditionally dated ca. 540 B.C.; the Book of Daniel was actually written ca. 165 B.C.) after whose time the Holy Spirit (the power of God that inspired prophets) had withdrawn, not to return and renew prophecy until the dawn of the Age to Come. Then a prophet, Elijah (Malachi 4.5, Mark 9.12) or the "prophet like Moses" (Deut. 18.15–18), was expected to appear.

The "Kingdom" or Reign of God. The teaching of Jesus centered on the Reign of God as a future hope and as a present reality. Neither aspect, futural or realized eschatology, can be rejected as inauthentic. His message was apocalyptic in its sense of urgency, in the motif of eschatological struggle with the forces of darkness, and in the expectation of a final judgment; but it was unlike much apocalyptic tradition in that he did not depict the future in detail, and formally rejected attempts to calculate when the New Age would arrive, calling instead (like the Hebrew prophets) for a response in the present to the royal power of God.

The Kingdom of God was present—where?—in the deeds and words of Jesus himself. That he performed miracles, most notably exorcisms and healings, is the unanimous testimony of the tradition, and there is now widespread agreement that a central element of the Gospels is expressed in the saying, "If it is by the finger of God that I cast out demons, then the Kingdom of God has come upon you" (Luke 11.20). In the eschatological perspective of Apocalyptic, the Present Age is ruled by the Angel of Darkness, the Evil Spirit, and by his overthrow the Age to Come will be brought in. The Kingdom was already present in Jesus' healings and exorcisms performed "by the finger of God" or "by the spirit of God" (Matt. 12.28). The very expression "finger of God," quoted from Exodus 8.19, contrasts the eschatological work of salvation with mere sorcery.

The forgiveness of sins was part of the eschatological hope, and Jesus proclaimed such forgiveness on his own authority, even to such particularly hated figures as Jews who had become tax collectors for the Romans. The Pharisees and Qumran sectarians strove for maximum purity through Torah observance (as their respective movements interpreted it), but Jesus, without directly opposing Torah, offered forgiveness of sins—a divine prerogative!— even to Samaritans and tax collectors.

Sacred meals were a common ancient institution, especially so in Judaism, and it is not surprising that Jesus brought his followers together for such meals, but here too the eschatological motif dominates, for these meals were anticipations of the Messianic Banquet (an expectation based on a prophecy in the Hebrew Bible: Isa. 25.6–8). The Qumran sect also had an eschatological sacred meal, to which only the pure, in terms of the sect's interpretation of Torah, were invited. But Jesus did not exclude the worst violators of Torah. Not that he condoned their actions; they too had to respond unreservedly to the proclamation of the Kingdom, in its manifestation as the forgiveness of sins. Their response, however, was not bound by the terms of Torah, and might even supersede the requirements of Torah.

The New Torah. Jesus offered no ethical system. He assumed the "great commandments" of Torah, love of God and neighbor, and allowed the particulars of their application to flow from the encounter with the Kingdom. Tax collectors and harlots would enter the Kingdom before the Scribes and the Pharisees not because they were tax collectors and harlots, but because in fact such people accepted the proclamation of the Kingdom and of repentence and forgiveness when the "righteous" rejected it. The Pharisaic oral Torah adapted Torah to current conditions, but here Jesus called for utter commitment in place of adaptation. In practice, he and his followers claimed exemption from Torah in regard to purifications and Sabbath observance, not out of disregard for Torah but out of regard for the extravagant righteousness of the eschatological Torah, whose reference was not to "current conditions" but to the coming Reign of God.

Jesus characteristically taught about the Reign of God by "parables," short, pithy similes illustrating its unpredictable coming, its hidden power, or its incomparable value, in terms of the common stuff of Galilean peasant life. He also employed two-part sayings contrasting the Present Age with the Kingdom, stressing the impossibility of living by both standards at once.

The Disciples and the Twelve. As Jesus travelled about Galilee, he gathered around himself from those who accepted his message a specially chosen group of "disciples" who abandoned all other concerns. These were sent forth as representatives of Jesus, sharing in his power and authority, to proclaim the Kingdom. Among them, a special role of leadership was given to twelve, the

"Twelve Apostles" of Christian tradition. The number is symbolic of the twelve tribes of ancient Israel, implying that the followers of Jesus were the New Israel ("new" in this context means generally "eschatological"). A Council of Twelve also governed the Qumran community, and either in addition to or among them was a special group of three priests, perhaps corresponding to the three Apostles (Peter, and James and John, the sons of Zebedee) who had a special role within the group of Twelve.

Summing Up the Ministry of Jesus

Jesus proclaimed the Kingdom of God as both present and future in various ways: teaching by parables and contrasts, performing wonders as signs of the presence of the Kingdom, proclaiming both the forgiveness of sins and a New Torah, establishing a meal anticipatory of the Messianic Banquet, to which he also invited persons who were (or had made themselves) obnoxious to followers of the Way of Torah, commissioning disciples to share in his prophetic work, and giving to their company a structure symbolic of the New Israel.

Into more detail we cannot go here, except to call attention to the best known of all the transmitted sayings of Jesus, the familiar "Lord's Prayer," as an expression of the eschatological understanding of his work and message:

> Our Father, who art in heaven,
>   hallowed be thy name,
>   thy kingdom come,
>   thy will be done,
>   on earth as it is in heaven;
>   give us this day
>   our daily bread
>   and forgive us our trespasses
>   as we forgive those who trespass against us;
>   and lead us not into temptation,
>   but deliver us from evil.

Still quite poetic in the Greek of the New Testament, it is even more so if retranslated into Aramaic. The Aramaic word for "Father" was almost beyond doubt not a formal style of address but the familiar, affectionate term (approximately "Daddy") used by children, indicating the "boldness" allowed to the eschatological children of the Kingdom. The opening petitions are a revision and intensification of an ancient Jewish prayer with eschatological reference, the Qaddish: "Magnified and sanctified be his great name in the world which he hath created according to his will. May he establish his Kingdom during your life and during your days, and during the life of all the house of Israel, even speedily and at a near time." The phrase translated into Latin and English as "our daily bread" contains in Greek a rare and puzzling word, probably a reference to "eschatological" bread (the Messianic Banquet). The forgiveness of sins is, as we have seen, eschatological in character. The "temptation" is the eschatological attack of the Evil Spirit, who is clearly mentioned in the Greek of the final petition ("the Evil One," not just "evil").

In the charged religious and political atmosphere of Palestine, the activities of Jesus and his followers aroused strong emotions and divided opinions. Jesus did not identify himself with any of the various movements and factions in Judaism, nor did he authorize any one form of Messianic hope as the proper interpretation of his person and actions. Torah-centered reforming and revolutionary movements (Pharisees, Essenes, and Zealots) were likely to be offended by his free attitude toward Torah and his willingness to associate even with tax collectors. Upholders of the status quo (Sadducees and Herodians) feared and disliked him as a radical critic and as a potential focus of rebellion as dangerous as the Torah loyalists. Herod Antipas, the ruler of Galilee, had John the Baptist killed, and wanted no trouble from any similar sectarian rabble-rouser.

The Turning Point. Jesus announced to his disciples that he would go to Jerusalem for the Passover, the feast of Israel's liberation from Egypt. The Gospels connect this event with two others: first, Peter's confession of faith in Jesus as "the Messiah, the Son of God"; and second, the Transfiguration, in which Peter, James, and John saw Jesus transformed in appearance by a heavenly light and talking to Moses and Elijah (representatives of "the Law and the Prophets," that is, the Hebrew Bible, and both connected with eschatological expectations). The Transfiguration is a puzzle to modern scholarship, which has tended to explain it away as a "misplaced post-Resurrection appearance." It is a theophany, a divine manifestation of eschatological significance in concrete form, an anticipation of the Resurrection appearances, perhaps, but its position in the Gospels marks the beginning of the climax of Jesus' career.

The Passover was a time of heightened messianic expectation, and consequently, political tension. When Jesus entered Jerusalem, the crowds of pilgrims hailed him in a demonstration of messianic hope, a hope that was encouraged by his "cleansing the Temple," driving from its courtyard the businessmen who exchanged foreign currency and sold animals for sacrifice. The authorities in Jerusalem became alarmed; Pilate, the Roman governor, was unpopular, and the Galileans who were present for the festival in great numbers were regarded as especially dangerous politically.

The Sadducees obtained an agent, Judas Iscariot, among the Twelve; he identified Jesus for them, and they had him arrested and tried (the nature and status of the trial and of the charges preferred have been discussed extensively and inconclusively). He was then handed over to Pilate, before whom he was charged with political subversion. He was put to death by crucifixion, a particularly painful and shameful method of execution used for "bandits" (including especially revolutionaries), and regarded by Jews as incurring a curse (Deut. 21.22).

The Resurrection. To the followers who had hoped that Jesus would be revealed as the Messiah, his death was a crushing blow. Afraid for their own lives, they scattered, some returning to Galilee, others staying quietly in and around Jerusalem. On the third day after the death and burial of Jesus, however, they were startled by reports that his tomb had been found empty, and that he had appeared alive to some of his disciples. (The "third day" is perhaps symbolic, the time when God acts for his people.) Eyewitness reports of Jesus having been raised from the dead and appearing to his followers originated both in Judea and in Galilee. The earliest preserved account is an established, traditional formula listing five of these appearances (1 Cor. 15.3–7); the empty tomb is specified only in somewhat later accounts, but it must have been taken for granted in the earlier ones, since a resurrection could hardly have been proclaimed had there been a corpse available to disprove it.

The Gospels recount several instances of Jesus' raising persons from the dead and restoring them to life in their previous condition. These are but foreshadowings of Jesus' own Resurrection, which his disciples understood not as the mere revival of a dead man, the resuscitation of a corpse and postponement of death, but as a definitive victory over death, a transition to eschatological existence, a resurrection to eternal life. The risen body, although continuous with the mortal body, is transformed and loses its characteristics of weakness and mortality. The expected resurrection of the dead was the center of a transformation of cosmic scope; that the Messiah should inaugurate it by dying and rising was no part of the Jewish Messianic hope, and all categories of that hope had to be revised to express the new thing that Jesus' followers claimed had been accomplished. The Reign of God in Jesus' proclamation had been both present and future, "already" and "not yet." Jesus' own passage into eschatological being, and the return of the Holy Spirit were now already accomplished; his return to bring about the resurrection of others, his "parousia" or "second coming" was still to be awaited.

The Ascension and the Coming of the Holy Spirit.   After appearing various times to his disciples, Jesus "was taken up into heaven, and sat down at the right hand of God," according to the ending appended to the Gospel of Mark (16.19); and he imparted to his disciples the Holy Spirit, according to several accounts in the New Testament. The chronology of these events is not specific in most of the accounts, and the detailed version of the first two chapters of Acts is the traditional and familiar one: Jesus appeared bodily to the disciples over a period of forty days, and was taken up into heaven at the end of this period; fifty days after the Resurrection, on the feast of Pentecost, the Holy Spirit was imparted, and this is also reckoned traditionally as the beginning of the Church. Pentecost, the Jewish feast falling fifty days after Passover, commemorated the Mosaic Covenant, and, like Passover, carried over from Judaism into Christianity, showing to Christians a pattern of foreshadowing and fulfillment, a "typological" relation between the Old Covenant and the New. The coming of the Holy Spirit was an expected eschatological event (Joel 2.28–32) associated with a New Covenant (Ezek. 11.17–20); 36.24–28; Jer. 31.31–34).

3
The Earliest Christian Communities

The Church in Jerusalem

The Church understood itself as the New Israel, the eschatological people of God. It was continuous with the community gathered around Jesus before his death, and continued to be led by the Twelve (with a replacement elected to fill the place of Judas), but it now saw in the death of Jesus, his rising and ascending to heaven, and the coming of the Spirit, an unexpected fulfillment of the eschatological hopes of Judaism. Jesus' family, who had not accepted his mission previously, now became part of the community, and his brother James became a leader of it. The Church in Jerusalem formed a sort of communal sect within Judaism, inviting fellow Jews to the New Covenant, and continuing to worship in synagogue and in the Temple while also meeting for its own worship and communal activities.

Sacramental Acts in the Primitive Church. The initiation of new members was by baptism, an act rich in the symbolic meanings of cleansing and rebirth, and was accompanied by other sacramental acts that in the Old Testament (and probably in sectarian Jewish practice of the first century) were used to convey spiritual power (*berākhā*, blessing): the laying of hands upon the head of the initiate, and (as seems probable in spite of the effort of interpreters to explain references to it as figurative) anointing with olive oil, an act used in ancient Israel to consecrate kings, priests, and prophets, and associated with the Holy Spirit (Isa. 61.1).

The meals of Jesus' followers were continued by the Church as the main element of its gatherings, with an additional special sacramental partaking of bread and wine. This rite had been instituted by Jesus at the "Last Supper," the celebration of the Passover with his disciples shortly before his arrest. He identified the bread and wine as his body and blood, and spoke of a New Covenant in his blood. The sacred meal was called the "Breaking of Bread" or the "Lord's Supper."

Jesus' disciples had been drawn from a broad cross section of first-century Judaism, with all its diversity, and they brought into the Church a variety of religious perspectives, all of which were inadequate to express their new understanding. The Jerusalem Church of the first generation included two distinct groups, the "Hebraists" and the "Hellenists"—Aramaic- and Greek-speaking Jews, respectively. The Twelve were Hebraists; the Hellenists had a corresponding group of leaders, the Seven, some of whom publicly voiced views that

15

seemed both religiously and politically treasonous to Torah-loyalists. One of them, Stephen, proclaimed that the Temple and its sacrificial cult were no part of the true Torah, but a false interpolation hardly better than idolatry. The origins of this view lie perhaps in an extremist Jewish sect with Samaritan connections. Jesus had given offense by speaking of the destruction of the Temple, which for large numbers of Jews was the main focus of loyalty—this may have been among the charges at his trial. Some of the Hellenists probably thought of him primarily as a prophet who had come to restore the true Torah, without the sacrificial cult. In any case, Stephen was stoned to death for speaking against the Temple, and the rest of the Hellenists were driven from Jerusalem. Under the leadership of Philip they moved into Samaria, where opposition to the Temple in Jerusalem was traditional, and began to baptize Samaritans. The Jerusalem Church, after some puzzlement, accepted this situation. Thus the Church began to move beyond the boundaries of Judaism.

The Galilean Church.   The Church in Galilee, although probably comparable in importance to its Judean counterpart, is not directly known from contemporary sources. It seems likely that its members came largely from Essene-like movements that emphasized baptism, a New Covenant, a priestly community, and asceticism based upon the Jewish institution of the Nazirate and upon the holy war customs of ancient Israel, features that were transmitted to the Church. It may also have contained a Zealot faction, but if so this disappeared after A.D. 70.

Saul of Tarsus.   Saul, a Pharisaic Jew from Tarsus (in Asia Minor, near Syria), educated in Jerusalem, fluent in both Greek and Aramaic, a holder of Roman citizenship under the name Paullus, and a zealous upholder of Torah, was among the most vigorous opponents of the Hellenists of the Church in Jerusalem. The attack upon God's Temple, the claim that a criminal who died under a curse was the Messiah, the pretense that the Holy Spirit had come to a disreputable sect—surely Israel must purge itself of such blasphemy if it hoped for God's merciful protection. He had a hand in the killing of Stephen and the expulsion of the Hellenists, and when the Hellenists appeared in Damascus, troubling the Jews there with their claims and bringing gentiles into their community, he was determined to root out the pernicious movement there. But on the road he had a vision of revelation (*gilluy shekinah,* in the Jewish theological term), in which Jesus appeared to him in the light of the divine glory. Saul's convictions were reversed: Jesus was the Messiah after all, and if so, then Torah had been superseded, the Covenant of Moses must give way to a New Covenant, the Resurrection of the Dead had begun, and the Holy Spirit had returned.

Blinded by his vision, Saul was healed and baptized in Damascus. After several years, he returned to Jerusalem, where Barnabas, a native of Cyprus with a background similar to Saul's and a respected member of the Jerusalem Church, introduced him to Peter and to James the brother of Jesus. Warned of a plot against him led by former associates, he returned to Tarsus and remained for about ten years.

Caligula's Statue. Relations between Jews and gentiles in Alexandria were quite bad during the reign of the emperor Gaius "Caligula" (A.D. 37–41). Following several public crises, riots broke out in which the Jews suffered greatly, and their enemies found a new way to vex them: statues of the emperor were set up in synagogues, and if the Jews removed them, they could be denounced for treason. Caligula was losing his sanity and becoming obsessed with his divine status. When a similar device, the erection of a public altar to Caligula, was employed in a Palestinian city, the Jews destroyed it, and the emperor ordered a statue of himself placed in the Temple in Jerusalem. He was talked out of this scheme at the last minute by King Herod Agrippa, and shortly afterwards assassinated by the Praetorian Guard, but Palestine was on the brink of war. The "abomination of desolation," as the apocalyptic writers referred to a pagan cult image in the Temple such as the one erected by Antiochus Epiphanes, was a sign of the last days. Apocalyptic fervor, centered about the Temple, was at a high pitch. The Jerusalem Church was increasingly regarded with suspicion by the Zealots, although the Hellenists were no longer to be found in the city itself.

The Gentile Church and Jerusalem. After their dispersion, the Hellenists baptized gentiles as well as Samaritans. The Jerusalem Church was unprepared for these developments, but eventually Peter and James bar Zebedee came out in support of a universalist mission to the gentiles. Peter devoted an increasing amount of time to missions, and James the Just, Jesus' brother, assumed more of the leadership in Jerusalem. Uncircumcised gentiles were now being accepted as full members of the Church, against the will of some Torah-loyalist members, and much to the dislike of some nationalistic Jews outside the Church, who induced Herod Agrippa to arrest those of the Twelve most involved with such activities, Peter and James bar Zebedee. James was condemned and killed; Peter escaped; and James the Just assumed leadership of the Jerusalem Church. Agrippa died shortly after. Barnabas moved to Antioch and had Saul—Paul, as we may now call him—come from Tarsus to join him.

The Church of Antioch was the earliest center of gentile Christianity, and the two Jews became its leaders. James was increasingly concerned that the gentile mission was hindering the spread of the Church among the Jews; a universalist in principle, he believed that the mission to Israel must succeed before the full measure of the nations would enter the New Covenant. Paul, in contrast, held that Israel's rejection of the Messiah was an element in the "mystery," the secret plan of God; the nations would turn to the God of Israel in the New Covenant, and only then would Israel as a whole accept it. So James put the interests of the Torah-following Jewish Church first, and Paul was equally strong for the gentile mission. Zealot pressure on the Church grew as

Zealot influence increased in Palestine. When Peter visited the Church in Antioch, James sent a message requesting that he and other Jews not eat with gentile "Christians"—a word that had recently come to be used in Antioch for those who claimed Jesus as Messiah, "Christ" being Greek for "Messiah." Peter and Barnabas complied, Paul refused, and a hot argument ensued. Paul left to go on a missionary journey to Cyprus and Asia Minor.

The "Apostolic Council."   Returning from his journey, Paul and some companions (including Titus, an uncircumcised gentile) went up to Jerusalem for a conference with James, Peter, and John to settle the controversies over the gentile mission. The results were satisfying to Paul: James agreed that full fellowship should be given to gentile Christians, stipulating only that they observe what amounted to the "Commandments of Noah." There was still room for divergent interpretations (is a marriage between first cousins incest? second cousins? is eating meat from animals sacrificed to idols, as much meat in gentile shops was, idolatry? is kosher butchering required?), and James may have had a stricter interpretation than Paul, but Paul was able to affirm that what was required was only what gentile Christians were doing as a matter of course already (Gal. 2.6–10). Those who insisted that gentile Christians observe the whole Mosaic Torah lost decisively, although they did not abandon their conviction and continued to oppose Paul and the gentile mission. Peter took charge of a mission to Jewish territories and Paul headed a similar mission to the nations. Contact with the Jerusalem Church was to be maintained by collections among the mission communities for the poor in Jerusalem. This last measure was designed to meet a practical need arising out of famines in Palestine, but it also had eschatological significance, for there was a prophecy (Isa. 60.5 ff) that in the last days the wealth of the nations would flow into Jerusalem. "Mission" in the ancient Church was the eschatological ingathering of the nations.

After the Jerusalem Council, Paul and Barnabas returned to Antioch. Barnabas later went to Cyprus, and Paul set out for Ephesus, but in a dream had a vision in which he was instructed to cross into Macedonia. He proceeded to travel from city to city along the Aegean coast to Athens, thence to Corinth, where he stayed for some months. He then returned to Jerusalem to fulfill a vow at the Temple. Shortly he travelled again through Asia Minor to Ephesus, where he stayed for several years, and then once more to Corinth and Macedonia. He returned again to Jerusalem with a delegation of gentile Christians from many provinces, bringing the collection for Jerusalem.

In his travels, Paul would go regularly to the synagogue in each new city and proclaim Jesus' death and resurrection. Sometimes he was well received, but more often he was expelled by the rulers of the synagogue, sometimes with a beating, or handed over to the Roman authorities on a charge of sedition. But some among the Jews and the God-fearers would accept the message, and Paul would then turn to the gentiles, who had a witness to God not in Torah but in the natural creation, and offer to them the New Covenant that Israel (the synagogue) had rejected. Often enough, this would offend adherents of the local civic cult and lead to new dangers. But in this way, a network of Christian communities around the Aegean Sea came into being. In addition to the dangers incurred, Paul also had to combat the proponents of rival versions of Christianity. Contact with all these communities was maintained by letter; Paul's surviving letters are the oldest "books" of the New Testament, and among the most difficult, for (with the partial exception of Romans) they are occasional writings dealing with complex local situations, and take for granted knowledge that the later reader does not have. They are characterized by an unmistakable immediacy and vigor.

Paul's Arrest and Death. Paul's enemies, probably both Jewish zealots and Jewish-Christian opponents of the gentile mission, were claiming that he encouraged Jews to abandon Torah. Even though Paul had gone so far as to have his assistant Timothy, the son of a gentile father and a Jewish mother, circumcised—an act which some found inconsistent with his insistence that circumcision was indifferent in the New Covenant—he upheld the table-fellowship of Jew and gentile in the churches, and this was enough basis to allow the charge to circulate. When the time came to take a collection to the Jerusalem church, Paul was warned not to go; but go he did. In Jerusalem James received the offering, but advised Paul to disprove the charge of abandoning Torah by undertaking another vow and fulfilling it in the Temple. To this Paul agreed, but when he entered the Temple his enemies accused him of bringing an uncircumcised gentile in with him, a profanation of the Temple that incurred the death penalty. Roman soldiers saved him from being lynched, and he was removed to safety at Caesarea, where in a hearing he denied the accusation regarding the Temple and insisted that all his activities were based on loyalty to Torah and to the purest Pharisaism, which was fulfilled precisely in Jesus. After some months of detention, Paul exercised his right as a Roman citizen and appealed to Caesar. He was sent to Rome and placed under house arrest. Here the account of the New Testament breaks off; later sources inform us only that Paul was beheaded at Rome under Nero.

No parallel account of Peter's activities and of the mission he headed survives, but postbiblical sources provided the information that he too died (by crucifixion) in Rome under Nero.

At this time there already was a Christian community in Rome, of unknown origin, containing both Jews and gentiles. It has been suggested that members of the anti-Pauline faction among the Jewish Christians were present here too, and were involved in the condemnation of Paul and Peter.

The Fate of the Church of Jerusalem. James the Just and his associates followed Torah scrupulously, but as political tension increased in Palestine, ultranationalist zealots determined to wipe out the Christian sect with its dubious loyalties. In an interregnum between Roman governors, James and some of his associates were stoned to death, to the regret of many non-Christian Jews who admired his uprightness and holiness of life. Those of the Jewish Christians who had never accepted the gentile mission now came to the fore, but no reconciliation with the Zealots was possible, and as war with Rome loomed nearer many of the Jewish Christians of Judea withdrew into Perea, where the Galilean Jewish-Christian Church was probably already established. War broke out shortly thereafter, culminating in the capture of Jerusalem in A.D. 70 by Titus, the future emperor (not to be confused with Paul's gentile assistant of the same name), and the destruction of the Temple.

Judaism Recovers . . . The Zealots were temporarily crushed, as were the sectarians who had joined the revolt (including those of Qumran); the Sadducees vanished with the collapse of their policy and the destruction of the Temple; and the major unifying factors in Judaism seemed to be lost. No longer could the Jewish community afford the diversity that had existed previously. The leaders who now emerged were Pharisaic teachers of the school of Hillel; they began the process of reorganization along the lines of the Pharisaic tradition of oral Torah. Out of this effort grew what has been called "normative" Judaism, the Rabbinic Judaism that in the period A.D. 200–500 codified the oral Torah into the Talmud. The task of holding Judaism together without the Temple was not easy. Jewish Christians and other sectarians began to be more rigorously excluded from the synagogues, and from about A.D. 90 one of the prayers of the synagogue service, to which all present responded with "Amen," was revised to include a curse on "Nazarenes and heretics." At the important council of Jamnia in A.D. 100, according to the traditional account, the rabbis standardized the list of books in the Hebrew bible, omitting many that had been regarded in apocalyptic circles as scriptural, and rejected the Septuagint version, insisting on Hebrew as the language of worship. They approved the anti-Christian prayer, eliminated some elements of the synagogue service to which Jewish Christians had given a Christian interpretation, and rejected Christian methods of scriptural interpretation. These measures gradually came to be accepted by almost all Jewish communities. Jerusalem began to be rebuilt, and early in the reign of the Emperor Hadrian (A.D. 117–138) there was talk of rebuilding the Temple. But eventually Hadrian turned against the Jews and forbad circumcision, a measure that led in the 130s to a new Zealot uprising under Bar-Kosibah (or Bar-Kokhba), whose followers accepted him as the Messiah. Jerusalem fell again to the Romans (A.D. 135), who now forbad Jews to go near it and founded a gentile city with a shrine to Jupiter on the site of the Temple.

. . . and Jewish Christianity Declines.   The Torah-following Jewish Christians were the dominant element in the Church before A.D. 70, and the future of the gentile mission looked dim after Paul's arrest, especially since his enemies gained influence after the death of James. The immediate effect of the events of A.D. 70 was to strengthen this element by the dispersal of Judean refugees, probably to Egypt, Syria, Asia, and elsewhere, where they were quite influential. Those who rejected the gentile mission took the name "Ebionim" ("poor" or "needy") or Ebionites. They looked on Jesus as a prophet who had restored the true Torah by excising the sacrificial cult, and accepting only the Pentateuch, thus revised, as fully authoritative Scripture. The true prophets were Adam, Enoch, and Noah; Abraham, Isaac, and Jacob; Moses; and finally Jesus, who became the Son of Man and would return to raise the dead. Their idea of prophecy has Samaritan features; from sectarian Judaism they inherited vegetarianism, renunciation of possessions, and an emphasis on ritual purity and ablutions. Qumran refugees may have entered the Church after A.D. 70, and if so they would have felt at home among the Ebionites. Relatives of Jesus were prominent among the Jewish Christians in Palestine and Syria. The movement was strong in Egypt; Peter and James were claimed as the true Apostles, and represented as holding Ebionite views. But the exclusivism of the sect, and the loss of Jerusalem as the center of Jewish Christianity, led to its decline. After A.D. 135, Pauline gentile Christianity was clearly predominant, and by the Middle Ages the Ebionites had vanished, along with other Torah-observing Christians.

4

Early Christian Worship and Doctrine

The Kerygma

What was the doctrinal content of primitive Christianity? To what—better, to whom—were those who accepted baptism committing themselves? Traditional Jewish categories had to be redefined: they conveyed little to gentiles, who took "Christ" as a proper name because they had no idea of a Messiah. The formula "Jesus is Lord" or "Christ is Lord," important as it was, presupposed a fuller understanding than it conveyed and remains cryptic without it. Several sorts of traditional formulations, surviving from the first generation of Christians, are communal in character, and may fairly be taken as representative statements. One of these is a summary form of preaching called "gospel" (*evangelion,* "good news") or *kerygma* ("proclamation"). "Gospel" soon came to mean a book, and "kerygma" is now used for the short formula. It occurs in several forms in the letters of Paul and in the Acts of the Apostles, and includes the following assertions:

1. The prophecies of the Hebrew Bible are fulfilled; the Messiah has come;
2. He was born of the seed of David;
3. He died, in accordance with the Scriptures;
4. He was buried;
5. God raised him from the dead;
6. He was raised to the right hand of God;
7. He will return as Judge and Savior of men.

References to the works of Jesus, to witnesses of his resurrection appearances, and to the sending of the Holy Spirit might also be included.

Worship and Doctrine.   In both Judaism and Christianity, worship is the act of ultimate self-determination. Doctrine arises out of it, rather than preceding it. The horror of idolatry characteristic of Judaism, Christianity, and Islam must be understood in this context; the misapprehension (shared by some members) that these traditions deny the religious value of the natural world is an erroneous inference from the same fact. Texts associated with worship are characteristically communal and traditional in nature. Ancient liturgical texts, at least, are often doctrinally rich. Can such texts be found among primitive Christian literary remains? They can, and they fill out the picture provided by the kerygma-form of the doctrine of the ancient Church.

Christological Hymns in the New Testament.   Recent scholarship has located a number of passages in the New Testament that can be identified more or less confidently as hymns or hymn fragments. They are usually quoted only in part or with interpolations or both, so that the exact form of the original is not quite certain. However, on the whole these studies offer convincing analyses and useful tentative reconstructions. One group of hymns refers specifically to Christ and his work, and a conspectus yields a remarkably coherent pattern:

1. The redeemer possesses unity or equality with God;
2. He is the mediator or agent of creation;
3. He is himself a part of or the sustainer of creation;
4. He descends from the heavenly to the earthly realm;
5. He dies;
6. He is made alive again;
7. He effects a reconciliation;
8. He is exalted and enthroned, and the cosmic powers become subject to him.

To what extent this pattern was adapted from pre-Christian sources and to what extent first-generation Christians originated it is not known; in any case, its application to Jesus was early and widespread. He is here not only an ethical teacher, a prophet, or a national Messiah; he is the protagonist of a cosmic drama of universal significance.

Such texts cannot be understood from bare outlines, so we here give tentative versions of several of them. In the case of liturgical texts, the language was not that of everyday conversation, but involved, exalted, and with many special conventions; the renderings seek to convey some of this flavor. In the first hymn, the meaning of the word translated "robbery" is much disputed, and the words "even the death of the Cross" are thought to be Paul's gloss, not part of the original. This hymn is quoted in Philippians 2.6–11.

> Being in the form of God,
>> he thought it not robbery to be equal to God,
> but emptied himself,
>> taking upon him the form of a servant.

> And being made in the likeness of men,
>> and being found in fashion as a man,
> he humbled himself,
>> becoming obedient unto death,
>>> [even the death of the Cross].

> Wherefore God also hath highly exalted him,
>> and given him a name that is above every name,
> that at the name of Jesus every knee should bow,
>> in heaven, and on earth, and under the earth,
> and every tongue confess that Jesus Christ is Lord
>> to the glory of God the Father.

Another is quoted in Colossians 1.15–20:

> He is the image of the invisible God,
>> the first-born of all creation;
> for in him were created all things
>> in the heavens and on earth.
>
> Through him, and unto him
>> were all things created,
> and he himself is before all things,
>> and in him all things hold together.
>
> He is the beginning,
>> the first-born from the dead;
> for in him all the fullness of God
>> was pleased to dwell,
>
> through him, and unto him,
>> to reconcile all things;
> and he is the head of the body, the Church,
>> that in all things he might become pre-eminent.

The Johannine Prologue.   With this group of hymns is also to be reckoned the famous prologue of the Gospel according to John:

> 1. In the beginning was the Word,
>> and the Word was with God,
> And the Word was God;
>> he was in the beginning with God.
>
> 2. All things were made through him,
>> and without him was not anything made.
> What was made in him was life,
>> and the life was the light of men.
>
> 3. And the light shineth in the darkness,
>> and the darkness hath not overcome it.
> He was the true light, that enlighteneth every man,
>> coming into the world.
>
> 4. He was in the world, and the world was made through him,
>> and the world knew him not.
> He came unto his own,
>> and his own received him not.
> But to all who received him
>> he gave power to become children of God.
>
> 5. And the Word was made flesh,
>> and dwelt among us,

and we beheld his glory,
> the glory as of the only-begotten of the Father,

6. full of grace and truth,
> and of his fullness
have we all received,
> grace upon grace.

The original contains subtle distinctions that no idiomatic translation can render. These include the following:

1. In the first stanza (as we have here divided the hymn) the word "God" has the definite article (literally, "the God") in the second and fourth lines, but not in the third. With the article, the word is equivalent to "the Father" (stanza 5); without it, it is applied to "the Word." The Word is God, but is not identical to the Father.

2. In stanzas 1 and 2, a distinction is made between the verb "to be," the subjects of which are God the Father and the Word, and "to become," the subject of which is "all things" (compare the hymn from Colossians quoted above), elsewhere "the world." Eternal, absolute being characterizes God; dependent, temporal being characterizes the world. But in stanza 5, the Word *becomes* "flesh" (here in the Old Testament sense of man, human nature as a whole, not in contrast to "soul" or even to "spirit"), he enters into the second, contingent mode of being.

3. Light and darkness are both possibilities for the world. The world as created is light, but as ignorant of the Word it is darkness. Only through the Word is it light (associated with life, glory, grace, and truth).

4. But "becoming," relative, contingent being, is not in itself darkness. The distinction "light/darkness" is not synonymous with the distinction "being/becoming."

These distinctions recur, with different terminology, in the history of doctrine. Doctrinal precision in liturgical texts seems odd to modern readers, but remained usual in Christianity for centuries.

Prayers in Early Christianity. The *berakah* (plural *berakoth*), a characteristic Jewish prayer form, begins normally with the formula: "Blest art thou, O Lord our God, King of the Universe." An apparent Christian adaptation found in the New Testament is "Blest be the God and Father of our Lord Jesus Christ" (perhaps in direct address "Blest art thou, O God, the Father . . ."). A variant of this formula, "We give thanks unto thee, O God. . . ." was also current among Christians.

Among the *berakoth,* some refer to a specific occasion and others are more general. So one finds in the New Testament a brief Christian *berakah* on comfort in trouble (2 Cor. 1.3-4). The Christian sacred meal, the "Breaking of Bread" or "Lord's Supper," was defined by a *berakah,* or a series of *berakoth,* pronounced over the bread and wine, and therefore itself came to be called "Eucharist," which is Greek for "Thanksgiving." Other sacramental acts were accompanied by similar *berakoth*.

Several *berakoth* found in the New Testament refer to the cosmic drama of salvation, resembling the New Testament hymns in content and language:

> We give thanks to the God of our Lord Jesus Christ,
> the Father of glory. . . ,
> according to the working of his mighty power,
> which he wrought in Christ
> when he raised him from the dead,
> and set him at his own right hand in the heavenly places,
> far above all principality and power and might and dominion,
> and every name that is named,
> not only in this age, but also in that which is to come;
> and put all things under his feet,
> and made him to be the head over all things
> for the Church, which is his body,
> the fullness of him that filleth all in all.
>
> (Eph. 1.16, 17, 19-23)

> Blest be the God and Father of our Lord Jesus Christ,
> who according to his abundant mercy hath begotten us again
> unto a lively hope
> through the resurrection of Jesus Christ from the dead,
> unto an inheritance incorruptible
> and undefiled and that fadeth not away.
> reserved in heaven, . . .
> unto a salvation
> ready to be revealed in the last time.
>
> (1 Peter 1.3-4)

The Christian communities that employed these and similar formulas regarded themselves as participating in the great cosmic drama of redemption; their very act of worship was part of the drama, a participation in the cosmic reconciliation effected by the Redeemer.

5

Early Christian Theologies and the New Testament

Diverse Tendencies

Because the book of the Acts of the Apostles aims at showing essential agreement between the Jerusalem apostles and Paul, and is less interested in other issues, it gives a more harmonious impression than do Paul's own letters. Conflict within Christianity was to be expected, for the movement was heir to the diversity of first-century Judaism, inheriting a number of sometimes conflicting categories that had to be assessed and modified to express the new reality that was seen in Jesus and the Church. With the loss of the centripetal institutions of Jerusalem in A.D. 70, Judaism had to produce unifying norms to prevent dissolution; a "normative Judaism" had to be specified. When the Church embraced gentiles outside of Torah on an equal basis, it was clear that participation in the new reality established by Jesus could not be defined in terms of Jewish institutions. But how was "normative Christianity" to be specified? The nature of the various tendencies operating in the first Christian generations is still in dispute, and only a sketch of one possible interpretation of the evidence can be given here.

The tradition of the sayings of Jesus was cultivated by some circles as a development of the "Words of the Wise" genre of Wisdom literature. Jesus came to be understood primarily or exclusively as the teacher of secret wisdom, whose words conveyed to those who were able to receive them knowledge of their own true being and an exclusively inner and spiritual "resurrection." Eschatology was individualized and regarded as wholly realized; the spiritual elite were thought to be beyond good and evil, exempt from ethical obligations. Because only the timeless truths of the teaching mattered, the historical Jesus of Nazareth soon dropped from view. Paul's opponents of 1 Corinthians and the "Gospel of Thomas" discovered in 1946 in Egypt exemplify this tendency.

Another tradition was more concerned with the acts of Jesus, especially the miracles. It drew on a Hellenistic literary genre, the *aretalogy*—a recitation of "the wondrous deeds of a deity or a divinely gifted human" (Moses Hadas). It was associated with the idea that Jesus was primarily the restorer of the true Torah, the revealer of a renewed and purified covenant. To this was added the notion that keeping this covenant by practicing circumcision and following dietary regulations and a liturgical calendar established communion with cosmic powers and enabled one to receive from them divine qualities, including mystical visions and the ability to perform miracles and interpret scripture

27

esoterically. Christ, the "divine man," possessed these superhuman powers to the highest degree; his true apostles should be able to prove themselves, by the exercise of the same powers, as possessing the Holy Spirit.

A third tendency developed out of Apocalyptic, presenting Jesus as a heavenly figure who appears to his disciples to answer questions about the origin and destiny of the cosmos. Here again the historical Jesus drops out of sight.

Paul opposed representatives of the first two of these three tendencies by insisting on the tension between realized and future eschatology, on the exemption of gentile Christians from Torah, and on the emptiness of boasting of spiritual knowledge and powers in a world ruled by the spiritual powers that crucified Christ, and in which rejection and persecution were the normal condition of his true disciples. He appealed to the kerygma—he called it the gospel—as a norm. The Gospel as a literary genre may be viewed as an expansion of the kerygma to book length. The Passion narrative was made the focus toward which the traditions of the deeds and sayings of Jesus were oriented. They are organized, as is increasingly recognized, in a pattern that is symbolic and theological rather than biographical. This is true already of the Gospel of Mark, written some time before A.D. 70; the biographical interest is only general, and the intention is to present not so much chronologically accurate facts as the eschatological conflict between Christ and Satan, the inability even of the disciples to understand Jesus' message before the Resurrection, and the rejection and martyrdom that his disciples must expect.

The Gospels

After A.D. 70 two Gospels were produced based on that of Mark but quite different from one another. The Gospel of Matthew incorporates much new material, especially parables and sayings used for teaching; it was probably written by a trained scribe for a Jewish-Christian, but not Ebionite, Torah-observing community; it presents Jesus in the role of a new Moses who reaffirms Torah by pointing to the love of God and humankind as its true center. A highly developed technique of Old Testament interpretation is used to refute Jewish critics of Christianity. To Mark's account (which began with Jesus' baptism), Matthew prefixes a narrative of the birth and childhood of Jesus, with a genealogy stressing the events of the Gospel as continuous with, and fulfilling, the history of Israel.

The Gospel of Luke was written by a gentile Christian who added to it a second volume, the Acts of the Apostles, an account of the Jerusalem Church and of Paul's activities down to his house arrest in Rome. Like Matthew, Luke also adds much material to Mark, including a genealogy and infancy narrative, but his sources are partly different and even material from a common source is differently arranged. Acts, like the Gospels, is at least as much based on symbolic patterns as on factual chronology. Luke emphasizes a theological periodization of history, the role of the Holy Spirit, and the injustice of the persecution of Jesus and his followers.

The Gospel of John follows the same basic pattern as the others, but if it uses common sources with them it reworks them so that they cannot be clearly identified. The other three Gospels are called the "synoptics" because of their common Marcan material. The interweaving of history and symbolism is more obvious in John, where it has always been recognized, than in the Synoptics. This gospel stresses "realized eschatology," the access to eternal life already made available in Jesus; it insists on the reality of Jesus' humanity, in opposition to a movement that denied it; it emphasizes conflict between Life and Death, Light and Darkness, Truth and Falsehood, Freedom and Bondage; it is often written on several levels at once, referring simultaneously to the historical events of Jesus' life, the conflict with Judaism and persecution experienced by the author's community, the opening of cosmic participation in divine life and love as the inner meaning of historical events, the sacramental rites of the Church as channels of such participation, and so on. Hebraic and Hellenistic elements are so interwoven that scholarly debates on the Gospel's background are frequent but indecisive.

The Gnostic Movement. Not everyone accepted the norm of the Kerygma set forth in these Gospels. These existed an influential movement composed of those who claimed to follow the teachings of Jesus, but who eliminated the historical figure of Jesus from their vision of salvation. They favored a doctrine of salvation through self-realization that developed in opposition to the biblical doctrine of Creation; they judged spacio-temporal existence quite negatively. The origins of this tendency among some Christians have been sought variously in Greek philosophy, in Oriental (mainly Chaldean) religious movements, in Jewish deviations, in the demoralization of apocalyptic circles after A.D. 70, and in various combinations of these forces.

Gnosticism regards the present world as bad by nature, the product of a failure in the divine world, a "tragedy in the Absolute." Humankind, or at least some persons, are beings from the divine world who by misfortune become trapped in the material world and forget their true origin and nature. The Redeemer descends from the divine world to reveal this knowledge to them; in some versions, the spirits of human beings are fragments of the Redeemer, who are rejoined to him. Knowledge (in Greek, *gnōsis*) of one's true nature is already salvation, assuring that one's destiny is to regain the divine realm. The Redeemer is not involved in the Creation, for here Creation and Fall are identical; he does not "become flesh," for the human condition is in its very nature bondage; he does not die as man to rise again, for salvation is not the salvation of man as such, but of fallen spirits from the condition of man. In some versions, he descends upon Jesus (a prophet but no more) at his baptism, making him the adopted Son of God, and departs again before the Crucifixion (adoptionism); in others, Jesus' humanity is unreal, a disguise adopted by the

Redeemer (docetism, from the Greek word for "seem": he only "seems" to be man). Eschatology is individual and realized only, for the cosmos as such cannot be saved, being evil by nature. This movement is of great importance, for normative Christianity defined itself largely in opposition to it. It was already at least beginning to develop in the doctrines combatted by Paul, and appeared in full bloom in the second century.

The Books of the New Testament

In addition to the four Gospels and Paul's letters, the New Testament contains other letters or "epistles" and an apocalypse. The letters to the Ephesians and to the Colossians, either late letters of Paul or, as many scholars suspect, writings of a follower of Paul, stress the cosmic scope of redemption, the heavenly being—already—of the Church as the Body of Christ (this is an adaptation of the idea of the cosmic man embracing all of humanity, current in the first century and also drawn upon by the Gnostic movement), and the necessity for vigilant struggle against the "world rulers of this present darkness," the demonic forces that still dominate the Present Age. Pastoral epistles, of similarly uncertain authorship, emphasize ethics and oppose gnostic tendencies. The Epistle to the Hebrews, a sort of homily by a pupil of Paul, correlates the Church with the wandering Israelites after the Exodus but before reaching Palestine, thus also emphasizing future eschatology, and depicts Jesus as the heavenly High Priest who definitively fulfills the redemption foreshadowed in Israel's sacrificial cult. The "Catholic" Epistles (meaning only "general" letters to the Church at large, rather than to the congregation in a specific city) are brief writings containing exhortations on various topics, ascribed to various apostles. The Revelation of John, traditionally ascribed to the Evangelist but regarded by many scholars as by some other writer, is an apocalypse with elaborate symbolism based largely on the Jewish festival calendar; it depicts Christ symbolically as "the Lamb that was slain," the center of the heavenly cult, who alone is able to open the sealed book of destiny.

"Delay of the Parousia." Some have theorized that the primitive Church expected Jesus to return and complete the transition to the Age to Come within a very short time, and that when this failed to happen eschatological hope was abandoned and compensated for by developments that underlie all of later Christianity, and explain the doctrines and institutions of the Church. Clearly many in the early years did expect an early return of Jesus, and there were problems—not a single Problem—occasioned by the "delay" (such as the fear that those who died in the interval would be at a disadvantage, and that the Church could not endure persecution), rather than an abandonment of expectation. Eschatological hope in Christianity has weakened at various times, and also reappeared in the form of intense apocalyptic fervor, often hard to reconcile with the Gospels' insistence that the end of the Present Age cannot be calculated in advance. That the "delay" was the one great crisis of the first Christian generations is an insufficiently founded hypothesis.

History of Salvation. The Kerygma formula centers on the death and resurrection of Jesus as historical happenings. Paul and the Gospels develop this emphasis in various ways; Luke lays great stress on it. The genealogies, for example, intend to show the Gospel events as continuous with and fulfilling the history of Israel in the Old Testament. This understanding is referred to as the History of Salvation; it regards God as acting in history for the salvation of humankind. This action may be hidden and unrecognizable, but one series of such acts is identifiable because it was accompanied by prophetic interpretation: the series of convenantal acts with Israel. Christians regarded the series as a preparation for the coming of Christ; the events of the Gospels are its culmination. Each new moment in the series reflects on the earlier ones, expanding the vision of salvation, until the definitive act occurs in the death, resurrection, and ascension of Jesus. Already present in the New Testament, this view of history was central to early Christianity. It figured in the struggle with Gnosticism, which cannot allow salvation to be essentially connected to anything in history.

In the Old Testament prophetic books and in Jewish theology, the future hope was described as a new instance of God's action as it had been known in the past, especially in the forms of a new Creation and of a new Exodus. Primitive Christianity already aimed to show that this expectation was fulfilled in Christ. A pattern of both progression and continuity was seen running through the events of the Hebrew Bible—in Christian terminology, the "Old Testament"—the events of Christ's life, the sacramental incorporation of the Church into Christ, and the still-to-come New Age. To find such a relation between events, persons, or things in the Old Testament and in the New is to employ "typology," relating an Old Testament "prototype" to a New Testament "antitype." Related both to prophetic prediction and fulfillment and to allegory, typology is not identical with either of these in spite of ambiguous borderline cases. It was the most important way of understanding the Bible as a consistent whole in Christianity through the ancient and medieval periods. A special branch of typology deals with sacraments and is prominent in liturgical texts. The most important model of salvation in the Jewish Scriptures, the Exodus, was basic to the understanding of Christ's work, the new Exodus.

Cosmic Liturgy. Among the New Testament books, Colossians and Ephesians, and especially Hebrews and Revelation, point to the motif of Cosmic Liturgy. In the broadest sense this motif includes three aspects: (1) the heavenly worship, the liturgy of the angels; (2) the rhythm of nature as liturgy; (3) the worship of the God of Israel by all nations. All three are already present in the Jewish Scriptures, and the traditional assignment of angelic overseers to the natural world and to the nations integrated them closely. This motif allowed the Church to regard its own worship as continuous with that of the hosts of heaven, to ascribe to the world of nature its proper religious value in a way consistent with the exclusivism of worship in the biblical tradition (as agent rather than object of worship), and to emphasize the universalism that was embodied in the incorporation of representatives of all nations into the Church, breaking down the wall between Israel and the gentile nations.

Apocalyptic as Christian Culture.   Cosmos and history as great alternatives are by now sufficiently well known to students of religion. Quite different models of time, space, and religious meaning are involved. But it is also increasingly clear that the biblical tradition, in introducing historical time as the locus of religious meaning, did not ever purge itself of the elements of the cosmic perspective, in fact could not do so. Apocalyptic is the most ambitious effort to extend history as the History of Salvation to cosmic dimensions, stretching from creation to eschaton and from the pit of Sheol to the highest heaven, embracing nature, human beings, and angels. History "demythologized" religion, and mythical categories expressed the transcendental import of historical events. Already used in the Old Testament (for example, God's fight with the Dragon, a creation motif in Mesopotamia, was applied to the Exodus), this method was the main vehicle of Christian doctrine until about A.D. 135. The element of "realized eschatology" kept Christianity from becoming a mere apocalyptic sect, even while it made extensive use of apocalyptic thought forms.

Symbolism and Apocalyptic.   The basic stock of human religious symbolism began to appear by the paleolithic period, flourished especially in the neolithic, and was essentially completed by the end of the Bronze Age. Later developments, including the "higher" religions, reinterpreted these symbols, arranging them in new patterns rather than generating new symbols. Their original context was cosmic; the biblical tradition adapted them to the History of Salvation, and through Apocalyptic they were available to primitive Christianity. The wheel, the tree of life, the axe, sun, moon, and stars, the zodiac, and so on, were all employed in this way, often in terms of typology. The gnostic movement, which denied positive significance to both cosmic and historical time, likewise drew on the same symbols, adapting them to the vision of salvation from materiality and from cosmic and historical time. Primitive Christian literature outside of New Testament, both gnostic (much of what is called the "New Testament Apocrypha") and normative (the "Apostolic Fathers"), reflects this apocalyptic atmosphere; its influence on the New Testament is also considerable. The cult has a special affinity for such symbolism. The modern reader is likely to find it a puzzling mixture of movingly beautiful and offensively bizarre elements.

Ethics and Spirituality

From sectarian Judaism Christianity inherited the "Two Ways" method of moral instruction: The Way of Light ("the Way" was a primitive self-designation of what was later called "Christianity") was contrasted with the Way of Darkness. The Church in the death-dominated Present Age was engaged in a spiritual Holy War against the dominant demonic forces, whose efforts (apparent especially in persecution) were redoubled as a result of the victory of Christ that guaranteed their ultimate doom. Like a mortally wounded wild animal, they were more dangerous than ever. The unification of the personality was opposed to the "double heart" or "double soul," simplicity to duplicity. The content of instruction given in connection with baptism was ethical and scriptural, consisting of knowledge of the fulfillment of the Old Testament in Christ and the Church (prophecy and typology) and of the "mysteries of the Kingdom," the knowledge of eschatological secrets based on oral and written apocalyptic lore. Baptism was "Illumination" or "Enlightenment," and the ancient hymn

> Awake, O sleeper,
> and arise from the dead,
> and Christ the Lord shall give thee light.
> The Sun of the Resurrection,
> begotten before the morning star,
> bestowing life with his rays.
>
> (Eph. 5.14; Clement of Alexandria,
> Protreptikos 8.84)

is probably from a baptismal rite. These observations on ethics and spirituality apply to normative Christianity; the gnostic movement presents a different picture which will be discussed later.

Worship as Normal Mysticism. The word "mysticism" is defined so diversely that it is often more trouble than help in discussing religious experience. If it is defined strictly in terms of purification, illumination, and unification as successive stages leading to complete identification with God, it is a marginal phenomenon in Christianity; if defined loosely as immediate awareness of relation with God, it becomes almost identical with personal religious experience in general. A Jewish author has coined the term "normal mysticism" for the experience of the presence of God in worship in the rabbinic tradition,* and it may be adopted also to refer to the corresponding experience in Christianity. That the sacraments essentially were believed to enable one to participate in some sense in the life of God seems a fair if yet vague assertion. The other elements of worship (prayers, hymns, and so on) direct the worshipper toward such a participation. They assist in bringing his or her life into the patterns of History of Salvation and Cosmic Liturgy. The Passover Seder enables the Jew, millenia later, to participate in the Exodus and to anticipate the New Exodus of the Age to Come; the Christian worship likewise overcomes

---

*Max Kadushin, in *The Rabbinic Mind* (third edition; New York: Bloch, 1972); and *Worship and Ethics: A Study in Rabbinic Judaism* (Chicago: Northwestern University Press, 1964.)

the separation of time; the worshipper participates in the New Exodus, anticipates the New Creation. He or she joins the heavenly spheres and the angelic
hosts in their ceaseless praise; space too no longer separates. Jewish worship
enables the worshipper, while retaining an individual identity, also to assume
larger identities, as either Israel the nation or all humankind, depending on
whether the Exodus or the Creation is in view. Christianity, likewise, knows
the larger identity, but here it is the Church, the New People of God, which
embraces in principle all humanity. The experience expressed in the Christian
berakoth quoted above (page 26) does not dissolve the worshipper into the
worshipping community or into God; it is personal but not individualistic,
corporate but not collectivist, mystical but not monist. The experience of incorporation into Christ and communion with God in worship, described in terms
of History of Salvation and Cosmic Liturgy, may fairly be called Christian
normal mysticism.

THE DEVELOPMENT
OF CHRISTIAN HELLENISM

6

The Church of the Martyrs

Christian Hellenism

The gentile Christianity that emerged as the mainstream of the movement in the second century lost contact with Torah-observing Christianity, Ebionite and non-Ebionite, but only gradually and partially moved away from cultural forms based on Apocalyptic (itself a product of the Hellenistic period), toward other forms adapted from Roman Hellenism.

Hellenism was itself an ambitious attempt to synthesize all human creativity and culture. Its success, of course, was only partial, but the achievement was tremendous by almost any standard. Christian Hellenism was nothing less than an attempt to convert and transform this massive synthesis, in spite of—and in full knowledge of—the elements incompatible with Christianity that permeated Hellenism. It was an effort to construct as a Christian culture "a great synthesis in which all the creative traditions . . . of the past were merged and integrated" (Georges Florovsky). Its success was likewise only partial; it nevertheless constitutes a major factor in human history, and a permanent major feature of Christianity.

The most noted single aspect of Christian Hellenism is probably the use of Hellenistic intellectual tools to define Christian dogma.

Even this path had already been partly traced out by Hellenistic Judaism, whose lead the Church followed in the initial stages of synthesizing the classical Christian doctrines in adapted Hellenistic terms. In fact, only a few of the basic terms of the classical statements of doctrine were already current in Greek philosophy, and even these were placed in a new context; what is truly Hellenistic is the use of a method of abstraction in which conceptual terms become objects of reflection, discussion, and definition. This was the technique used to define Christian *dogma*. But the very idea of dogma needs clarification: in modern usage, the word usually means a proposition accepted blindly on the basis of authority, something negative and restricting; but it was not so regarded in antiquity ("dogma" comes from the Greek word for "think"). In the present chapter, we will try to penetrate more adequately the ideas of "dogma," "schism," "heresy," and "orthodoxy."

The transition from Jewish to Greco-Roman Hellenistic culture was matched in importance by the other great social transition of Christianity in the ancient world: from illegal sect to the state religion of the Roman Empire, its "establishment" as a state church (the current expression "the establishment," in the sense of the dominant elements in society, comes from this use of the word for the condition of a state religion). These two transitions condition all of the later history of Christianity. What we shall call "Christian Hellenism" is not a long dead stage of history; the cultural and doctrinal synthesis is a perennial aspect of Christianity, and the state church era is only now breaking down.

Salvation in Early Christianity

Religion is the means for the ultimate transformation of life, involving both a vision of ultimate reality and a way of realizing this ultimacy. It is a vision and a way of salvation, where "salvation" is defined precisely as ultimate transformation. Textbooks sometimes give the impression that in its first millennium Christianity had no serious doctrine of salvation ("soteriology" is the technical term), but more recent studies have shown that this proposition is false. The doctrine of salvation was not so much the object of discussion and definition as its presupposition. It remained more closely tied to apocalyptic imagery than did the doctrines of the Trinity and Incarnation, the main foci of attention in Christian Hellenism; it was expressed in several complementary sets of images, without much systematic organization. The major motifs are present already in the New Testament, and are developed in terms drawn from the Old Testament and Apocalyptic. Four main motifs or models may be distinguished.

Christ the Victim: Juridical Terminology.   Juridical terms for sin and salvation are found in both the Old and the New Testaments and in postbiblical writings. They are perhaps most prominent in the context of apocalyptic, with its Last Judgment: the Present Age must come to an end before God's power, and those who will not experience that power as grace must know it as wrath. Paul speaks of "Jesus who delivers us from the wrath to come." (1 Thess. 1.10) Legal terms referring to the work of Christ as the payment of a debt and the like are frequent; Latin writers occasionally speak of Christ's sufferings in terms of "satisfaction," or as somehow filling the role of a punishment. But one does not find much in the way of later substitutionary theories: death is not thought of as a punishment inflicted by God on all people for Adam's transgression, sin is not biologically inherited guilt, the crucifixion is not Christ's innocent suffering of penal torments inflicted by God. The idea of salvation as "appeasing the angry God" cannot be identified with any prominent statement of atonement in early Christianity.

Christ the Victim: Sacrificial Terminology. Sacrificial images of salvation are closely linked to juridical images; both belong to the concept of covenant. The idea of sacrifice is utterly distorted in modern popular culture, where it is taken to mean painfully giving up some good thing for a higher, usually altruistic cause. Parents "sacrifice" to send their children to college, not by offering goats or bullocks upon an alter, but by foregoing a new car or television set. "Victims" of natural disasters, accidents, or crimes are those who suffer or die to no good purpose. But the living rite of sacrifice is most typically an occasion of joy; often a part of the victim (a neutral word meaning only an animal to be sacrificed) is eaten by the worshippers, with good appetite.

Already in the Old Testament, the sacrifices are not something God needs, but a means he freely provides for maintaining, and when necessary restoring, communion between himself and his people. They included: (1) the holocaust, in which the entire victim (except the hide) is burnt on the altar; (2) the expiatory sacrifice, offered to remove an inability (incurred by breaking covenant) to participate in normal worship: here the parts of the victim not burnt are eaten by the priests but not by the person(s) requiring expiation; (3) the communion sacrifice, in which the unburnt parts are eaten by the priests and by the offerer and his guests (who must be in a state of ritual purity); and (4) the Passover, which is not part of the Temple cult and requires neither priest nor altar: all of the Paschal Lamb (except, of course, the hide and such) is eaten, the blood only being poured out. Christians regarded all of these as foreshadowing, and being replaced by, the sacrifice in which Christ is both priest and victim. As already mentioned, the Eucharistic bread and wine are identified with the body and blood of Christ (without any precise theory of how this was accomplished) truly made available for the participation of the faithful in the being of Christ; not *a* sacrifice, but the one sacrifice of the New Covenant, the only Christian sacrifice, Christ himself. The Last Supper, the Cross, and the Eucharist are here aspects of one single sacrifice. The sacramental acts linked the sacrifice motif to the idea of participation, which will be discussed more fully below.

Christ the Illuminator. We have already seen that baptism was called "illumination" or "enlightenment" in early Christianity. The image includes, but is not restricted to, moral and intellectual instruction. From the beginning, Christian instruction preparatory to initiation (called "catechesis" or "catechism") involved the "Two Ways" teaching, with catalog-like lists of virtues and vices, and ethical duties. Humankind's plight includes ignorance, but (except for the Gnostic movement) it is more than that. The "mysteries of the kingdom" into which Christians were initiated were teachings, not comprehensible to the world at large, concerning the cosmic drama of salvation. For the Jewish Christian, scripture (the Old Testament) was fulfilled and thereby newly comprehensible; for the gentile Christian, the way was opened to a new philosophy based on the doctrine of Creation. For both, there was a new knowledge of God's mercy and love for humanity:

> O the depth of the riches
>   and wisdom and knowledge of God!
> How unsearchable are his judgments,
>   and how inscrutable his ways!
>   (Rom. 11.33)

> Through [Christ] we gaze into the heights of heaven,
>   through him we see the reflection of God's . . . countenance,
> through him the eyes of our heart were opened,
>   through him our . . . darkened mind blossoms towards the light
> through him the Lord desired us to taste the immortal knowledge,
>   (1 Clement 36.2)

The content of the "mystery" is nothing less than the cosmic drama of salvation:

> Without doubt, great is the mystery of our religion:
>   He was manifest in the flesh,
>   he was vindicated in the spirit,
>   he was seen by angels,
>   he was proclaimed among the nations,
>   he was believed on in the world,
>   he was taken up into glory.
>   (1 Tim. 3.16)

This is one of the redeemer hymns, here referred to as a "mystery," the same word that from the second century designated in Greek what Latin (and English) came to call a "sacrament." Apprehension of this mystery is consciousness-transforming illumination; it is already participation in the mystery, in the struggle against enslaving powers and in normal mysticism.

(3) **Christ the Giver of Immortality, and Deification.**   Writers of the third and following centuries speak of "deification," a disconcerting term, to designate what to them was a sacred reality and what some modern writers pejoratively call the "physical theory of redemption." But this model of salvation is present under various terms from the earliest period, and is absolutely crucial for an understanding of Christian Hellenism.

What is distinctively Christian about Christian Hellenism is, firstly, the doctrine of Creation. For pagan* Hellenism, the cosmos itself is in some way eternal. Alongside or with the eternal cosmos is the realm of origin and decay. These are the two orders of being and becoming. Philosophy desired to "save the phenomena," to justify the realm of becoming by somehow relating it positively to the realm of immutable being. Plato spoke of "participation" in

---

*"Pagan" here and in the following pages designates the pre-Christian religions of the Mediterranean world, northern Europe, and so on. It should be understood as a neutral term, without any pejorative nuances. "Non-Christian" will not do in this context—there was also a Jewish Hellenism.

this sense. But all of pagan antiquity would have subscribed to the Buddha's dictum that whatsoever is an arising thing is also a ceasing thing. As we saw in examining the Johannine prologue, Christianity also knew the tension between being and becoming, but with a difference: being is proper to God, and becoming to "all things," the cosmos. The participation of "all things" in the Logos, the Word, is life and light; it is the participation of becoming in being. The nonparticipation of becoming in being is death and darkness. Both are cosmos—"cosmos" in early Christianity has two senses: the creation of such, and the creation as dominated by Death. Immortality, in this view, is not an inherent characteristic of any created being, including angels and souls; the Christians of the first centuries were not willing to call the soul "immortal," for they regarded God as

> . . . the blessed and only sovereign
> the King of (all) the kings who reign,
>   and Lord of lords who rule
> who along hath immortality,
>   and dwelleth in light unapproachable,
> whom no man hath seen,
>   whom none can ever see,
> (1 Tim. 6.15-16)

but whose

> divine power has given us all things that pertain to life and godliness,
> through the knowledge of him who called us to his own glory and excellence,
> by which he has given to us exceeding great and precious promises,
> that through these [we] may become partakers of the divine nature,
> having escaped the corruption that is in the world . . .
> (2 Peter 1.3-4)

Human beings are not inherently immortal in soul or body, but were meant to participate in immortality (love, truth, light, eternal life); at the Fall they lost this participation and became subject to death and corruption. Endowed with reason, moral freedom, and a physical body, a human being is a microcosm, placed in a crucial position in the world (in this rather special sense only, the doctrine of creation is anthropocentric); his Fall was a cosmic disaster, by which Death gained control of the cosmos, and the created order was frustrated in its very essence. Modern writers have called this a "light doctrine of the Fall and its effects" because it does not subsume everything under the categories of guilt and punishment. Rather, it sees the created order as threatened with slipping, or even jumping, back into nonbeing—one wonders how any estimate of the Fall could be "heavier." Humankind is aware of the threat of ultimate death, and struggles to evade it and to establish individual being, but inevitably without success and at the expense of others; human capacity for love is destroyed by futile self-interest.

The Incarnation of the Son of God is seen as a triumph over this threat. The Word became flesh, and the humanity he assumed is the most intimate possible union of becoming to being. It is the point at which created beings can return to their intended participation in God. The Buddha's dictum no longer holds universally. Whatever is an arising thing is also a ceasing thing *unless* it participates in the union in Christ of being and becoming. In the Incarnation, flesh and spirit, man and God, created and uncreated being, are indissolubly united in a single identity. In the Ascension, Jesus in his humanity is "enthroned at the right hand of God;" human nature shares eternally in the being of God. By participating in the deified humanity of Christ, human beings are enabled to partake of the life of God, and thus are "deified," without ceasing to be human. They are, indeed, restored to full humanity, for in this view a person is incomplete if he or she is cut off from participation in the life of God. This is what orthodox Christian writers mean by "deification": not the obliteration of the distinction between humanity and God, not humankind's ceasing to be human, but rather becoming fully human by sharing in the love and eternal life of God, by receiving the gift of immortality and incorruption, which becomes the new principle of life already within the Death-dominated Present Age, and will be fully realized in the Resurrection and the Age to Come.

Much space has been devoted to this model of salvation because it is a main motivating force behind the development of Christian Hellenism, which insisted on the integral humanity of Christ within the one identity of God the Son. One should add that it is a mistake to interpret this model, as some have done, as implying that salvation becomes operative automatically or mechanically. The former, false principle of life must be utterly rejected morally (repentance) and a hard struggle must be waged against the enslaving powers, including accepting the very real possibility of martyrdom.

Christ the Victor. In addition to the "physical theory," textbooks sometimes refer to a "ransom theory of atonement," namely that Christ's death was a ransom paid to Satan for the human race. This is, however, but a variant of a basic model of salvation, that of Christ as victor over the powers that enslave the cosmos.

Apocalyptic Judaism was familiar with an elaboration of the account of the Fall in Genesis: Satan was identified as the angel who was appointed ruler and guardian of the cosmos after the creation. He therefore bears the title "Prince (or King, or God) of this World." But when Adam was created in God's image, the angels were ordered to show him honor, and Satan became enraged with envy and instead contrived to bring about Adam's ruin, subjecting him to death, by which Satan now rules (parasitically) over the cosmos. Apocalyptic thought included the hope for the Age to Come (or Reign of God) in which this rule of death would be overcome.

Christians held that it had already been overcome by the incarnation, death, resurrection, and ascension of the Redeemer. The "Gospel of Nicodemus" (in the New Testament Apocrypha) dramatically depicted the "Harrowing of Hell": after his death, Christ entered Hell (Sheol, Hades, the realm of the dead, conceived as a place of imprisonment rather than of penal torments) and broke its gates, freeing the souls of Adam and Eve and the righteous dead. The New Testament already depicts salvation as a victory over the "world-rulers of this present darkness" (Eph. 6.12):

> For this purpose the Son of God was manifested,
> that he might destroy the works of the devil.
>
> (1 John 3.8)
>
> Forasmuch as [men] are partakers of flesh and blood,
> he also himself likewise took part of the same;
> that through death he might destroy him that had the power
> of death, that is, the devil;
> and deliver them who through fear of death
> were all their lifetime subject to bondage.
>
> (Heb. 2.14–15)

It was through the "mystery" or "mysteries" of the cosmic drama depicted in the New Testament hymns that this liberation took place, through

> the three mysteries to be cried aloud,
> wrought in the silence of God and hidden from the Prince
> of this world;
> the virginity of Mary, her giving birth, and the Lord's death,
>
> (Ign. Eph. 19.1)
>
> the hidden wisdom which God ordained before the ages for our
> glorification;
> none of the Rulers of this Age understood this,
> for had they known it, they would not have crucified the
> Lord of Glory.
>
> (1 Cor. 2.7–8)

Ignatius of Antioch (about A.D. 115) quotes what is probably a hymn on this theme:

A star shone forth in heaven
    more brightly than all the stars
and its light was greater than words can tell
    and its newness caused astonishment.

And all the other stars, with the sun and the moon,
    formed a chorus around this star;
but the star surpassed them all in brightness,
    and there was perplexity, whence came this new thing so unlike them.

From that time all magic began to be dissolved,
    and every spell of wickedness to vanish away;
ignorance began to be removed,
    and the Ancient Kingdom to be destroyed.

For God was manifest as man
    for the newness of life eternal;
that which had been prepared by God
    began to come into being;

and so all things were disturbed
    for the overthrow of Death was being planned.

                  (Ign. Eph. 19.2–3)

The *Odes of Solomon,* a collection of hymns dating perhaps from the first century, contains references to the Harrowing of Hell:

Sheol saw me and was in distress;
    Death cast me up, and many along with me.
I was gall and bitterness to it,
    and I went down to its lowest depth. . . .

And I made a congregation of living men
    among the dead of it,
and I spake to them with living lips,
    for my word shall not be void.

And those who had died ran toward me and cried,
    and said, 'Son of God, have mercy on us,
'and do with us according to thy kindness,
    and bring us out from the bonds of darkness,

'And open the door through which we can come out to thee,
    for we perceive that our death doth not hold thee,
'let us also be redeemed by thee,
    for thou art our Redeemer.'

And as for me, I heard their voice,
    and I placed their faith within my heart,
and my name I sealed upon their heads,
    for they are free men, and they are mine.

The Church, like the Qumran community, thought of itself as a militia engaged in war with the world-rulers, the demonic powers of the Present Age; the definitive victory must be appropriated anew by each individual.

Christianity as an Illegal Sect

Although the Way of Torah included features that offended many in the Roman Empire, all agreed that it was praiseworthy to follow the ways of one's ancestors, and the apolitical practice of Judaism was usually tolerated. Gentile Christians were guilty of the same offenses as Jews, in the view of the Roman Empire. True, the gentiles did not circumcise males or refuse to eat pork, but they did reject the civic cults and the imperial religion, and for this they could not plead loyalty to ancestral custom—that was exactly what they had renounced. Judaism was a national religion, but Christianity spread to all nations, infecting them with what was thought of as the Jewish "hatred of the human race." As is well known, the emperor Nero (reigned A.D. 54–68) had many Christians in Rome killed in spectacularly cruel ways. During the first century, Christianity was still thought of as a Jewish sect, but as it separated from Judaism it came to be recognized as a distinct and illegal religion, characterized by recent origin, stubbornness, extremism, and superstition, and incompatible with beneficial religion and with loyalty to the Empire. Just what law Christians were held to have broken is unclear, but the practice of their religion was a capital crime. Intelligent people disbelieved, and official investigations revealed as groundless, popular rumors that the Christians met at night for orgies (did they not call their meetings "love feasts"?) and murdered and ate babies (did they not practice the ritual consumption of flesh and blood?). Conscientious officials tried to assure due process for persons accused of Christianity. Anyone who denied being a Christian or who would renounce his adherence to the sect could prove his innocence by paying homage in some token way to the gods of Rome or to the emperor. Until A.D. 250, persecutions were sporadic and local in character. Much depended on whether the local governor thought of the Christians as dangerous subversives or as harmless cranks.

The Age of the Martyrs. From the point of view of the Christians, the issue was precisely worship as the act of ultimate self-determination. If Christ's cosmic victory had freed them from slavery to death and led them to a worship that was itself a new life, then love (God's love for his creation, in the first instance) is stronger than death. The fear of death is the instrument of enslavement. To renounce the new life and freedom publicly out of fear of death would then be a return to slavery; and to bear witness to the truth in the face of death was to participate in the most real way in Christ's victory. The rite of baptism included an utter renunciation of Satan and the ruling powers of the Present Age, and an oath of allegiance to Christ ("sacrament" was the Latin term for a soldier's enlistment oath, and in Christian use acquired the sense of "an act that brings forth sacred power"):

> Let the candidate for baptism make Renunciation thus:
> "I renounce Satan, and his works, and his pomps,
> and his service, and his angels, and his inventions,
> and all things that are under him."
> And in his Oath of Enlistment let him say:
> "And I adhere to Christ."
>
> (*Apostolic Constitutions* 41.1–3)

The Christian was not supposed to seek martyrdom by provoking the authorities (occasionally enthusiasts staged protest demonstrations with no other foreseeable result); he or she was permitted to flee persecution, but once brought before a magistrate, had the inalienable duty to bear witness ("martyr" means "witness" in Greek) publicly to the truth—basically, to refuse to worship idols or deny adherence to Christ—whatever the consequences.

Charisma, Eschatology, Mysticism and Martyrdom. In the period before A.D. 135, charismatic prophets, often wandering ascetics, had played an important role in the Church. They tended to disappear in the milieu of Hellenistic gentile Christianity, but the principle of charismatic ministry did not disappear: it was continued by ascetics living within the local church communities, and by the martyrs and confessors (those who risked death and suffered imprisonment or torture, reckoned also with the martyrs). The eschatological nature of Christianity, not accepting "current conditions" (which are always more or less a reflection of the "Ancient Kingdom of Death") but living by an absolute, as yet unrealized standard, is clearest in the witness of the martyrs. The whole Church accepted both the risk of martyrdom and a voluntary exclusion from public life, which was inextricably bound up with civic cults that were in Christian eyes front organizations for the dominion of Death. The entire Church was the Church of martyrs. But in it the actual martyrs and confessors were the charismatic leaders. The "acts" of the martyrs exhibit what might be called a "mysticism of martyrdom": martyrs endure with a strength not their own because of Christ's presence in them, and enjoy the deifying vision of Christ in his divine glory at the time of martyrdom.

The Sacrament of Martyrdom. Baptism was regarded as the initiation into the death and resurrection of Christ:

> you were buried with [Christ] in baptism,
> in which also you are risen with him
> through faith in the working of God,
> who raised him from the dead.
>
> (Col. 2.12)

Believers preparing for baptism ("catechumens" or "candidates") who suffered martyrdom before being baptized were regarded as having received the "baptism of blood"; for other martyrs, it was a renewal and fulfillment of baptism.

The sacramental meal of bread and wine in which Christians partook of the body and blood of Christ, the sacrifice of the Cross, was called "eucharist" ("thanksgiving") from the prayer of thanksgiving chanted by the bishop over the bread and wine. The martyrs were believed to participate in the sacrifice of Christ also, fulfilling in their own persons the offering of his body and blood. Ignatius, bishop of Antioch (about A.D. 115), condemned to die at Rome, feared that the Roman Church would try to have his sentence commuted, and wrote:

Grant me nothing more than that I should be poured out as a libation to God, while there is still an altar ready . . . I am God's wheat, and I am ground by the teeth of wild beasts, that I may be found pure bread . . . Entreat Christ for me, that through these beasts I may be found a sacrifice to God . . . The Prince of This World wants to carry me away, and to corrupt my resolution toward God. Let none of you help him . . . I desire the bread of God, which is the flesh of Jesus Christ, . . . and for drink I desire his blood, which is love incorruptible.

(Ign. Rom. 2.2; 4.1, 2; 7.1, 3)

The association of martyrdom with eucharist goes even farther than this. An early example of the eucharistic prayer (Hippolytus [?], early third century) runs as follows:

We give thanks unto thee, O God,
through thy beloved Child Jesus Christ,
whom in these last times thou didst send to us,
the Savior and Redeemer, and the "Angel of thy Counsel,"
who is thy Word inseparable (from thee),
through whom thou didst make all things
and in whom thou art well pleased

whom thou didst send from heaven into the womb of the Virgin
and who, dwelling within her womb, was made flesh,
and was manifested as thy Son,
being born of the Holy Spirit and the Virgin;

who, fulfilling thy will,
and acquiring for thee a holy people,
spread out his hands when he came to the Passion
that he might free from passions those who believe in thee;

who, when he was betrayed to his voluntary Passion
that he might destroy Death, and break the chains of the devil,
and tread hell under foot, and give light to the righteous,
and set up the boundary-post, and manifest the resurrection,
taking bread, and giving thanks to thee,
said, "Take, eat, this is my body, which is broken for you"
and likewise also the cup,
saying, "This is my blood, which is shed for you;
as often as ye do this, do it for my memorial."

Remembering, therefore, his death and resurrection,
we offer to thee this bread and this cup,
giving thanks to thee that thou hast counted us worthy
to stand before thee and minister to thee;
and we pray thee that thou wouldest send thy Holy Spirit
upon the offering of thy holy Church,
and gathering together into one all who partake of thy holy things,
grant that they may be filled with the Holy Spirit,

> that their faith may be confirmed in truth,
> that we may praise and glorify thee
> through thy Child Jesus Christ,
> through whom be glory and honor to thee
> with the Holy Spirit in thy Holy Church
> both now and ever, and for ages of ages.

This remarkable text should be compared with the prayers of martyrs recorded in ancient sources, for example, that of Polycarp, bishop of Smyrna, martyred about A.D. 155:

> O Lord God Almighty,
> the Father of thy beloved and blest Child Jesus Christ,
> through whom we have received knowledge of thee,
> the God of Angels and powers and of all creation,
> and of the whole clan of the righteous, who live before thee:
> I bless thee that thou hast deemed me worthy of this day and hour
> that I may take my share, among the number of thy martyrs,
> in the cup of thy Christ,
> for the resurrection to eternal life both of soul and of body
> in the incorruptibility of the Holy Spirit;
>
> may I today be received among them before thee
> as a precious and acceptable sacrifice,
> as thou hast prepared beforehand, and manifested, and fulfilled;
>
> O faithful and true God,
> for this cause, and for all things,
> I praise thee, I bless thee, I glorify thee,
> through the eternal and heavenly High Priest,
> thy beloved Child Jesus Christ,
> through whom be glory to thee
> with him and the Holy Spirit,
> both now and for ages to come.

The account goes on to say that the martyr's body in the flames was "not like flesh burning, but like a loaf baking" and was "like the smoke of incense or precious aromatics"; that the Christians of Smyrna wanted to take his body for burial and thus "have communion with his holy flesh"; and that they

> took his bones, more valuable than precious stones and finer
> than gold, and put them in a fitting place, where the Lord
> will permit us, as may be possible, to come together with joy
> and gladness to celebrate the birthday of his martyrdom, both
> in memory of those who have already fought, and for the train-
> ing and preparation of the [martyrs] to come.

The martyr's remains or "relics" are precious, having been offered to God as a pure sacrifice, a new manifestation of Christ's one sacrifice. The striking phrase "to have communion with his holy flesh" seems to mean more than just to have contact with it; it may refer to the celebration of the Eucharist on his tomb, so closely is his sacrifice bound to Christ's.

Another notable passage of martyr literature recounts that the North African martyr Felicity (ca. A.D. 200) gave birth to a child while in prison awaiting her death. Seeing her labor pains, a jailer asked how she could hope to endure the pains of martyrdom. "I suffer alone now," she replied, "but then there will be one in me who will suffer for me, because I shall suffer for him." Worship as ultimate self-determination culminates in the martyr's incorporation into the sacrifice of Christ.

Perfectionist Schisms. Certain actions, including murder and blasphemy (in this context meaning the renunciation of Christ to escape persecution) were regarded as breaking the baptismal covenant. The Lapsi, those who "lapsed" before the threat of martyrdom, often repented and sought readmission into the Church—that is, participation in the worship of the Church. For several centuries, the possibility of readmitting such persons was a center of controversy. The poles of the dispute are designated "rigorism" and "laxism." The decision eventually taken, to readmit such persons under quite severe conditions, allowing (once only) a recognized repentence after baptism, seemed too lax to perfectionists and caused some communities to break away from the majority of Christians on the grounds of upholding the purity of the Church. This is what is called a *schism* or "splitting"; it is disciplinary rather than doctrinal in character. Another kind of perfectionist schism was Encratism, which required celibacy for all members of its communities. Montanism, a movement originating in Asia Minor, rejected such "lax" practices as any restoration of lapsi, or the remarriage of widowed persons, but it was especially characterized by its claim to new revelations from the Holy Spirit to charismatic prophets, and by apocalyptic fervor. All such movements regarded the majority of Christians as having compromised their baptismal covenant. "Rigorism" and "laxism" are relative terms: the entire Church was quite rigorous by later standards, and it would be an error to identify rigorism with the perfectionist schisms. Even the stringent standards of the church of the martyrs were regarded by the perfectionists as insufficient.

The Gnostic Movement

The Gnostic movement, referred to in the previous chapter, flourished during the second and third centuries. It was especially strong in Egypt and Syria; in some cities, it appears to have been established earlier than normative Christianity and to have been numerically stronger for several centuries. It was never a unified or uniform entity, but rather a general movement including a number of schools in competition with each other as well as with normative Christianity. The surviving literature of the movement ranges from moderate documents that sound not unlike Colossians or the Gospel of John to fantastic speculations about the emanations of divine beings and the Fall that produced the cosmos. To some extent, the movement attempted to exist within the "Great Church" (as the normative Christian community is sometimes called). Gnostic teachers claimed to possess a higher, esoteric Christian teaching, to which, for those capable of enlightenment, normative Christianity was only a transition (although for others it might be the highest attainable level). But the attempt was not ultimately successful, as we shall see. The Gnostic movement was the stimulus for self-definition on the part of the Great Church. It was virtually identical with "heresy" during the second century. "Heresy" means a "sect" or "faction" separated from the Great Church for doctrinal reasons. The Great Church adopted for itself the Greek words "catholic" ("universal") and "orthodox" ("right-believing" or "right-worshipping"). The ideas of "heresy" and "orthodoxy" arise in some form in every movement that embodies a definite point of view. They presuppose only a norm of true teaching and a community responsible for transmitting it. "Schism" and "heresy" both designate disunity within Christianity (the terms are commonly employed also to designate similar phenomena in Islam, Buddhism, Marxism, etc.); in keeping with the view we have adopted of the relation between worship and doctrine, schism might be viewed as an impairment of the unity of the worshipping community, and heresy as a misdirection of ultimate self-determination. The historical success of a given "orthodoxy" may lead, in modern usage, to acceptance of the term as a designation even by those who are in fact not committed to the judgment it implies.

Gnostic Ethics.   It is difficult to generalize about the Gnostic movement, owing to its lack of uniformity. It tended to adopt in ethics either an extremely permissive view (having attained to knowledge, the Gnostic cannot be affected by anything in the cosmos and can do as he pleases), but it must be acknowledged that this libertinism is from documented anti-Gnostic writers, who may be unduly influenced by polemics, or, more commonly, a very rigorous one (the Gnostic must renounce everything having to do with time and matter, especially sexuality). At least some Gnostic schools permitted their members to escape persecution by renouncing Christ and participating in the civic cult, a reasonable policy for docetists who believed that Christ's body, and consequently the Crucifixion, were unreal.

The Great Church Combats Gnosticism

The doctrine of Creation in orthodox Christianity (and orthodox Judaism) affirms the essential goodness of time and matter, of the realm of "becoming." That death and corruption now dominate it was of course generally accepted, but was regarded as a distortion, not as the inherent character of the cosmos. The tragedy occurred within the cosmos; it was not its cause. On so basic an issue, the Church could not compromise; the entire vision of salvation was at stake. Several writers have accurately pointed to three main weapons against the Gnostic movement: scripture, the bishop, and the rule of faith.

Scripture. The Church inherited the Old Testament and for some decades had only this as "scripture." The Gnostic movement tended to reject it, and along with it, of course, the orthodox ideas of Creation and History of Salvation. The various books of the New Testament were collected and arranged in a form parallel to that of the Old: Gospels, Acts, Pauline epistles, and other epistles plus Revelation corresponding to Torah, historical books, prophets, and "writings." The orthodox doctrines of Creation, Incarnation, and Resurrection were safeguarded by the books of the two Covenants (or "Testaments," as it is somewhat inaccurately rendered in English). The books of the New Testament were accepted as being written by Apostles or their direct pupils and reporting apostolic teachings, being of inspired composition, and generally accepted by Christian communities everywhere. For some centuries writings of the period A.D. 90–135 (the "Apostolic Fathers") were considered borderline cases, accepted as scripture in some areas. As noted in the previous chapter, the books of the New Testament, like those of the Old, represent different perspectives, but Gnostic writings were excluded and writings rejected by Gnostics were accepted.

The Bishop. Writings of the first and early second centuries contain only ambiguous and incomplete information about the offices and orders of the ministry. The Twelve and such figures as James the Just and Paul were unique to the first generation. Jewish Christianity knew charismatic prophets, teachers (scribes), travelling missionary apostles, and regularly appointed and instituted leaders of local communities. It is this last category that retained importance in gentile Christianity. It seems likely that some local communities were led by a college of presbyters (elders) similar to the *zeqenim* (elders) who governed the synagogue. Among them, would presumably be the *proestos* (president), corresponding at least in part to the Jewish *archisynagogos* (ruler of the synagogue). In other Christian communities, the leadership was patterned after that of the Qumram community, whose *paqid* and *mebaqqer* correspond to the Christian bishop (*episkopos,* "overseer"). The bishop was assisted by deacons (*diakonoi,* "servants" or "ministers"). During the second century, these systems were merged, producing a threefold ministry in each community: bishop, college of presbyters, and deacons; in addition, other functions might be fulfilled by specially selected and ordained persons, depending on local traditions. In any case, this threefold ministry prevails from the later second century almost everywhere. The bishop was the pastoral overseer of the community, responsible for instructing persons who requested baptism, supervising teaching, interpreting scripture, and presiding in worship (in which only he addressed formal prayers to God). The presbyters handled practical administrative matters and sat in benches near the bishop's seat at worship (in which they had no active role); the deacons assisted the bishop, especially in matters of "charity"—seeing to the welfare of the needy of the Church and, as far as possible, of the entire locality—and led the congregation in worship, addressing instructions to them and so on.

The bishop was regarded as the successor of the Apostles of the first generation, who appointed the first heads of the local communities they founded. The consecration of the bishop by the "laying on of hands" (the consecrating bishops laid their hands on the head of the bishop elect while saying the prayer of ordination) was the outward sign of this legitimate succession from the Apostles, deriving from a sacramental act of Judaism whereby spiritual power (berākha) was transmitted. The bishop was responsible for the continuity of teaching from generation to generation, so that the authentic teaching of the Apostles would be preserved. The claim that the Gnostic movement was a later perversion of the true teaching of the Apostles, and that the agreement of the bishops everywhere on the content of that teaching was a reliable test of authentic Christianity, was another major defense against Gnostic claims.

The bishop was also the representative of his community to other Christian communities. Questions and problems that could not be resolved at the local level were dealt with by the bishops of entire districts meeting in councils. Some kind of order was necessary in determining how and by whom such councils were to be called and who should attend them. Two principles were employed to establish this order. Under the "principle of accommodation" the Church, for the sake of convenience, followed the administrative boundaries of the Roman Empire, the bishop of the capital of each province (the "metropolitan" bishop) being a sort of president of the bishops of his province. The councils followed the rules of order used in the Roman Senate. The "principle of apostolicity" gave special importance to those local communities that had been established directly by an Apostle, for all other local churches were their "daughters," founded by representatives of the apostolic churches.

Both of these principles served to give a special position to the church of Rome: Rome was the capital of the entire Empire; Peter, the head of the Apostles, had presided over the church there and her bishops were regarded as his successors; and he and Paul had both been martyred there. No other local church in the western part of the empire had a serious claim to apostolic foundation; they were "daughters" of the local church of Rome. And finally, Rome exercised de facto leadership against the Gnostic movement, and against later heresies. Roman leadership was acknowledged everywhere, but not defined, and in general it was less emphasized in the eastern part of the Empire, where a number of local churches claimed apostolic foundation.

The Rule of Faith. The bishops were especially responsible for preserving the Apostolic faith. "Faith" in the Old Testament and Judaism is trust in God's promise; God's existence and his covenant with Israel are presupposed. "Faith" in Christianity is not essentially different, but the Church, an international, persecuted minority competing with Gnostic claims to the true revelation, had to make the presuppositions explicit. The rite of baptism included a threefold formula, originally in the form of questions asked the person being baptized before each of the three immersions, in the second century perhaps in some simple form such as:

> Dost thou believe in God the Father?
> Dost thou believe in Jesus Christ, the Son of God,
>   who was incarnate, died, and rose again?
> Dost thou believe in the Holy Spirit of God?

Instruction prior to baptism may have been the context in which such Trinitarian formulas were combined with something like the *kerygma* form to produce a summary of the doctrinal content of Christianity, the "rule of faith" or "rule of truth." Basically the same everywhere (there was no standardized text; the outline was the same but the exact wording varied), this rule of faith and the "creeds" that developed from it at least by the third century were the norm for interpreting scripture (the Gnostics often having their own interpretations); it was regarded as a third safeguard of Apostolic tradition along with the Scriptures and the bishops. Further consideration will be given to their function in connection with the Nicene Creed.

The Gnostics were firmly entrenched in some areas; they also had books ascribed to Apostles, and they had their own traditions about the teachings of Jesus. But they lacked the cohesiveness necessary to prevail against the "three weapons." Normative Christianity defined itself against Gnosticism not only in doctrinal statements but also by emphasizing its character as a self-conscious, unified community. This self-awareness of the "Great Church" was expressed in the words "orthodox" ("right-believing" or "right-worshipping") and "catholic" ("universal," referring not only to the much-prized unity over geographical space, but also to continuity through generations), in contrast to "heresy," a word that points to the division of the Gnostics into rival schools and to the charge that their doctrines were thought up by various clever teachers, whereas the unity of the Catholic Church was both the result and the sign of its faithfulness to Apostolic teachings and to Christ himself.

Faith and Gnosis

Faith is already a gnōsis, a spiritual understanding. In the ancient period, *gnōsis* always meant true knowledge, and the "gnostic" was the one who possessed it, the "man of knowledge." Orthodox opponents of what we now call "gnosticism" spoke of "pseudognostics" or "so-called gnōsis." The true gnosis was the possession of the Catholic Church. The chariot-throne of God (*merkabah*), in Judaism a symbol of the mystical vision of God reserved for the most advanced spiritual elite, became in Christianity a baptismal symbol. The claim that there was a higher, esoteric knowledge different in content from the baptismal faith was steadfastly rejected. Yet there was a higher gnosis in orthodox Christianity. We have already encountered the "mysticism of martyrdom." Paul, referring (as all scholars agree) to his own experience, refuting the claims of his opponents to advanced spiritual powers and mystical knowledge, used the imagery of Apocalyptic to describe a mystical vision:

> . . . [about] visions and revelations of the Lord: I know a man in Christ who fourteen years ago was caught up to the third heaven (whether in the body or out of the body I cannot tell; God knows) . . . ; he was caught up into Paradise . . . and heard inexpressable things, which a man may not utter. Of such a man I will boast, but of myself I will not boast, except of my weakness.
>
> (2 Cor. 12.2–5)

The seer, caught up to the highest heaven, perceives divine secrets that may not be communicated; here is something more than the degree of knowledge possessed by all baptized Christians. Some Christian writers of this period distinguish between "faith" and "knowledge," or between "faith only" and "knowledgeable faith." Orthodox "gnōsis," unlike that of the Gnostic "heresies," is continuous with the rule of faith in the sense that it is still knowledge of the "mystery" or "mysteries" of the kingdom and of the fulfillment of scripture, assisted by oral and written apocalyptic traditions. It also involves freedom from the "Passions," the drives that control and pervert human actions; usually it entails a teaching responsibility; and it also includes the cultivation of prayer to obtain a stable condition of unceasing prayer and realization of God's love, and—at least for some—the vision of God that transforms the beholder into the likeness of God through participation in love.

Middle Platonism and Logos Theology

The philosophical movement known as Middle Platonism flourished in the period 100 B.C.–A.D. 200. It was a revival of Platonic philosophy that drew from Plato the idea of the cosmos as a copy of eternal forms, molded by the "demiurge" or Craftsman out of chaotic formless matter. From Aristotle, Middle Platonism derived the idea of a single transcendent God, the Unmoved Mover of the cosmos, the eternal Mind. These ideas were combined by identifying the demiurge with a second divine being who is the mediator between the transcendent God and the cosmos, the "second God" or "Mind," in whom the Platonic forms are contained as ideas. An increasingly positive evaluation of the material world developed among Middle Platonist philosophers, and they and the Stoics became the main supporters of belief in God's providential care for the world.

Philo (30 B.C.-A.D. 50), a leader of the Alexandrian Jewish community, recognized that Middle Platonism, unlike other varieties of Greek philosophy, had important similarities to the Jewish scriptures in its doctrines about God and the world. He set about adapting it to express biblical theology in the setting of Hellenistic culture. The personified Wisdom of Judaism was close enough to the cosmic mediator to allow Philo to accept this feature of Middle Platonism, which he preferred to call Logos. The term means the rational structure of things and was occasionally used by philosophers for the "Second God," but might also mean "word," recalling the creative Word of God of the Jewish scriptures. Like Wisdom, Philo's Logos is a personified power of God, the exact understanding of which is disputed among scholars. Philo also adapted the allegorical method of interpretation, used by Greeks to extract edifying lessons from Homer's epics, to the scriptures and the Jewish liturgy, to find in them a symbolic account of the soul's progress toward the vision of God. After A.D. 70, Philo had little influence within Judaism, but he directly influenced some Christian writers, and his general approach to the theological use of Middle Platonism recurs in Christianity.

The New Testament Christological hymns already present the Redeemer as a sort of cosmic mediator in the creation, and in one case (the prologue of St. John's Gospel) name him "Logos." From about A.D. 150, Christian writers refer the Logos idea to Christ, designating him as the ordering principle of the cosmos and its *telos,* the end to which it is ordered. This Christian Logos theology may conveniently be considered the first stage of Christian Hellenism. It proved to be a valuable beginning, although not a sufficient conceptual structure. The Holy Spirit had no organic place in the Logos idea, and the distinction of persons in the Godhead is affirmed only in relation to the creation, so that one might infer that it depends on the creation at least in an anticipatory way.

The first Christian writers to employ the Logos theology were the so-called "Apologists" (in the etymological sense of "those who reply," not in the modern sense of "apologizers"), writers of the period A.D. 135–180, who addressed the hostile pagan world, defending Christianity against both popular and legal accusations, and criticizing pagan culture from a Christian viewpoint. They were not dealing with internal Christian concerns (as the Apostolic Fathers had done in the period A.D. 90–135), nor were they attempting a complete account of Christian doctrine (no one in the ancient Church did that). For their purposes the Logos doctrine was adequate and useful. Among them were several philosophers who had become Christians, much to the annoyance of some of their colleagues; probably the most important of these was Justin Martyr (about A.D. 100–165), who wrote a defense of Christianity addressed to the Roman government and also a (reconstructed) account of his dialogue with the rabbi Trypho (probably identical with the famous Tarphon mentioned in Jewish sources). Christianity was by now quite separate from Judaism, and the dialogue is a sharp but still basically respectful and friendly discussion between two scholars; in writing it, Justin was probably aiming not only at Jewish debating opponents but also at the Gnostic Marcion, who rejected the Old Testament entirely. The pagan philosopher Celsus wrote an anti-Christian work, *The True Logos,* probably against Justin.

After the time of the Apologists, the Logos doctrine was generally accepted by orthodox writers; its emphasis on creation made it a useful counter to Gnosticism, and two rival theologies that appeared at the beginning of the third century were rejected vigorously. One of these was "adoptionism," the doctrine that Christ was a man adopted by God as his son, which the Ebionites and some Gnostic sects also professed; the other was "modalism," the doctrine that Father, Son, and Holy Spirit are forms of appearance of a single divine person. The rejection of these doctrines expanded the category of "heresy," which had almost been synonymous with Gnosticism, and strengthened orthodox adherence to the Logos doctrine.

Why were modalism and adoptionism so vigorously combatted? The doctrinal disputes of Christian antiquity were primarily about the *identity* of Jesus Christ, whom the Church worshipped, in terms of the distinction between God and creation, absolute and contingent being. Three premises characterize the orthodox position: (1) there is only one God, and he alone is to be worshipped; (2) Jesus Christ is the Son of God and is properly worshipped in the Christian cult; (3) God the Father and God the Son are not simply identical with one another. All three of these are implied already in the New Testament Christological hymns, and the intellectual tension contained in them supplies much of the dynamics for the development of Christian doctrine. Observe here again the primacy of worship in matters of doctrine; the Church's vision of Christ was given in worship, and subsequently defended and described in doctrinal formulations. Adoptionism violated the second of these premises, and modalism the third.

Some Early Christian Theologians

Improvements in the formulation of doctrine were being made. Ireneus (A.D. ca. 140–ca. 200), bishop of Lyons in the later second century, writing against the Gnostics, emphasized the History of Salvation and typology, depicting humankind as free, responsible, and capable of fulfillment only by growth. He balanced the Logos doctrine with a fuller emphasis on three identities in the Godhead, the "Trinity." Clement of Alexandria (ca. A.D. 150–ca. 215) suggested that each nation has a traditional body of genuine wisdom (philosophy, in the case of the Greeks) that is a preparation for Christianity, but is mixed with distortions and falsifications owing to the dominion of death in the Present Age. Origen of Alexandria (A.D. 184–250), the greatest scholar of ancient Christianity, wrote an enormous number of works, including commentaries and notes on every book of the Bible, a comparative edition of the Old

Testament with six versions in parallel columns, books on prayer and martyr-dom, a reply to Celsus' *True Logos,* and several highly original books on philosophy and theology.

Among these last was *On First Principles,* in which he proposed that the world in its original, spiritual form is from eternity; it consisted of a large (but finite) number of absolutely equal and alike spiritual beings, immaterial but in some sense corporeal, who perpetually beheld God. Through some fit of irrationality, they all (except one) turned away from God and separated them-selves from him to a greater or lesser extent, thus introducing variety, and lost their spiritual faculties. The material world was created as a compensation, and the fallen spirits became angels, human beings, and demons. Through a long (but finite) series of world ages, in each of which each spirit is embodied in an appropriate state of being, they are reeducated and gradually led back to their original state. The incarnation of the Logos (in which the one unfallen spirit, united to the Logos, became the soul of Jesus) is the central event in this process. It will culminate in the "Restoration of All Things," and time and materiality will be no more. Unlike the Gnostics, Origen evaluated time and materiality positively, but they were still only of provisional value, and not ultimately included in salvation; humanity as such will not be included in the Restoration of All Things; even the humanity of Jesus is only a stage on the way.

Origen followed the traditional Logos doctrine, even to the point of supposing that the Logos is subordinate in power to the Father, and the Spirit to the Logos ("subordinationism"). But he was able to clarify one aspect of it by insisting explicitly that the "generation" of the Son, and the "procession" of the Holy Spirit, from the Father, are eternal relations described in terms borrowed from temporal processes, rather than processes with a time-sequence. This specification, when divorced from Origen's idea of an eternal creation, was employed by later theologians to clarify the distinction between (1) the origin of the Son and the Holy Spirit within the Godhead and their distinct identities, and (2) the role of the Son and Holy Spirit in the creation, and in the relations of God to the cosmos. Before Origen, the same terms had been used for both, causing confusion in the fourth century, as we shall see.

Origen's theory of an eternal spiritual creation and a provisional, temporal material creation was too foreign to the Church's tradition to be accepted, although it took centuries to work out the problems involved. On the other hand, his spiritual teaching was not entirely consistent with this theory, for its focus of devotion was Jesus, the incarnate Logos. This aspect of his work was accepted and cultivated, especially among monks. Origen's influence is to be seen in the subsequent Christian acceptance of a modified form of the Platonic doctrine of the immortality of the soul.

Origen's contemporary, the pagan philosopher Plotinus, founded a new school of philosophy, Neo-Platonism, that superceded Middle Platonism. It too was based on the idea of the "Great Chain of Being," but emphasized the transcendence of God more than Middle Platonism had done. Increasingly, Neo-Platonism is recognized as a brilliant, but ultimately unsuccessful, attempt to save philosophy from becoming dominated by Christians. It will be discussed more fully in a later chapter.

The Last Roman Persecutions

A severe persecution of Christians in some parts of the Roman empire at the beginning of the third century was followed by a long period of relative peace. In A.D. 235 the empire was plunged into decades of political and economic chaos (the "military anarchy"), but only sporadic persecutions and lynchings occurred until the persecutions of A.D. 250–253 and 257–260, under the emperors Decius and Valerian. These were, for the first time, systematic and empire-wide, designed to eliminate a movement that conflicted with unreserved loyalty to the Empire. In the eyes of these emperors, such loyalty was the duty of all citizens and was needed to save the empire from collapse. The role of the bishops was by this time well understood by the government; a special effort was made to eliminate them. Adherents of a violently anti-Christian neo-Platonic religious movement guided government policies during this decade. The *lapsi* were numerous; a half-century of relative security had preceded, and the Church was off guard. The reaction of the bishops was twofold: they readmitted the lapsi more readily than before, although still under strict conditions; and they made the preparation of candidates for baptism more stringent than ever. After A.D. 260, the persecutions were again abandoned by the government.

The military anarchy lasted until about A.D. 285, when the emperor Diocletian (reigned 284–305) restored stability and organized administration on a new plan, designed for efficiency and orderly transfer of power. This plan did not succeed in preventing a power struggle among Diocletian's successors: a new persecution occurred in the years A.D. 303–313, slackly enforced in the western provinces but exceptionally cruel and thorough in the eastern part of the empire.

The situation changed dramatically when Constantine, one of the contenders for power, turned to Christianity in A.D. 312, on the eve of a victory that made him emperor in the western half of the Empire (he was sole emperor from A.D. 324). He assured the Church not only toleration but favor. Thus began an era in the history of Christianity that was to last from the fourth century to the twentieth. Constantine and his successors were quite sincere in their profession of religion; they felt responsible for the unity and welfare of the Church, and they expected the blessing of strength and prosperity for the empire that turned to the worship of the true God. The Apologists and their successors had called upon the Roman government to cease persecution in the name of justice; thanks to Constantine, the request was granted.

Christian Worship in the First Three Centuries

As they were excluded from the synagogues, the Christians began to hold their own synagogue services, celebrated at sunrise and in the evening, and composed of readings from scripture, psalms, hymns, and prayers. These were in principle daily services, sanctifying the rhythm of the day, although not necessarily actually observed every day. The sacramental meal of bread and wine, the Eucharist, originally celebrated in the context of a complete sacred meal, was detached from this setting, associated with a service of readings on the synagogue model, and celebrated chiefly on Sundays in the morning. The Eucharist was a memorial of the death and resurrection of Jesus and an anticipation of the Age to Come, an eschatological reality already present; Sunday, the first day of the week, was also the eighth day, the symbol of the New Age, just as the seven-day week, ending on the Sabbath (Saturday), symbolized the creation and the Present Age under the aspect of creation. Wednesday and Friday were generally kept as fasts by the Christians, and marked with special services. Easter and Pentecost were carried over from the Jewish calendar, but in most provinces always kept on a Sunday by Christians. On these days only were new Christians baptized (except for the seriously ill, who might be baptized "out of season"), anointed, and for the first time allowed to participate in the Eucharist. Only baptized Christians could attend services of worship; candidates for baptism could be present for readings from scripture, but had to leave afterwards.

Prayers from this period have been quoted above (pp. 45–46). Several hymns serve to show the importance of the Cosmic Liturgy motif. One is quoted in Justin's *Dialog with Trypho*:

> Come together, O ye nations, and let us glorify God,
> for he hath looked upon us also;
> let us glorify him through the King of Glory,
> through the Lord of Hosts,
> for he hath been gracious to the nations also
> and our sacrifices [hath he received from our hand].
>
> (Dial. 29.1)

A hymn fragment of the third century, from an Egyptian papyrus, is the oldest known Christian hymn with musical notation. Its text, with missing words supplied by conjecture, runs as follows:

> May none of [the works of God's hand]
> be silent [by night or day],
> the light-bearing stars, [the high mountains,
> the deep seas], the roaring rivers,
> may they all join as we sing hymns
> to Father, Son, and Holy Spirit;

may all the powers [of heaven
    and hosts of angels] respond: Amen, amen,
power and praise, [glory and thanksgiving],
    to the giver of all good. Amen, amen.

An evening hymn of the third century or earlier, still in use:

Joyful light of the holy glory
    of the immortal Father,
heavenly, holy, blessed,
    O Jesus Christ.

Having come to the setting of the sun
    and seeing the evening light,
we sing to God,
    Father, Son, and Holy Spirit.

Worthy art thou at all times
    to be hymned with thankful voices,
O Son of God, who givest life;
    therefore doth the world glorify thee.

This hymn was sung at the evening service, in connection with the lighting of
an oil lamp and the recitation of a prayer of thanksgiving over it.

7

The Church and the Christian Empire

The Fourth-century Dispute about the Trinity

Origen's version of Logos theology was influential, especially in the eastern provinces of the empire, but his idea of an eternal world of spirits was too atypical of Christian tradition to be widely accepted. Arius (A.D. 256–336), a prominent presbyter of Alexandria, drew on Origen's subordinationism and also on an overliteral understanding of the old tradition that applied to Christ the Old Testament title "Angel of the Lord" or "Angel of the Great Counsel"; he held that God created out of nothing (1) the Logos or Son of God, and (2) through the Logos, the cosmos, or "all things." This created Logos was incarnate as Christ; he was not a mere man, but the first-created and greatest of angels. Arius could interpret, sometimes rather convincingly, the language of the New Testament and the Logos theologians.

A controversy over this teaching (soon called "Arianism") broke out in Egypt and Syria about A.D. 320. Alexander, bishop of Alexandria from ca. 313 to 328, rejected it entirely: the Logos, possessing with the Father eternal being and worshipped in the Church, cannot be a creature, even a very special one. But other bishops, followers of Origen's subordinationism, without entirely endorsing Arianism, defended Arius against Alexander. Constantine convoked a council of over three hundred bishops from all over the empire, at Nicea (in Asia Minor) in A.D. 325, to deal with this and other problems. One of the defenders of Arius, Eusebius (A.D. 263–339), bishop of Caesarea in Palestine, proposed a settlement in terms of the traditional baptismal creeds, knowing that Arius could interpret them in his own sense. The council did adopt such a creed as the standard of teaching in the Church, but only after adding to it several phrases that Arius could not accept, most importantly describing the Logos as "of the same being" (in Greek, *homo-ousios*) as the Father. All but two of the bishops subscribed (some reluctantly); Arius refused and was deposed.

Arianism and Political Theory. At first, Constantine was pleased at the degree of unity achieved. But Eusebius, a friend of Constantine's, pointed out some political implications. For Eusebius, the emperor's acceptance of Christianity and his restoration of political unity and order were part of the History of Salvation: the Logos was acting through Constantine, who embodies Christ's kingship and inaugurates a golden age on earth, an age of "realized eschatology." A subordinationist or Arian view of Christ lessened the distance between Christ and emperor, allowing more scope for such claims. Constantine turned against the Nicene settlement; his son Constantius espoused a form of Arianism.

59

So it came about that Church and Christian emperor were soon at odds. Could the emperor, having accepted Christianity, determine its doctrinal content in the way most favorable to his own interests?

Eusebius of Caesarea represents one possibility. He was a noted scholar; he compiled the first history of the Christian Church, a famous work invaluable for its extensive quotations from otherwise lost sources. He was the author of an unreliable, propagandistic account of Constantine's conversion; an account of the recent persecution in Palestine; and refutations of Neo-Platonist and Jewish attacks on Christianity, in which he develops an unhistorical distinction between Hebrews (the Old Testament saints) and Jews (the iniquitous race that rejected Christ), setting the stage for later anti-Jewish and eventually anti-Semitic attitudes, not based on any real knowledge of Judaism.

Monasticism.   Eschatological tension with the Present Age almost vanished in Eusebius. But how could it be maintained when the Church was suddenly made part of the establishment? The Church of the martyrs had been an eschatological countercultural community; what was the Church of the Christian Roman empire to be? Unable to prevent a lowering of standards, a degree of compromise, when Christianity became a safe and even advantageous religion for Roman citizens, the Church had several means of safeguarding her integrity. The three defenses against Gnosticism (scripture, the bishopric, and the rule of faith) continued to serve this purpose—the Gnostic movement was on the decline, except for the followers of the Chaldean Gnostic teacher Mani (A.D. 216–276), whose teachings had spread from the Persian to the Roman Empire.

The defense against gnosticism was reinforced by a new development of asceticism, originating among the peasants of Syria and Egypt. Ascetics and consecrated virgins had existed in the Church from the earliest times. Having its prehistory in sectarian Judaism, this form of religious life offered freedom from the cares that bind one to self-interest and to the standard of the Present Age: the ascetic strove for complete freedom from "passions" and free self-consecration according to the standards of the Age to Come. In the later third and early fourth centuries, Christian hermits living solitary lives in the wilderness came to the attention of Christians in "the world" and their example was followed by many; at the same time, monastic communities appeared, allowing the eschatological life to be lived in common. Minimizing needs, simplifying life as far as possible, the hermits and monks centered their lives around the reading of the Scriptures and ceaseless meditation and prayer inspired by it. The large numbers of Christians who were dissatisfied with the comfortable conditions and laxity that was inevitable after Constantine were strongly attracted by this form of life. Charismatic leadership, which had been exercised largely by the martyrs, passed now to the hermits and monks. It is not surprising that in the provinces where monasticism was strongest—Egypt in particular—monks played an important role in resisting the government's efforts to impose Arian doctrine.

Modalism Again. In addition to imperial support, Arianism gained another important advantage when an anti-Arian bishop in Asia Minor, Marcellus of Ancyra (died about A.D. 374) published a work in A.D. 334 claiming the support of the Council of Nicea and its creed for a refined form of modalism combined with a "two-stage" Logos theory: the unitary God emanates forth his Logos-power for the purpose of creating; the Logos becomes the Son in the incarnation, and before his ascension breathes forth the Holy Spirit; but Logos and Spirit remain only powers of the divine Monad, which expands into a Dyad and a Triad without a differentiation of identities; at the end of history, Logos and Spirit will be reabsorbed into the divine Monad. Adherents of the traditional Logos theology were totally opposed to any form of modalism, which they thought was a greater danger than Arianism; they became suspicious of the Council of Nicea.

The Arian Controversy: First Phase. Athanasius (A.D. 295–373), Alexander's successor as bishop of Alexandria, became the leader of those who resisted the emperors and held to the Council of Nicea; the bishops of Rome consistently upheld the Council in the West. Constantine fell increasingly under the influence of Eusebius, and in A.D. 335 Athanasius was sent into exile for the first time (he was banished from Alexandria five times during the controversy). From about this time the Christians were divided into two fronts, an anti-modalist front that included the Arians dominated in the eastern provinces, and an anti-Arian front that included Marcellus and his followers dominated in the West. Neither front had much real unity, but the issues were not yet sufficiently clarified to permit a more adequate alignment. Many inconclusive councils met and issued creeds of their own. The term *homo-ousios* was replaced in some of these creeds by the vaguer terms *homoi-ousios* ("of like being") or just *homoios* ("like") to describe the relation of the Logos to the Father. The emperors of the period wanted unity and favored vague formulations, sometimes trying to forbid discussion of the issues.

The Arian Controversy: Second Phase. The artificial alignment of the two fronts began to break up in the 350s when followers of Marcellus produced such explicitly modalist statements that the anti-Arian leaders repudiated them, and extreme Arians, insisting that the Son is anomoios ("unlike" the Father) awakened the antimodalist front to the Arian danger. The supporters of the formula "of like being" (*homoi-ousios*) began to work for an alliance with Athanasius in a center opposed to modalism and Arianism both; this movement was crushed by a pro-Arian emperor, but the supporters of the homoios formula (the Son is "like" the Father) came under the leadership of a remarkable group of bishops in Asia Minor, the "Cappadocian Fathers," who interpreted the formula to mean "like the Father in all things," and agreed to Athanasius that this was just another way of stating what the Council of Nicea meant.

The Cappadocians' Theology of the Trinity. The Cappadocians were able to do this because they interpreted the Council of Nicea in an unmistakably antimodalist way, beginning with a real distinction among the identities of Father, Son, and Holy Spirit. Although there are really three identities, one does not speak of "three gods," they held, because the three persons share entirely in all actions, being one in will and power, and do not distribute the divine *ousia* or being as a generic category (as in the case of human beings sharing a common humanity). The distinctions of identity refer only to the relations of origin designated by the names Father, Son, and Holy Spirit; the Son and the Spirit, originating eternally from the Father, are distinct from him, but never separated from him. In the Incarnation, all three persons participated in their common will and power, and the Son alone was incarnate by identity.

The Holy Spirit received specific attention only when a small faction accepted the uncreated and divine being of the Son, but not that of the Spirit. The Cappadocians, aware that Scripture contains no explicit exposition of the doctrine of the Trinity, observed that according to the New Testament (especially the Gospel of John), the Son is the image of the Father, and reveals the Father; so too the Spirit is the image of the Son and reveals the Son; however, the Spirit is not revealed by any other identity, but remains, in the present Age, an eschatological mystery. It is the Spirit who brings the Church to participate in the saving acts of Christ, and who makes eschatological realities present already in this age—who, in Paul's term, is the "down payment" (not "guarantee" as translations of the New Testament have it) of the Age to Come. The tradition of worship of the Church, from which doctrine arises, is guided by the Spirit as God and recognized the Spirit as God, for example in the biblical baptismal formula (Matt. 28.19) and the ancient hymn *Joyful Light* (see above, p. 58).

The Trinitarian Victory. Arianism collapsed rapidly after the death of the last Arian emperor in A.D. 378 (except among the German barbarian tribes that had recently been converted to Christianity by a moderate Arian missionary, and retained this doctrine for several centuries). The great majority of Christians accepted the formulations of Athanasius and the Cappadocians, and the doctrine of the Trinity as sketched above was affirmed in a revised version of the Nicene Creed at a council in Constantinople (A.D. 381). This is what is usually called the Nicene Creed.

Constantinopolitan

The Nicene Creed. The Nicene Creed, a classic Christian text, deserves some attention.

> We believe in one God the Father almighty,
>   maker of heaven and earth,
>   and of all things visible and invisible;
> and in one Lord Jesus Christ,
>   the only-begotten Son of God,
>   begotten of the Father before all ages,

(God from God); Light from Light; true God from true God
begotten, not made,
[who is] of one substance (homo-ousios) with the Father,
[and] through whom all things were made;
who for us men, and for our salvation, came down from heaven,
and was incarnate by the Holy Spirit of the Virgin Mary,
and was made man;
and was crucified also for us under Pontius Pilate;
he suffered and was buried;
and the third day he rose again
in accordance with the Scriptures,
and ascended into heaven,
and is seated at the right hand of the Father;
and he shall come again, with glory,
to judge both the living and the dead;
[and] his kingdom shall have no end;
and [we believe] in the Holy Spirit, the Lord, the Life-giver,
who proceeds from the Father, [✓]
who with the Father and the Son together
is worshipped and glorified,
who spoke through the Prophets;
and [we believe] in one holy catholic and apostolic Church;
we acknowledge one baptism for the remission of sins;
and we look for the resurrection of the dead,
and the life of the Age to Come.

Amen.

Based on a baptismal creed and revised by the councils of A.D. 325 and 381, this text was soon widely accepted as a uniform baptismal creed, finally supplanting all others except the so-called "Apostle's Creed" (probably a seventh-century revision of the ancient form used in Rome). The baptismal creeds were intimately associated with the rites of initiation into the Church, that is, into participation in the divine-human eschatological life in Christ. As such, they are more than summaries of orthodox Christian belief in propositional form, although they may serve that function also. The creeds are not stated in the form: "I (or we) believe that . . ."; but in the form: "I (or we) believe *in* . . .", in the sense of having faith in, putting trust in, someone (not something), namely, Father, Son, and Holy Spirit. Athanasius and the Cappadocians consistently argued against Arianism on the grounds that God himself is the redeemer who alone can destroy the Ancient Kingdom of Death and restore his creation to participation in his own life, by himself participating in its life, including even the conditions caused by its alienation from him. In either the baptismal or the conciliar context, affirmation of the creed is a participation in the "mystery," the cosmic drama of salvation. *Dogma* is the conceptual outline of the mystery. In its original context, it is the intellectual form or outline of a mystical reality apprehended in worship. The Nicene Creed does not repeat of the Holy Spirit (as it might have done) the terms it applies to the Son (*homo-ousios* and so on), but states that the Spirit is worshipped and glorified together with the Father and the Son, leaving the rest implicit.

Dogma and Knowledge

Since the concept "dogma" is often currently understood as an (arrogant) attempt to define divine realities in terms of philosophical concepts, it is worth stressing that the dogma of the Trinity as defined in the Nicene Creed served an opposite function. The extreme Arians who insisted that the Son is *anomios,* "unlike" the Father, held the belief (widespread in antiquity) that language belongs to the essence of things. They held that God, like other beings, has a name that expresses his essence. To know the essential name of something is to know the essence of the thing. God's essential name is "unbegotten"; since everyone agreed that the Son is begotten, he is not God, is of another essence, is unlike God in being. Against this argument, the Cappadocian Fathers appealed to an old tradition that emphasized the unknowability of God: nothing that can be said or thought about God is adequate to him. Created beings (even angels) cannot know God's essence, not because of a defect in their intellect but because of his utter transcendence and boundlessness. Knowledge of God is not knowledge of his essence, but of the power and activity by which he reveals himself, called in Scripture energy, power, will, authority, rule, kingdom, righteousness, wrath, light, glory, wisdom, reason (logos), spirit, truth, grace, life, love, and so on.

Athanasius had already stressed this distinction against Arius: the creation, the realm of becoming, has to do with the *will* of God which causes it to arise out of nonbeing; the Son is of the very essence of God, the absolute being in which there is no "before and after," known only negatively to created minds (it is not anything that can be thought). The Cappadocians, and after them the entire Eastern Christian tradition, emphasize the distinction: the prophets and martyrs have a vision not of God's essence but of his energies, and this vision (unlike the Platonic vision of forms in God's mind) transcends conceptual knowledge just as it transcends sense perception. It is a participation of the whole man, body as well as mind, in the divine energies, which create in him the capacity to know them; and this is the participation in God's being that is humankind's proper destiny. It is in the context of this attack upon the claim to know God conceptually that the doctrine of the Trinity received its formulation. Therefore, no speculative system was elaborated. The element of paradox or antinomy, for example in the assertion that God is both three and one, remains. It cannot be resolved at the level of conceptualization, for its function is to point to a supraconceptual experience. No less than the Zen *koan,* Christian dogma in this context aims at leading the mind to such an experience. The conceptual framework, like the dramatic imagery of apocalyptic origin, supports and guides it; the dogmas are the landmarks by which it orients itself, without which it would be endlessly misguided and lost. The struggle against Arian rationalism imbued Christian Hellenism, and all of Eastern Christianity down to the present day, with a habitual distrust of grand conceptual systems.

Pentarchy and Papacy

In keeping with the principle of church order already discussed, the bishops of provincial capitals ("metropolitan" bishops) had jurisdiction over the other bishops of the province. The metropolitans, in turn, were under the jurisdiction of "patriarchs," the bishops of the great cities of the empire. In the fifth century, the system took the form of five patriarchates: Rome, Alexandria, Antioch, Constantinople, and (for honorary reasons) Jerusalem. This system is called the "pentarchy."

The ancient Christian referred to his own bishop affectionately as "papa." In the western part of the empire, this came to be understood as an honorary title, borne by the metropolitans. When the provincial capitals were overrun by barbarians, they declined or vanished as ecclesiastical centers, leaving only the bishop of Rome with the title—in English, "pope"—from the sixth or seventh century. In the eastern provinces, on the contrary, the title finally came to be applied to every parish priest.

All agreed that the Pope (in the western sense!) had special authority and leadership, but its character was not defined. In the west (especially in Rome itself), it was felt to belong to the essential structure of the Church, but in the eastern provinces it was thought of more as a historically conditioned convention.

Christian Worship after Constantine

The structure of Christian worship remained basically the same after Constantine as before, but four new factors appeared.

1. Features of court ceremonial were adapted to the services, making them more colorful and impressive.

2. The bishops' prayers had been addressed to God the Father, through the Son, in the Holy Spirit, although hymns and acclamations—and, of course, private prayers—were often addressed directly to Christ. During the Trinitarian controversy, the catholics insisted against the Arians that prayer can be properly addressed to any of the three persons of the Godhead or to the entire Trinity; from this time on, the public prayers of the bishop might take any of these forms, although in Rome the older custom continued to be followed.

3. Jerusalem became an important pilgrimage center. The church of Jerusalem developed the custom of commemorating specific events of the Gospels with annual services, on a fixed day, on the actual or supposed site of the original event. Other churches then adopted this practice, although of course they could not celebrate on the original site. Thus in addition to the few great Christian festivals of the first centuries a number of festivals commemorating specific events came to be celebrated.

4. The monks developed short prayer services for midmorning, noon, midafternoon, bedtime, midnight, and in some places predawn, in addition to the original morning and evening services. They also cultivated the custom of chanting all 150 psalms in order every week (or twice a week, or every day!), and of reading the entire Bible through every year. All of these customs were later adopted, in many areas, by the local churches, although of course only the clergy could participate in so many services; the laity attended much as before.

Church, State, and Society after Constantine

The Arian controversy established the limits of the emperor's power over the Church. He could intervene in doctrinal disputes, and could depose and exile bishops who opposed him; but he could not impose his wishes in respect of doctrine, or interfere with the sacramental life of the Church. The area of social ethics remained more ambiguous. At no time could the Church realize perfectly in all its members the life of selfless love, the eschatological new being for which it strove; but as an illegal countercultural community it could reach a much closer approximation than could be expected of the vast realm that was not embracing Christianity. Monasticism provided for the continuation of the Christian counterculture, but could not include the entire Church.

Christians had brought legal disputes among themselves, not before the (pagan) courts, but before their own bishops (see 1 Cor. 6.1-6). As was natural, the Roman state regularized this situation under Constantine by recognizing the bishops as magistrates, and therefore as state officials. Bishops like Eusebius were willing to go a long way toward tailoring doctrine into a state ideology, but this possibility was closed by the Arian controversy. Other bishops avoided dubious doctrines, but enjoyed moving in high society; and inevitably the Church was drawn into the politics of the empire and came to own a great deal of land.

But it was exactly the leadership of the bishops that prevented the Church from being totally absorbed, both because the structure of orders of bishops, presbyters, deacons, and so on remained distinct from the state bureaucracy due to its sacramental character, and because the great fourth-century bishops, imbued with the independence of the monastic movement, not only defeated Arianism but went on to state without compromise the eschatological social standards that would characterize a truly Christian society—including the disappearance of private property!

The Cappadocians, Ambrose (339-397) in Milan and John Chrysostom (ca. 350-407) in Antioch and Constantinople, are the best known of these fierce defenders of social justice. To their credit, they did not make the typical utopian error of rejecting the imperfect but attainable good in the name of an unrealizable ideal. It was not possible to prevent the empire from moving in the direction of a police state; certainly, it would have been futile to attempt to impose pacifism by denying that the state had the right to defend itself; the "just war" theory that gradually grew up was intended to set limits to the occasions for waging war, and to the means that might be employed in war. Possibly opportunities were lost; for example, no direct and concerted effort was made to eradicate slavery, or the interrogation of political prisoners by torture. What was done in such areas? The freeing of slaves was encouraged, facilitated, and in cases of special need was financed by the Church. A trend toward humanitarian legislation had already appeared under the influence of Stoicism; this was pressed further, and the fourth and following centuries saw a series of legal reforms designated to protect prisoners, slaves, the poor, women, and all the needy and disadvantaged in general. Public and private welfare institutions that cared for orphans, the aged, the sick, and the poor appeared on an impressive scale. The bishops mentioned above were reformers by preference, but employed radical public criticism and confrontation when necessary: John Chrysostom died in exile largely as a result of such protests.

The Suppression of Pagan Worship.   After Christianity became the official religion of the empire (only at the end of the fourth century, not under Constantine), the pagan cult was outlawed; unfortunately for paganism, a usurper who led an uprising against the emperor Theodosius (reigned 379–395) proclaimed himself its champion; when he was defeated in battle, the coercive power of the state was brought into play throughout the empire in favor of Christianity, which was by now the majority religion. To their credit, the Christians did not persecute pagans as the pagan state had persecuted them; the elimination of the civic cult was applauded, but pagans were not forced to participate in Christian worship, nor subjected to the death penalty.

On the whole, the fourth-century transition from counterculture to establishment was neither the glorious triumph that Eusebius had welcomed, nor the fall into corruption that later sectarian theories have made of it, but an inherently ambiguous process through which opportunities and dangers were interwoven.

The Dispute about the Incarnation.   The Nicene Creed does not reject the Logos theology; it does set the doctrine of the Trinity in a context larger than that of cosmology, bringing the transcendence of the Son and Holy Spirit into sharper focus. In answer to the Arian argument that Christ's human characteristics involve finitude and prove that he is a created being, the orthodox emphasized his humanity as a voluntarily assumed condition, not to be read back into his eternal being. The weak Arian argument was bolstered by the view of at least some Arians that the Logos assumed only a human body and simply took the place held in other people by the human soul, and that consequently no human soul was involved in the incarnation.

In Syria, some anti-Arian circles had believed that the human plight is primarily due to the mutability and instability of the mind, and its consequent failure to control passions and pathological imaginations. Two rival views of

Christ developed in these circles. One was that of Apollinaris (ca. 310–ca. 390), who agreed with the Arians that in Christ the Logos fulfills the function performed in others by the human soul, but held the catholic and anti-Arian view that the Logos is fully God. Thus the unstable soul is eliminated, and men and women can attain stability by participating in Christ's humanity. The Cappadocians objected to this, that Christ is not half man and half God but fully God and fully man, and only so the redeemer of the whole man, in whom human nature in all aspects receives the gift of immortality and incorruption. When their teachings were thus rejected, Apollinaris and his followers formed a sectarian church that eventually died out.

But Apollinaris was also opposed by some who agreed with him that the human problem is an unstable mind: Theodore (ca. 351–428), bishop of Mopsuestia, was the most important figure in a movement that was much influenced by the conviction that what is done by nature is necessary, and what is done by will is free. At this point some Arians would have agreed; they had argued that the generation of the Son of God from the Father had to be by will (and so of the same order as the creation of the world), because otherwise it would pertain to the nature of God (as Athanasius held), and would be an involuntary, necessary emanation that the Father could not help. The Cappadocians had replied that God is free both by will and by nature, and that man and woman likewise become free by will and by nature when they participate in the deified humanity of Christ. But Theodore and his followers thought of salvation as attaining an immutable will through moral effort; freedom is essentially freedom from mutability, on this view. Jesus, united to the Logos from the moment of his conception, forms one person with the Logos by a perfect agreement of will, maintained before his death by moral effort, but after the Resurrection by perfect immutability. In spite of his real desire to maintain that there is only "one person" in the Incarnation, Theodore could not avoid a duality of identities, the Logos and Jesus.

Theodore's doctrine of Incarnation did not become controversial until after his death. His follower Nestorius (ca. 380–ca. 450) became bishop of Constantinople in the year of Theodore's death. He soon started a controversy by objecting strongly to a customary title given to the Virgin Mary: *Theotokos* (accent on the third syllable), "she who gave birth to God," more or less equivalent to "Mother of God." Mary, he held, was the mother of the man assumed by the Logos; God the Son cannot be born of a woman any more than God the Father can. The issue came into sharp focus: who was it who was born of the Virgin Mary and died on the Cross?

The Council of Ephesus.   Cyril (?–444), bishop of Alexandria, attacked the views of Nestorius, insisting that there is only one identity in the Incarnation, that of the Logos made flesh, God the Son. From Cyril's point of view, everything that had been successfully defended against the Arians was endangered again by Nestorius: the Nicene Creed attributes both human and divine predicates and actions to a single identity, "one Lord Jesus Christ." At the

Council of Ephesus, the Third Ecumenical Council (A.D. 431), Cyril's teaching was affirmed. Nestorius would not concede, and was deposed and exiled. The followers of Theodore of Mopsuestia later withdrew to Edessa in Mesopotamia, and subsequently to Nisibus, in the Persian Empire; their doctrines became the accepted teaching of the Church of the Persian empire, the "Assyrian" Church or "Ancient Church of the East," also called "Nestorian."

The Council of Chalcedon.   Cyril emphasized the unity of Christ's person: Christ is the Son of God, *homo-ousios* with the Father in his eternal, divine being; and the same Christ is *homo-ousios* with humankind in the humanity he assumed, a full, integral humanity, body and soul. He used a phrase taken from a book thought to be by Athanasius, but in fact written by Apollinaris, to express his doctrine: "the one incarnate nature of God the Logos." But after Cyril died, some of his followers, misunderstanding this phrase, interpreted it to mean that Christ is not consubstantial with human beings. A council called to settle the resulting controversy in A.D. 449 was dominated by Cyril's successor as bishop of Alexandria, Dioscurus, who was not one of the extremist Cyrillians (called "Eutychians" afater their spokesman Eutyches) but did not want their doctrines to be denounced, for political reasons. His rough treatment of their opponents and his high-handed tactics caused another council to be called shortly thereafter, the Council of Chalcedon (A.D. 451), the Fourth Ecumenical Council. Here the *Tome,* a statement of Leo, bishop of Rome from A.D. 440–461, was read; Leo spoke of two *formae* or natures in Christ, each performing the actions proper to it. The majority of bishops at the council were firm supporters of the tradition of Cyril, and at first suspected Leo of "Nestorianism," dividing Christ into two identities. But the Roman legates explained that what Leo wanted to assert by such phrases was the permanent integrity of both the divine being and the human being in Christ; he accepted the title "she who gave birth to God" (in Latin *Dei genitrix*) of the Virgin Mary, and proclaimed that the Son of God was crucified and buried. The bishops then accepted Leo and the *Tome* as being in agreement with Cyril, and drew up a formal declaration including phrases from Leo: "in two natures" and "the properties of each nature being preserved."

> Following the holy fathers,
> > we all with one voice teach that it should be confessed
> that our Lord Jesus Christ is one and the same Son
> > the same perfect in godhead, the same perfect in manhood,
> truly God and truly man,
> > the same [consisting] of a rational soul and a body;
>
> consubstantial (*homo-ousios*) with the Father as to his godhead,
> > and the same consubstantial (*homo-ousios*) with us as to
> > > his manhood
> in all things like unto us,
> > sin only excepted

begotten of the Father before the ages as to his godhead,
    and in the last days, the same
[begotten] of the Virgin Mary, the Theotokos, as to his manhood
    for us and for our salvation;

one and the same Christ, Son, Lord, only begotten,
    made known in two natures
which exist without confusion, without change,
    without division, without separation;

the distinction of the natures having been in no wise taken away
    by reason of the union,
but rather the properties of each nature being preserved
    and both concurring into one person and one hypostasis,

not separated or divided into two persons,
    but one and the same Son and only-begotten,
God the Word, the Lord Jesus Christ,
    even as from of old the prophets have spoken concerning him,
and as the Lord Jesus Christ himself has taught us
    and as the symbol of the Fathers has handed down to us.

This is another classic text of Christianity. It is often denounced today as an example of an extreme Hellenization of Christianity, employing static concepts, especially "nature" in the phrase "in two natures." Such a criticism results from considering the statement out of its context, as an independent formula. The official statement of the Council presents it as a sort of analytic footnote to the Nicene Creed; the "holy fathers" mentioned at the beginning and end of the text are the bishops of the Councils of Nicea and Constantinople, along with those of the Council of Ephesus; the "symbol of the fathers" is the Nicene Creed. Already at this time there was a strong reverence for "the fathers" of the Church. Bishops and teachers were thought of as spiritual fathers from a very early time (see 1 Cor. 4.15). The "Fathers of the Church" are the Christian writers of the ancient world recognized by the Church as contributing to the growth of the Church by holiness of life and orthodoxy of teaching. From the Greek and Latin word for "father," the study of their writings is called "patristics," and the ancient period of Christianity, "the patristic age."

The "two natures" formula, in Christian use, is to be understood in the context of the basic distinction between God and creation, absolute and contingent being. The Chalcedonian formula asserts that the *distinction* remains ("without confusion, without change") even in the most intimate union of the two, the Incarnation, where there can be no thought of *separation* ("without division, without separation"). It specifies the idea of "deification"; in fact, each of these terms should be seen in relation to the other: "two natures" is the stable context or framework of the transformational process "deification."

The Chalcedonian formula thus belongs to the tradition of the New Testament Christological hymns. It includes the eschatological (nonstatic) reference to the Incarnation "in the last days," the omission of which in the Nicene Creed has occasioned some criticism. The unity of Christ's person is asserted by the phrases "one and the same" (repeated three times), "the same" (five times), and "in one person and hypostasis (identity)"; Cyril's insistence on this point is safeguarded and the misinterpretation of it as impairing the humanity of Christ is excluded.

Nestorius hailed the Council of 451 as a vindication of his views. Some of his former associates had avoided his fate, but continued to reject Cyril's conviction that it was none other than God the Son who was crucified, and were regarded by many as Nestorians; they obtained approval from the council. Therefore many of Cyril's followers rejected the Council and its formula, and insisted on speaking of "one nature" (which they understood as synonymous with "one identity") in Christ. This party came to be called "monophysite" (from the Greek for "one nature"); it continues at present in the Coptic Church of Egypt, the Church of Ethiopia, the "Jacobite" Church of Syria, and the Apostolic Church of Armenia. The followers of Theodore of Mopsuestia and the monophysites both regarded the Council of 451 as favoring the views of Theodore, and the latter party rejected it for that reason.

"Neo-Chalcedonianism." Another interpretation existed, which took more seriously the council's adherence to Cyril; this has recently come to be called "neo-Chalcedonianism" (often with pejorative intent, by historians who favor Theodore's views); an older term is "theo-paschitism," the doctrine that God has suffered as man, that the "one hypostasis" of the Chalcedonian definition is the identity of the second person of the Trinity, God the Son, who is the one and only subject of all the actions described in the second article of the Nicene Creed. "Neo-Chalcedonianism" ultimately prevailed in the eastern Roman empire, and it may reasonably be regarded as the culmination of Christian Hellenism.

The Imperial Dilemma

In the fifth century, the western half of the Roman empire collapsed under the pressure of invading barbarians, mostly Germanic tribes who were Christians, but could not be integrated into the framework of the empire because they were Arians. The Church of Rome was firmly committed to the council of Chalcedon, and remained strong when the empire collapsed in Italy. The emperors had to rely on their eastern provinces, but in these, especially in Egypt and Syria, monophysitism was strong; and in addition Christianity, with its universalist perspective, had served as the catalyst for a renascence of national culture and national consciousness. The emperors were in an unenviable position between supporters and enemies of the "two natures" formula.

Early in the sixth century, an additional difficulty appeared, or reappeared. Evagrius of Pontus (345-399) had developed and systematized the
teachings of Origen. His methodical presentation of prayer and means of
spiritual progress was both ardent and orderly; it had wide appeal, especially
in the monasteries. But along with it went Origen's teachings about the two
creations, and all the elements of his thought that were proving themselves
unacceptable to the Church, in a new and even more intense form: Christ, for
Evagrius, is not the Logos incarnate, but the one unfallen created spirit, united
to the Logos by perfect knowledge. This Christ presided over the second,
material creation, and voluntarily became incarnate; but only the soul, the
spiritual part of man and woman, is in God's image, and at the end of time
the material creation will vanish and all the spiritual created beings will be
restored to equality with Christ. Evagrius insisted that prayer ought to be pure
and without forms or images. What does this mean? Orthodox monks accepted
it in the sense that the vision of God is beyond concept—the energies of God
are not Platonic forms or ideas. But Evagrius, it seems, meant not only this;
because the body is only second best and destined to vanish, the spiritually
advanced no longer need the Incarnation; their spiritual life is no longer formed
by the History of Salvation.

In Egypt, these views caused a controversy among the monks. They were
vigorously opposed by those who, seeing the world in terms of Cosmic Liturgy,
had a positive attitude toward bodily and material existence, and toward the
world of nature. The hermit, Aphu "the Antelope," so-called because he lived
with a herd of antelope in the wilderness during the week and served as bishop
of a village on Saturdays and Sundays only, travelled to Alexandria to attack
the ideas of Evagrius before the bishop there. Aphu's views finally prevailed
in Egypt, but Evagrius remained influential, and in the early sixth century his
teachings were stirring up a major controversy among the monks in Palestine.

The Age of Justinian.   The Neo-Chalcedonian theologians had two major
tasks to accomplish: first, they had to vindicate the faithfulness of the Council
of Chalcedon to the teachings of Cyril (and if possible to convince the monophysites of it); and second, they had to assess the heritage of Origen, assimilating the valuable elements and isolating the dangerous ones.

The east-Roman emperor Justinian (reigned 527-565) felt a great responsibility for maintaining the unity both of the Church and of the Roman empire;
he thought of them as forming a single community under the guidance of two
harmonious, divinely ordained institutions, the imperial power and the priesthood. Justinian's accomplishments include a (short-lived) restoration of Roman
rule in Africa and Italy, a major legal reform with emphasis on social justice
and welfare, reorganizations of the government, and an ambitious building
program that initiated what is called "Byzantine architecture" and produced
the great Church of the Holy Wisdom (Agia Sophia) in Constantinople, a
marvel of architecture.

Agia Sophia. The minarets were added after the Turkish conquest of 1453, when the church was converted into a mosque.

Justinian came to support the Neo-Chalcedonians, and attempted to gain the approval of both the Church of Rome and the monophysites as a means of securing unity. He also took steps to have the teachings of Evagrius condemned as heresy, and eventually hit on the questionable policy of condemning troublesome figures as heretics after their death. He called a council at Constantinople in 553, and persuaded the bishops to condemn Origen and Evagrius; he then induced them to condemn Theodore of Mopsuestia, and secured the reluctant agreement of the pope of Rome by coercion. The positive achievement of this council was its approval of the Neo-Chalcedonian insistence that the "one person and identity" of the Chalcedonian formula was none other than the identity of the Logos and Son of God, the second person of the Trinity: "one of the Trinity has suffered in the flesh," as the contemporary slogan expressed it.

But the monophysites refused to be convinced. They were divided internally; extremists who thought of Christ's humanity as having been transformed into something utterly unlike that of human beings in general were struggling with moderates who fully accepted its being *homo-ousios* with the humanity of others. Justinian tried conciliation, then coercion, and at the end of his life compromise, but nothing availed to commend Chalcedon to the monophysites. Unintentionally, his interventions did assist the moderate monophysites against the extremists; and from that time on the Chalcedonian Eastern Orthodox and the monophysites, formally separated, have been theologically very close to one another. Both accept and use a hymn composed during this period (according to the Chalcedonians, by Justinian himself) that expresses the vision shared by moderate monophysites and neo-Chalcedonians:

> Only-begotten Son and Word of God,
>   who art immortal,
> and who, for our salvation, didst will
>   to become incarnate of the Holy Theotokos
>   and ever-virgin Mary,
> and without change didst become man;
> thou wert crucified, O Christ our God,
>   trampling down Death by death:
> thou who art one of the Holy Trinity,
>   glorified together with the Father and the Holy Spirit;
> save us.

The Chalcedonians accepted the Council of 553, the Second Council of Constantinople, as the Fifth Ecumenical Council.

The Later Disputes about the Incarnation. Justinian's failure to reunite monophysites and Chalcedonians led to a new effort by several seventh-century emperors, based on the assertion that there is in Christ, the incarnate Logos, only one energy, or, in a revised formulation, only one will. This was not formally contrary to anything previously set forth by Chalcedon or the other ecumenical councils. It could therefore (its promoters hoped) be accepted by Chalcedonians, and could also make Chalcedon palatable to monophysites by emptying the distinction of natures of any important content; and, at one stroke, appeal to the Assyrians as well, since it seemed to define Christ's unity as a unity of will—as they had always thought!

The great opponent of this doctrine was Maximus the Confessor (580–662), a layman and monk, who pointed to the traditional teaching that Christ must be fully man to be the redeemer of the whole man. Therefore, he held, Christ must have not only a divine but also a human energy and will. His opponents implied that two wills means opposed wills, the division of mind and heart that the traditional spiritual discipline aimed to eliminate—in the Son of God! Maximus responded that Christ's human will was in perfect agreement with the divine, being free of that indecision and wavering that characterizes human nature, not in its essence, but as it exists enslaved by Death.

Maximus drew together all the great themes of Christian theology: History of Salvation, Cosmic Liturgy (the phrase is borrowed from the title of a modern book on Maximus), and deification in the sense of the salvation and fulfillment of the creation by its participation in God. In the Present Age, diversity, time, and space divide created beings from God and from each other; when participation in God is restored, these factors do not disappear, but cease to separate. Man, as a synthesis of intellect and body, is a microcosm; at creation, he was given the task of securing unity in the cosmos, with its diversity. With the fall, he failed, and the five essential distinctions in the cosmos—male/female; paradise/inhabited earth; heaven/earth; material creation/intelligible creation; and God/creation—all became separations, divisions, oppositions. Christ, the incarnate Son of God, "recapitulates" human history, and becomes himself the mediator who restores cosmic unity and participation.

Maximus proposed a correction of Origen's doctrine of the Restoration of All Things, from the perspective of Neo-Chalcedonianism: there will be an eschatological restoration of *nature,* including human nature; the divine glory will be revealed to the entire cosmos; but the revelation will not be received uniformly, but will be determined by *will.* Those who are conformed to the divine life of selfless love, the way of Life, will experience it as grace, light, and life; but those who choose the way of death cannot participate in it, but experience it against their will as "wrath"; and it is this experience to which apocalyptic imagery refers in speaking of the fires of hell and of the "outer darkness."

Maximus underwent gruesome tortures for refusing to accept the "one will" doctrine. But at the Third Council of Constantinople, A.D. 680–681 (The Sixth Ecumenical Council), he was vindicated, and the "one energy" and "one will" doctrine rejected. The monophysites, of course, were not involved in this council and never recognized it.

The Rise of Islam.   During the seventh century, a force both political and religious appeared in the world, the dynamic, aggressive community of Islam. Within a few decades of its birth, it became an empire. Roman rule in Egypt, Syria, and Palestine, lacking support from the indigenous population, crumbled before it. Shortly all of North Africa, and then Spain, were brought within its domain; the Persian empire was totally overthrown by it; Constantinople itself was besieged. The old Mediterranean-centered Christian world vanished forever, and in the following centuries Christianity itself died out altogether in North Africa (except for Egypt), and was reduced to minority status in Egypt and Syria. Three of the five great patriarchates, Alexandria, Antioch, and Jerusalem, were henceforth (except for brief interludes) under the Muslim government, as were the centers of Syrian and Egyptian monophysitism and of the Assyrians.

John of Damascus (ca. 675–750), a monk living in Muslim-ruled Syria, summarized the mature synthesis of Christian Hellenism in *The Fountain of Knowledge,* the nearest approximation to a "handbook of doctrine" produced by ancient Christianity. It has annoyed modern scholarly readers: because it emphasizes technicalities and precise definitions, it lacks systematic structure, and omits such central issues as the doctrine of salvation. The reader will by now recognize that these characteristics are normal in Christian Hellenism: the vision of salvation is the motive for discussing Trinity and Incarnation, but does not itself receive extensive examination; concepts are elaborated and defined, in great detail if necessary, but they are supposed to eventuate not in a system but in a transconceptual experience. John of Damascus provided the classic exposition of "hypostasis" as involving two aspects, existence and identity. The humanity of Jesus exists, not in an identity of its own, but only in the identity of the Logos.

The Icons.   John of Damascus was also the outstanding theologian of the "Iconoclastic Controversy." Christians had always made use of wall paintings, at first of Christ under the form of the shepherd or the teacher, along with biblical events interpreted as referring to Baptism and the Eucharist and various symbols; after the time of Constantine, a characteristic art style was developed, combining Hellenistic naturalism with the sacral formalism of the eastern provinces. By the sixth century, the interiors of churches were lavishly adorned with breathtaking mosaics, and panel paintings of Christ and the saints were used for devotional purposes, as "windows" through which Christians could communicate with the heavenly world.

For a variety of cultural, political, and religious reasons, the government of the eastern Roman empire attempted to prohibit use of such images in the period A.D. 725–780 and 813–843, substituting the use of symbols (for which there was a long Christian tradition). A variety of arguments were employed on both sides, but the theological impulse behind "iconoclasm" (Greek for "image-breaking," the standard term for the attempted prohibition) seems to have been a conviction that Christ and the saints should not be depicted in human form, especially not for purposes of religious contemplation, because in salvation human nature is transformed beyond recognition. Here we encounter again the influence of Origen and Evagrius.

John of Damascus provided the necessary defense of the icons, distinguishing between *worship,* which is reserved for God alone (but is rightly given to Christ in his humanity, because of the unity of person), and *veneration,* which may be given to the saints, in whom God's image is restored and revealed, and to material objects that depict or represent the Incarnation: icons, the cross, the book of the Gospels, and so on. Neo-Chalcedonianism, far from denigrating the humanity of Christ, emphasized the traditional insistence on its integral and complete character as the basis of human participation in the life of God.

The Second Council of Nicea of A.D. 787 (Seventh Ecumenical Council) endorsed this defense of the icons, marking the maturation of the neo-Chalcedonian phase of Christian Hellenism.

Subsequently, the icons were thoroughly integrated into the Church's liturgy in the East Roman empire, although not in the West. The true icon, which may properly receive veneration (the phrase "image-worship," still frequently used for such veneration, ignores the careful distinction referred to above), follows with great strictness an archetype that in some cases is regarded as being of miraculous origin. The iconpainter must prepare himself by prayer and fasting; only certain kinds of paints are allowed; and the finished icon, especially if it is to be used in a church, is consecrated with special prayers by a priest. Only rarely does a new icon-type arise. Icons cannot be governed by fashions in style or by individual preferences, because they must channel the devotional life of the Church.

These observations about icons suggest a further step in the understanding of dogma, especially of the immutable character it possesses once it has risen to expression. A dogma is an icon in concepts. It faithfully reproduces its archetype in order to make it present to the worshipper.

III

THE MEDIEVAL STRUGGLE
FOR A CHRISTIAN SOCIETY

8
The "Dark Ages"

The western part of the Roman empire collapsed during the fifth century; it was overrun by tribes of barbarians who spoke Germanic dialects and who had been converted to a moderate form of Arian Christianity during the fourth century. The resulting "dark ages" lasted for several centuries, until the situation stabilized as the barbarians settled and gradually abandoned Arianism for Catholic Christianity.

During these "dark ages," the eastern provinces of the empire held off the barbarians and remained essentially intact. But in the early seventh century the eastern empire experienced its own "dark ages." Syria and Egypt, where both nationalism and monophysitism had alienated much of the population from the empire, were overrun by an invasion from the Persian empire; the Balkan peninsula was invaded by pagan tribes of Slavs and Avars. Unlike the barbarians in the west, however, those in the east could not capture the important cities. So the empire survived, and through clever diplomacy and military reform regained most of the lost territory.

A more permanent blow to both east and west came with the appearance of the Muslim Arabs, who in the seventh century conquered Syria and Egypt, and also North Africa, formerly part of the western Roman empire. They also destroyed and supplanted the Zoroastrian Persian empire. In the eighth century, the wave of Arab conquest continued through Spain and into what is now southern France, and in the east penetrated to the very walls of Constantinople. Decisive defeats were finally inflicted upon the Arabs in the east (at Constantinople) in 717 and in the west (at Tours) in 732, but the southern and eastern coasts of the Mediterranean were left in Muslim hands.

The Franks, who defeated the Arabs in the west, were a Germanic tribe that had been converted to Catholic (not Arian) Christianity at the beginning of the sixth century. They were able to consolidate and reorganize much of the former western Roman empire in the later eighth and early ninth centuries, coming into conflict with the eastern empire ("Byzantine empire," as it is now called), which was still large and powerful, and which had more internal unity after the loss of Egypt and Syria.

These tumultuous events profoundly affected the lives of all Christians, establishing very different political and cultural circumstances for most of them. It is usual for books and college courses on church history to deal only with the Christians of western Europe, with perhaps a minimum of reference to the "Byzantine" or east Roman empire, in covering the medieval period. This is understandable, but a bit misleading: the plurality of Christian cultures in the middle ages is badly underestimated. Divided by the Christological controversies, all of these various Christian cultures shared common roots in apocalyptic symbolism and in Christian Hellenism.

The "Assyrian" Church

The "Assyrian" church of the Persian empire, officially Nestorian in doctrine, was fiercely persecuted by some of the Persian rulers. Muslim conquest brought more favorable conditions at first, for on principle the Muslims tolerated Judaism, Christianity, and some forms of Zoroastrianism. Assyrian scholars at Nisibus translated Greek philosophical works into Syriac, and from Syriac into Arabic, giving rise to Arab philosophy and philosophical theology. Although they were sometimes persecuted by the Muslims also, the Assyrians flourished for some six centuries, sending Syriac-speaking monks to India, Central Asia, and China. These missionaries were remarkably successful in adapting their presentation of the Christian Gospel, without distorting it, to indigenous cultural forms.

In Kerala, on the Malabar coast of India, Syrian missionaries established a Christian community some time before the sixth century. It struck deep roots and exists down to the present day, although (like the Jain and Sikh communities) its spread was limited by the encapsulating power of the Hindu caste system.

In Central Asia, various tribes accepted Christianity as a result of Assyrian missions. The Central Asian churches were destroyed at the end of the middle ages.

In China, the Assyrians made extensive use of Taoist, Confucian, and Buddhist traditions. At first, they had considerable success. But contact with Persia was difficult and often impossible: after a time, some writings indicate, Christianity was threatened with absorption into popular Chinese religion. Whether the Assyrians would have averted this danger is unknown, for persecutions instigated by rival Taoist and Buddhist factions caused the Chinese church to disappear after about A.D. 900.

The "Monophysite" Churches

The so-called "monophysites," who rejected the Council of Chalcedon, were mostly under Arab rule after the seventh century. The Coptic Christians in

Egypt and the Jacobite Christians in Syria and Mesopotamia experienced alternations of fortune, and were gradually reduced to minority status, but they continued to produce outstanding writers, scholars, and architects through the middle ages. Their literature has not yet been studied adequately.

The Armenian Apostolic Church, established as the national religion at the beginning of the fourth century, suffered from Arab and Greek imperialism, but nevertheless developed a flourishing national school of art and architecture—it has been claimed that some basic features of Byzantine and western architecture are of Armenian origin—and of literature, represented by the devotional poetry of Gregory of Narek (ca. 945–ca. 1010).

In Nubia (modern Sudan), Egyptian missionaries converted the local kingdoms to Christianity probably in the sixth century. The churches there flourished through most of the middle ages, but in the end they vanished and the country became almost entirely Muslim.

Ethiopia, never a part of the Roman empire, had accepted Christianity in the fourth century. Dependent upon Egypt for its *abuna* (patriarch), Ethiopia was otherwise largely isolated from 650 until 1270, and often threatened by Muslim and pagan invaders. Here a remarkable Christian culture, with many Judaic and African elements, developed. A unique kind of ritual dance by priests and cantors enhances festival worship down to the present. Church architecture developed remarkably (the Ka^cbah at Mecca owes its present form to a reconstruction in A.D. 608 by an Ethiopian architect); the most striking examples are the monolithic churches of Lalibela, carved out of solid granite (?ca. 1200). After 1270, the ancient dynasty, claiming descent from King Solomon, returned to power; in the fourteenth century, the national epic, the *Kebra Nagast* ("Glory of Kings") was composed. "The *Kebra Nagast* is not merely a literary work, but—as the Old Testament to the Hebrews or the Koran to the Arabs—it is the repository of Ethiopian national and religious feelings, perhaps the truest and most genuine expression of Abyssinian Christianity."*

Other Christian Communities

A community of Syrian Christians who probably originated in connection with the "monothelite" Christology of the seventh century, the Maronites withdrew to the remote Lebanon mountains to escape the wars between the Arabs and Byzantines. During the Crusades, they accepted papal leadership, keeping most of their indigenous Syrian culture.

Some mention should be made of the Georgians, although, as Chalcedonians, they came to accept in large measure the religious culture of Constantinople. Like the Armenians, they are a nation in the Caucasus Mountains who went over to Christianity at the beginning of the fourth century. Their culture retained distinctive elements, for example in music and architecture, while accepting Byzantine models for painting and forms of worship.

---

*Edward Ullendorff, *The Ethiopians* (London: Oxford University Press, 1960), p. 144.

The Plurality of Christian Cultures

All these communities developed their national cultures in conjunction with their respective churches, which came to embody their ethnic identity to a remarkable degree. Visual arts, architecture, and crafts primarily served the needs of worship. Literature and music were likewise developed primarily within the life of the church. Beginning with the later middle ages, most of these communities suffered persecution and impoverishment, and were deprived of educated leadership; some of them also suffered great numerical loss. Therefore, in modern times, they have often been regarded (also by Western Christians) as unimportant little remnant groups of superstitious peasants. In the earlier middle ages, when such a description might have seemed to many to fit western Europeans, the various Christian ethnic communities of Asia and Africa were intellectually and culturally second to none in the world.

At the center of the life of Christian communities was worship. Its basic patterns and elements have been described in the preceding chapters; the Christian of the middle ages followed the traditions established in antiquity, with some additions and with some amount of distortion. These patterns everywhere included life-cycle rites such as baptism (infant baptism being normal in the middle ages), marriage, and burial, and calendrical rites including a daily cycle, a weekly cycle (sometimes elaborated with cycles of two or eight weeks), and yearly cycles regulated by the moon (the movable feasts, Easter being the chief) and by the sun (the fixed feasts such as Christmas or saints' anniversaries). The basic outline of the services was also much the same everywhere. But in the choice of scriptural lessons to be read, in the prayers, and in the hymns, there was much divergence from country to country and from province to province. Only gradually during the middle ages did the majority of Latin Christians abandon their own liturgical forms for those of the city of Rome, and the eastern Chalcedonians likewise replace other local traditions by those of Constantinople. The other communities described above, however, retained their national rites, which were an essential element in their ethnic identity.

Another universal feature of medieval Christianity was the leading role of monks in the churches and, to a considerable extent, in society in general. Thus there was posed within monasticism itself the very problem that it had partly solved in the fourth and fifth centuries: the tension between the Present Age and the Age to Come, between acting to reform and reorder society in the light of the standards of the Age to Come, at the price of inevitable compromise and even distortion and corruption, and withdrawing from society to live a more truly eschatological life, that of the Kingdom of God. Neither solution could be entirely satisfactory.

Celtic Christianity

In the fifth century, pagan Anglo-Saxon invaders destroyed Roman Britain and pushed Christianity into the western extremities of the island, Cornwall and Wales. There it flourished and spread to other Celtic-speaking areas, Scotland and Ireland. Developing largely in isolation, Celtic Christianity evolved distinctive cultural patterns. Monasteries dominated all aspects of the life of the Church. Abbots and not bishops were the true leaders. Rigorous asceticism was practiced; at the same time, a high standard of learning was maintained by the monks. Celtic monks wandered far abroad. Some reached then uninhabited Iceland in small boats; others travelled as missionaries to Gaul, northern Italy, and eastern Europe, where they established churches and monasteries in the sixth and seventh centuries.

Celtic Christianity was marked by an intense love of nature, rooted both in pre-Christian Celtic tradition and in the legacy of hermits like Aphu of Egypt. The Irish legend of Tuan mac Cairill contains a Christianized form of the idea of a magical transformation into, or rebirth as, an animal. Irish hermits, thinking of themselves as brothers to the wild animals, befriended deer, boars, and wolves, according to the traditional accounts. They regarded the natural world as less corrupt than human society. The ancient Cosmic Liturgy motif appears in the spirituality of the Irish monks, with its emphasis on harmony with nature.

Celtic Art. The peoples of northern Europe, unlike the Greeks and Romans, avoided naturalistic representations of the human form in their art. They preferred either wholly abstract, geometric forms, or a highly stylized, abstract

The Ardagh Chalice, ecclesiastical altar vessel of the eighth century.

use of plant and animal forms. They especially loved intricate, rich jewelry and metalwork, and excelled at making it. The Celtic church used this tradition to enhance Christian worship and spirituality. The eighth-century Ardagh chalice is a masterpiece of the jeweler's craft. Monastic artists applied the Celtic sense of design to manuscript illumination, covering whole pages with fantastically intricate patterns. These seem to be pure decoration, but recent studies indicate that they combine Mediterranean and indigenous traditions to depict symbolically the Cosmic Mystery of Redemption. Some writers now speak of a Christian transformation of a magical image of the world expressed in a symbolic "code." Celtic monks "baptized" pre-Christian megalithic cult pillars by carving crosses on them; out of this practice there gradually evolved the great stone "high crosses," covered with panels of scenes representing the History of Salvation, and abstract forms symbolizing the Cosmic Liturgy.

The Other Western Churches.   In the east, each ethnic community used its own language for worship, but in the west, everyone except the Arian barbarians employed Latin; and all the Latin churches, which belonged to the patriatchate of Rome, accepted the Chalcedonian christology, although they tended to be a bit uneasy about the neo-Chalcedonian understanding of it.

The Latin churches were thus not divided into rival communities by doctrine, as were those of the east. On the whole, there was also less cultural diversity among them, owing to the use of Latin. But each region had its own traditions of art, liturgy, and chant; diversity at this level was comparable to that of the east. The Roman church, with its acknowledged primacy in the west, still represented only one local tradition in the sphere of culture.

Augustine and Neo-Platonism

Western Christianity owes many of its distinctive features to currents set in motion by, or at least channeled through, Augustine of Hippo (A.D. 354–430). The son of a pagan father and a Christian mother, Augustine was raised as a Christian but not baptized. He revolted against the unreflective Christianity of his childhood and at age 19 joined the adherents of the Persian-Babylonian prophet Mani (A.D. 216–276), the Manichees. Their religion was a variety of gnosticism; it claimed to offer an esoteric "true Christianity" of which the Catholics were ignorant, based on a dualism between a pure, good, but passive light-substance (of which the soul is part), and an active, coarse principle of evil that invades the realm of good and traps fragments of it. Salvation is attained when the soul is awakened to its true nature and purified through prescribed rituals.

Augustine broke with the Manichees in 383 when he went to Italy, where he became a professor of rhetoric at Milan and studied Neo-Platonic philosophy. Neo-Platonism depicted the world not as a dualistic mixture of good and evil substances, but as a graded series of levels of reality originating in the One,

In an example of Celtic art, St. John is depicted from the Book of Kells.

the first principle of all things, which is beyond being, form, or mind. Inherently productive, the One spontaneously emanates the form-containing Mind. Mind, in turn, produces Soul, which on the one hand contemplates the forms contained in Mind, and on the other, as Logos, orders the visible, material world in the likeness of the forms. Matter, the last stage in the unfolding of the One, is capable only of being ordered; it is non-productive, close to non-being, and negative in value. Individual souls are embodied by regrettable necessity to make the material world as good as it can be made. But the soul's true good lies in turning away from matter, back toward Mind, and ultimately toward the One.

In contrast to the Manicheans, then, the Neo-Platonists taught that God and the soul are entirely incorporeal; that the world-process as a whole is good, and that the soul's true good lies in the intellectual contemplation of immutable realities, ultimately of God himself. Augustine heard the sermons of Ambrose in Milan, and found in them many of the same teachings, together with an allegorical interpretation of Scripture that explained seeming crudities in a profound and spiritual way. He returned to his native religion and was baptized in 387, becoming a monk under the influence of Athanasius' biography of the Egyptian hermit Anthony. He returned to Africa, and became bishop of the town of Hippo Regius.

The Donatist Controversy.   Augustine was soon engaged in controversy with an African perfectionist schism, the Donatist church. The Donatists believed that the Catholics had accepted *lapsi* as bishops and had thus incurred a sort of ritual impurity. They concluded that the true Church existed only in Africa, among those who rejected these bishops; some writers have seen them as anti-Latin Berber nationalists, but the dispute seems to have cut across both ethnic and class lines. The Donatists wanted to maintain the pre-Constantinian front between Church and world; Augustine fully accepted the ambiguous situation of the post-Constantinian Church, embracing in principle if not in fact the whole society, and serving as the context in which the soul is guided, corrected, and nourished. He argued from the traditional Cosmic Liturgy motif that the Catholic Church alone is the fulfillment of the promise that all nations will turn to the God of Israel.

The Donatists' case was rather weak historically; at a hearing involving hundreds of bishops from both sides, the Roman government decided in favor of the Catholics, penalizing the Donatists (who had been the first to take the dispute to the government!) with fines and confiscations.

Such controversies were often occasions for disorder. Donatist extremists had resorted to violence, and the Catholic bishops felt it legitimate to call for force against them—as Athanasius had already done against a similar movement in Egypt. Augustine approved of the sanctions used. In 385, some bishops in Spain had been involved in securing the execution of the leaders of an allegedly gnostic ascetic movement, the Priscillians; the bishops of Gaul and Italy reacted by excommunicating them. The ancient Church was quite clear that physical violence, torture, and death were not admissible against heretics; Augustine upheld this consensus, and in fact such means were not used. But the rather malicious legal device of classing the Donatists as heretics, together with Augustine's theological arguments in favor of compulsion, were centuries later to be twisted into support of such measures.

The Pelagian Controversy.   In his later years, Augustine was engaged in a controversy with Pelagius, a British monk who had a considerable following in

Italy and Africa. Pelagius held that apart from Christ, human beings inevitably sin because they are born into a world where "everyone does it"—they learn by bad example, and none can escape this conditioning. After Christ has come and demonstrated sinlessness, however, man and woman have the ability to accept God or not. They do need "grace," the active gift of God's influence, and this is given in their inherent natural powers, in the Christian revelation that calls them to a new life, and in the gift of baptism that allows them a new beginning. These are graciously given by God; the rest is up to man and woman.

Augustine knew that this is too simple. The human will is often divided; humankind's motivations are confused and contradictory. God must somehow give the will also. Will is, in Augustine's view, the very seat of sin: all its other bad effects come from the perverse, rebellious will. In the present human condition, free will is reduced from true self-determination to mere wishing. It is the elect, whom God endows with grace, who are free to choose him (not, it seems, to reject him, which would be spurious "freedom" in Augustine's eyes) and who are further given the "gift of perseverance" to keep them from defecting. The rest of humankind are incapable of attaining salvation. No one can attain to perfection in this life, or to the certainty of his or her own salvation.

Pelagius thought of God mainly as a law-giving ruler who punishes in hell those who break his clearly stated laws. Augustine was contemptuous of the fear of hell as a motivation. He argued from the already common practice of infant baptism that humanity is weighed down and corrupted, not only by individual sins, but by a burden of guilt borne by the whole race, manifest in concentrated form in sexual drives. This "original sin" results in the just and inevitable condemnation of all but the elect. The elect are all baptized (or martyred), but by no means are all the baptized among the elect. The present sufferings of humankind are the products of God's righteous wrath; his decrees are inscrutible but utterly just.

Augustinian Wisdom.   Augustine's idea of "wisdom," together with his teachings on sin and predestination, became characteristic of most of western Christianity but had much less effect in the east. Augustine regarded the world from a Neo-Platonic perspective, as a sort of reflection of the being and essence of God, a strong reflection in the soul, but a weak one in matter. The soul, as being, knowledge, and will, is analogous to the trinitarian structure of the Godhead, in Augustine's interpretation, as Life, Light, and Love. God the Son is the perfect expression of the Father's self-knowledge; the Holy Spirit is the perfect expression of the mutual love of Father and Son.

The soul can direct itself either toward God, or toward matter and the world of the senses. Augustine was profoundly sensitive to beauty in nature and in art, but found enjoyment of such beauty hard to justify; one should *enjoy* God, but *use* created beings. He knew that one should not *use* other persons. One should love them, but not simply in themselves; rather, one should love God through them. In fact, it is this love that holds the Church together, whereas the rest of humanity is held together by sin. But only the elect know this love, and in the Present Age the Church contains many others. Therefore, it must function as an authoritative institution within which elect individuals can turn from transitory to immutable things.

Wisdom, or contemplation, is for Augustine "the intellectual cognition of things eternal." The discursive reasoning process of intellect is a lower function; the intuitive grasp of eternal and universal ideas is intellect's higher function, its wisdom. These ideas in God's mind have a reflection in the soul; but the human mind grasps the universal ideas only by divine illumination. It is the intellect that may reach the height of contemplation in momentary ecstasy, in "the flash of a trembling glance," and grasp the Unchangeable God; but the vision is not coldly intellectual, for it is the "enjoyment of God" in rapturous love. It is not yet the heavenly beatific vision of saints and angels, the vision of the essence of God; that is not attained in this life (except by Moses and Paul).

The vision of eternal truth seems to relegate normal mysticism. Cosmic Liturgy and History of Salvation can have only a limited role. Incarnation and Church ("the whole Christ, head and body," in Augustine's own striking phrase), along with nature and history, are lost to sight in a contemplation that "knows nothing but God and the soul." "It is not the mystery of God in Christ that [Augustinian wisdom] has directly in vision, but the mystery of ourselves, which God, which Christ, aid us to unravel."*

The Later Pelagian Controversy.   The Pelagian controversy continued for a century after Augustine's death. In the east, the Pelagians found natural allies in the party of Theodore of Mopsuestia; it has been aptly said that "a Nestorian Christ is a sufficient savior for a Pelagian man." Most of the Christian east rejected the Nestorian-Pelagian theology in 431, but without approving Augustinianism. In the west, too, many regarded Augustine as a teacher of dangerous, unfounded novelties, depicting God as an arbitrary tyrant who coerces some into his kingdom and cruelly excludes others. A series of councils on the subject culminated in the Council of Orange (529), which affirmed much of Augustine's doctrine: that the entire human race is infected with sin from Adam on, that no one can claim merit independent of grace, and that grace is not just natural ability plus external information and exhortation, but is an "infusion" of spiritual influence and power that enables the will to choose the soul's ultimate good. The Council did not accept the idea that grace is irresistible, and condemned the notion of a "predestination to evil." With papal confirmation, these decisions came to be accepted throughout the West.

Differences Between East and West.   Eastern and western Christians agreed that human nature in the Present Age is radically distorted, that the distortion is much deeper than the balance of particular good and evil acts committed by

*Louis Bouyer, *The Spirituality of the New Testament and the Fathers* (New York: Desclee Co., 1963), p. 493.

individuals, and that no human being can overcome it through his or her own power. From the time of Augustine on, certain differences in emphasis increasingly separated the two churches in their understanding of these principles. "Original sin" in the west has been conceived as an inheritance of guilt; in Greek, the term used is "ancestral sin," and it has been understood as the inheritance of death and corruption that causes human beings to commit guilt-incurring actions. Western theology has regarded "grace" as a created energy, added to human nature by the Holy Spirit, that enables persons to overcome the moral impotence of that nature and for the first time to achieve a supernatural goal;* eastern theology has understood grace as the very life of God, the "deifying" divine energies, in which humankind can participate. Ontological categories retained primacy over legal categories in eastern theology, but not always in western. Introspective, subjective, and individualistic aspects of spirituality became increasingly prominent in the west. The doctrine of the Trinity was also increasingly understood in diverse ways, as will be seen later.

The Survival of the Western Church.   The position of the church as an institution in society was affected by the political collapse of the western empire. In some border areas, Christianity was temporarily obliterated. On the whole, however, the church survived, while political order, education, and Roman-Hellenistic culture largely vanished. The bishops, especially, were called on to provide leadership, for no one else was capable of it. Consequently they had not only to uphold orthodox doctrine under difficult circumstances, but also to preserve education and literacy, and often to function as political leaders. They succeeded at least well enough to ensure both the survival and recovery of Catholic Christianity, and the preservation of much of classical civilization.

Rome was sacked by the Goths in 410. Although the city had ceased to be the real political center, its symbolic value was still great. This was the first time in history that Rome had fallen to an enemy, and the shock was great in the west; the eastern empire, with its capital intact, was less disturbed by the event, while western writers like Augustine correspondingly drew no comfort from the fact that a Roman emperor reigned as before in the unconquered "New Rome," Constantinople. In popular feeling, the empire had already ceased to be a unity.

Justinian still thought of it as a unity, and reconquered North Africa from the Vandals and Italy from the Goths. But the Goths were soon succeeded by the more hostile Lombards, who pushed the imperial forces into a few enclaves and largely isolated Rome. The papacy had to assume responsibility for maintaining political order and for averting famine. Gregory the Great, pope from 590 to 604, was a former government official who combined spiritual and political leadership. The Church of Rome had received by donation extensive land holdings throughout Italy; Gregory administered these skillfully enough to

---

*This idea of grace was generally rejected by the sixteenth-century Reformation in the West, however.

supply the needs of the poor in Rome and elsewhere. He wrote a number of works on pastoral care, spirituality, the miracles of the saints of Italy, and similar topics; he revised the texts of the Mass (the service of the Eucharist, Latin *missa*) for use in the specialized "stational" services, celebrated by the pope in various churches in Rome according to a fixed annual schedule, at which officials of the city government attended. He laid "the foundations of the new structure of the medieval Papacy that was to govern the western world after the . . . wars and invasions of the sixth century.*

*Berthold Altaner, *Patrology* (New York: Herder and Herder, 1960), p. 556.

9

Early Medieval Europe

The Benedictines

Among the refugees in Gregory's Rome were monks from Monte Cassino, south of the city. Their monastery, founded some 75 years earlier by Benedict of Nursia (ca. 480–ca. 545), had been destroyed by the Lombards. Benedict had provided as a constitution for the community a Rule, abridged and revised from an earlier anonymous work. The community was a sort of spiritual family under the guidance of an abbot whose authority was practically unlimited. The asceticism was moderate (for the period!); much emphasis was laid on "stability": a monk should never, except for the gravest reasons, leave the monastery. Gregory (a former monk himself) welcomed the Benedictines, but gave them a new task, as missionaries to distant lands. From this time on, Benedictine monasteries appeared throughout western Europe. The Benedictines and other monks (Celtic monks and those from Gaul had their own rules and traditions) were another major factor, along with the bishops, in the survival of Christianity in the dark ages, and in the preservation of literary culture as well.

Hierarchy. The orders of bishop, presbyter, and deacon had been universally accepted at a very early time. Other, "minor" orders varied with local tradition; there was a tendency to multiply them, to establish a number of different "roles" in worship services (readers, psalm-singers, cantors, door-keepers, etc.), partly for practical purposes and partly because of the unifying effect of what is now called "division of labor." According to the ancient Roman prayer for ordaining deacons, the Church is

> "distinguished [meaning both 'diversified' and 'adorned'] by a
> variety of heavenly gifts,
> bound together by [not 'in spite of,' as modern translations
> imply] the distinction of its members,
> united by the marvellous law of the whole structure."

The existence of the various orders in the Church is what is called "hierarchy." Today understood to mean "the rule of priests" (*tōn hiereōn archē*), more or less synonymous with "clericalism," its true meaning is "sacred order" (*hiera archē*), and it was originally a barrier against clericalism: when functions are distributed among a number of orders, no one of them can attain excessive power, for all are mutually interdependent.

The Parish System

From the fourth century on, however, newly founded country churches were no longer given a bishop. Instead, the functions of saying the formal prayers of the community at services, and of pastoral oversight, were delegated to the presbyters, who began also to bear the title of "priest" (*hiereus, sacerdos,* etc.— terminology was not fixed until rather late). The duty of bestowing ordinations (initiations into the hierarchy), the bishops reserved for themselves.

As Christianity spread into the countryside, communities much like the older village churches, but without a bishop, were established. The various functions were divided among the orders of presbyter, deacon, "minor" orders, and laymen. When the terminology was finally fixed the communities without bishops were designated "parishes," and the territory for which a bishop was responsible was called a "diocese." Every larger town still had its bishop, and was the center of a diocese of which the parishes were the constituent parts. The bishop was to hold responsibility for all the parishes in his diocese, and to visit them frequently. The hierarchical principle was largely preserved in the parishes. It is referred to in an ancient Roman prayer:

> Almighty and everlasting God,
> by whose Spirit the whole body of the Church
> is governed and sanctified,
> receive our supplications and prayers
> which we offer before thee
> for all estates of men in thy holy Church,
> that every member of the same,
> in his vocation and ministry
> may truly and godly serve thee.

Parishes and Monasteries in the "Dark Ages."   Around the Mediterranean Sea, dioceses were small and bishops not distant from their parishes. Farther north, where the population was very thin, parishes were much larger, and dioceses immense; their boundaries often faded out into unknown lands. Here, monasteries were often the true centers of Christianity (and of literacy and what existed of classical culture). A parish church might be attached to a monastery or women's convent. Where it was not, the members of the hierarchy, the "clergy," often lived a communal, celibate life much like that of the monks, although married priests were not unusual. The parishes were supported by endowments, mainly of land in the "dark ages," including farmlands worked by the clergy. Church laws forbade clergy to engage in business or to have a regular profession, but, like the monks, they were often part-time farmers.

The northern parishes were too large for a single center to serve everyone, so "oratories" (chapels) were built in villages and on landed estates, and large wooden or stone crosses erected in the open in hamlets. Clergy from the parish would go out to celebrate services of worship, preach, and teach at these places, but only at the parish church was there a baptismal font or a graveyard; except for emergencies, all "parishioners" (Christians living within the parish) were baptized and buried there. There, too, was the school, which served mainly to train clergy, as the monastery schools trained monks. Bishops in the north could not visit remote parishes with any frequency, so the parish clergy bore a heavy responsibility. Along with the bishops and monks, the usually forgotten parish clergy were a third factor in the survival of Christianity.

The Anglo-Saxons and Franks

In England, the pagan Anglo-Saxon invaders were divided into small kingdoms. In 596, Gregory the Great sent 40 Benedictine monks as missionaries. About the same time, Celtic missionaries began to visit the northern Anglo-Saxon kingdoms. The two missions met in the seventh century. The Romans were perplexed by the outlandish peculiarities (from their viewpoint) of Celtic Christian culture; the Celts concluded (not without reason) that the Romans were haughty and intolerant. The Romans prevailed in England, and in the following centuries the Celts also gradually conformed to Roman custom, not without much resistance. The English retained a strong attachment to Rome and the papacy for centuries, but the Celtic traditions in art, and a particular love of nature, remained as evidence of Celtic influence.

The Franks, a Germanic tribe in what is now France (named for them), were converted from paganism to Catholic, not Arian, Christianity at the beginning of the sixth century. In spite of vicious, bloody dynastic disputes, they established a stable kingdom in northwestern Europe. But the churches were plagued by corruption; just as the lords of estates held the estate chapels as private property, so the Frankish rulers treated the churches in their domain, misusing property and having unqualified and often unworthy friends and relatives ordained as priests and bishops and given endowed pastoral positions. In remote areas, Catholic doctrine was not taught. When English missionaries began to appear among the pagan eastern German tribes, hoping to reach their Saxon fellow-tribesmen in Germany, Pope Gregory II assigned to the most able of them, Boniface (ca. 680–753), a commission to reform the Frankish church by enforcing canon law (church laws established by councils or, in the west, by the popes). Boniface labored tirelessly and with much success to persuade the Frankish rulers to respect the integrity of the churches and to bring the churches under effective papal control. The alliance between papacy and northern reformers was the characteristic pattern of the medieval church from this time on.

The Carolingian Theocracy. The emperor in Constantinople was too busy fighting the Arabs to do more in Italy than collect taxes and draft soldiers. In the middle of the eighth century, in return for papal approval of a change of royal dynasty among the Franks, the new king, Pippin the Short, attacked and overthrew the Lombards in Italy, and "returned" their lands—much of which had previously belonged to the Byzantines—to the papacy. The new Frankish dynasty, the Carolingians, supported the papal program of reform. Pippin had himself anointed in imitation of the ancient Hebrew kings.

His son Charlemagne, after suppressing an attempted Lombard revival, was crowned Roman emperor by Pope Leo III in Rome in 800, over three centuries after the title and office had disappeared in the West. He regarded himself as the true Christian emperor, the Lord's anointed, the head of a theocratic state. He carried out a further extension of the reform now known as the "Carolingian renaissance," assembling an international team of scholars at his court to guide it. Latin learning was reformed; the language was henceforth taught according to more classical standards. The copies of the Latin Bible available in northern Europe had come to contain confused and erroneous readings; a good text was established and new copies made. Church services were a confused hodgepodge of the native rite of Gaul and imported Roman forms; books were requested from Rome to provide a standard type. What finally came were "Gregorian" books intended for the papal stational services, poorly adapted to parish use and lacking many necessary items. These were filled in by the court scholars, and this edition was accepted in the Frankish kingdom and later in Rome itself (rather to the detriment of parish worship). Monasteries had been following a variety of rules, especially the Irish "Rule of St. Columba"; Charlemagne made the Rule of St. Benedict obligatory on all. Councils were called to condemn a reappearance of the adoptionist heresy. The Roman tradition of figurative art, depicting biblical scenes and persons, was officially sponsored among the Franks, partly supplanting the abstract, symbolic northern forms. In general, Charlemagne sought to raise standards and at the same time to impose a high degree of uniformity, based largely on Roman models.

Two "Roman Empires"—Frankish and Byzantine.   The emperors in Constantinople never regarded themselves as anything other than Roman emperors; their subjects were "Romans." The term "Byzantine" is a modern usage that in most contexts any true "Byzantine" would have resented and rejected. The Frankish-papal alliance was already inimical to Byzantine interests in Italy, and Charlemagne's claim to the title of Roman emperor was totally unacceptable—not even the pope could make a barbarian king into a Roman emperor! In the west, on the other hand, the reputation of Constantinople was badly tarnished by the series of schisms and heresies that had prevailed there—monophysite, monothelite, and most recently iconoclast—all of which had sent refugees flocking to Rome. The Frankish Roman empire was utterly free of such lapses.

The Icons and the Western Churches.   The Roman Church had long sponsored representational art; since at least the time of Gregory the Great it had formally defended it as a means of instruction, especially necessary for the illiterate. The papacy rejected iconoclasm, and the Frankish state followed its lead.

On the other hand, the dominant influence in western theology was Augustinian Neo-Platonism, which tended to be a bit uneasy about figurative art. The Seventh Ecumenical Council rejected iconoclasm in 787, thus ending the schism between Rome and Constantinople, and posing a threat to the Frankish-papal alliance. The acts of this council were known in the west in an incompetent translation that missed the essential distinction between "worship" and "veneration." Frankish propaganda immediately attacked the Byzantine theology of icons; a Frankish synod at Frankfort (794) was claimed to be the true Seventh Ecumenical Council. The devotional (as distinct from didactic) use of icons was condemned and forbidden. The papacy refused to join the Franks in condemning the Council of 787, but neither did it condemn the Frankish Council of 794, and for some three centuries the latter, with its ban on devotion to (more accurately, by means of) icons, rather than the former, was recognized in most of the West.

The "Filioque"

An unidentified writer of sixth-century Gaul had composed a didactic summary of doctrine attacking Arianism and Nestorianism that came to be called (mis-leadingly) the "Athanasian Creed." Where the Nicene Creed simply quotes John 15.26, stating that the Holy Spirit "proceeds from the Father," the "Athanasian Creed" asserts that

> the Holy Spirit is from the Father and the Son,
> not made, nor created, nor begotten, but proceeding.

Anti-Arian in intention, this phrase is based on Augustine's interpretation of the doctrine of the Trinity.

When the Visigothic kingdom in Spain abandoned Arianism for Catholicism (587–89), the phrase "and the Son" (in Latin, *filioque*) was added to the Nicene Creed for anti-Arian emphasis. This version of the Nicene Creed was adopted by the Franks.

The eastern theologians, beginning with the revelation in the history of salvation of three divine identities, regarded it as the distinctive character of God the Father to be the source of the Son and of the Holy Spirit, to be the only "causal principle" in the Godhead, both of the distinction of the Three Persons (for the Son and the Spirit each derive their particular mode of being from the Father) and of their unity (for it is from the Father, as a single source, that they derive). Were there two divine "causal principles," there would be two Gods; were Father and Son together the single source of the Spirit, a modalistic confusion would result.

Latin theologians, beginning with the oneness of God, emphasized the single divine essence; they tended to identify the entire being of God with that essence, and to regard the Holy Spirit as the mutual relationship of Father and Son, the mutual bond of love. The three persons are thus identified as relations within one essence. Augustine himself, in his formal statements, had not gone much beyond the usual Greek view: the Spirit proceeds eternally from the Father, principally, but also, by the gift of the Father, from the Son: the Father remains the sole ultimate source. But his novel use of "proceed" to designate the Spirit's relationship to the Son, together with his idea of the Spirit as the expression of the mutual love of Father and Son, underlies the *filioque,* which thus became usual among the Latins, while the Greeks regarded it as unfounded and dangerous speculation.

Here again, Charlemagne seized the initiative, and a Frankish council of 809 specifically approved the phrase in the Nicene Creed. Pope Leo III had no objection to the *filioque* as doctrine, but held that only a full ecumenical council could even consider altering the text of the Creed. In Rome, the Creed was not part of the Eucharistic service, to which it had been added elsewhere; Leo had the text without *filioque* engraved in Greek and Latin on silver tablets and placed in St. Peter's Basilica in Rome.

Christianity Spreads in Europe

The Christian mission had traditionally been addressed to free peoples, and had been accepted by sovereign states in Armenia, Georgia, and Ethiopia. The Celtic and English missionaries had the same understanding, although the latter sometimes found themselves among border tribes subdued by the Franks. But the Carolingian theocracy introduced a policy of forcibly converting conquered tribes, thus associating the Christian mission with imperialist expansion, and, in the eyes of the warlike pagan tribes, subjugation and virtual enslavement. "Conversion" was at sword point, and was enforced by savage laws: eating meat during the Lenten fast was punishable by death. The eastern Germanic tribes conquered in this way later became the heirs of Charlemagne and his policy of forced conversion.

The pagan Slavic tribes in eastern Europe were the object of missions sent by the Franks, by Rome, and by Constantinople. The political implications were unavoidable: a successful mission established a "sphere of influence." Disputes over the Adriatic coastlands, the natural base for such missions, was a major factor in a temporary schism between Rome and Constantinople in the ninth century. The Franks conquered the weaker tribes on their borders (unlike the German tribes, the conquered Slavs could expect only harsh oppression: the word "slave" comes from "Slav"), and tried to bring the stronger ones into their sphere of influence.

It was in this setting, surprisingly enough, that the traditional conception of missions was not only reasserted, but formulated with new clarity and power. The mission to the Slavs from Constantinople was entrusted to two brothers, Cyril-Constantine (d. 869) and Methodios (d. 883). Following the eastern custom, the brothers (who were expert linguists and masters of Slavonic) translated the liturgical books and much of the Bible. They devised an alphabet, or perhaps two of them, for the Slavs.

Frankish missionaries attacked these activities, insisting that Catholic Christians must use in their worship one of the three languages of the inscription on the Cross (see John 19.20): Hebrew, Greek, and Latin. Cyril and

Methodius countered this attack with a remarkable development of the traditional Cosmic Liturgy motif, asserting that (1) all languages are of equal value; all attain their fulfillment as sacral languages precisely by their use in Christian worship, as means of participation in the Mystery; (2) not just an elite, but the whole of each nation, should be able to understand Scripture and liturgy, to participate fully in "normal mysticism"; and (3) the diversity of languages and cultures is a blessing, a positive good for the human race, a divine gift. The two brothers won the approval of Pope Hadrian II for this teaching.

The destiny of the various Slavic peoples was diverse. Those conquered by Germans remained in an oppressed condition until most of them finally disappeared into the German-speaking population. Several principalities accepted Latin Christianity as free peoples, and received bishops of their own nationality (the decisive factor in attaining recognized national status in the middle ages). Among them the teachings of Cyril and Methodius were never entirely forgotten; although Latin was normally used for worship, a Slavonic translation of the Roman services was able to survive in a few places. The eastern Slavic principalities received Christianity from Constantinople, using Slavonic translations from the Greek.

Latin and Vernacular Languages. When Benedict founded his monastery, his monks were mostly ordinary peasants whose daily language was a late form of Latin. By Charlemagne's time, early forms of the modern Romance languages had supplanted Latin in southern Europe; the language of worship was no longer intelligible to most people (of course, it never had been to Celtic- or Germanic-speaking Catholics). The Carolingian scholars cultivated a classicizing, correct, and rather artificial Latin. Participation in "normal mysticism" was inevitably hampered.

Sermons were provided in the spoken language. Everyone knew by heart and chanted a number of brief responses, acclamations, and hymns in Latin. The dramatic, nonverbal, ceremonial elements in worship, such as the "kiss of peace" or various processions, or the striking changes in the interior decoration of churches during the Lenten fast, were not dependent on language. Avenues of participation remained open in worship in the early middle ages, even in the Latin west; at the same time, Latin had a universality that no vernacular language possessed; it certainly aided the cultural integration of western and central Europe.

Vernacular culture was not much recognized in the Carolingian state, but the Celts cultivated it, and the English followed their example. Prominent among the poems written in Old English are vivid paraphrases of Latin liturgical texts; bridges were thus established between Latin and vernacular culture. English missionaries transmitted this tradition to the continental Germans, and from this beginning German literature takes its rise. But no formulation comparable to that of Cyril and Methodius appeared to ground vernacular culture in religious awareness.

The Dark Ages Return

The Carolingian empire disintegrated during the course of the ninth century, as new dangers threatened the west. Renewed Arab assaults in the south coincided with the appearance of the Vikings in the north and the invasion of the Magyars in the east. An unscrupulous faction of Italian nobles gained control of the papacy. As central power declined in the north, feudalism grew. Church property, including monasteries, was drawn into the feudal system, and many of the old abuses reappeared. The proprietary rights of landowners and nobles over church property and appointment to endowed posts went unchecked; bishops and abbots became feudal lords in their own right, and some of them differed from other warring barons in title only.

The papacy, under the thumb of Roman politicians, was often occupied by corrupt and unworthy men. The reformers in the north could no longer expect leadership from Rome; instead, they were led by certain influential monasteries, such as Brogne, Corze, and Cluny, which became the centers of loosely knit "families" of monastic communities, sometimes numbering in the hundreds. A reform party among the bishops assisted, but on the whole the bishops absorbed themselves in feudal concerns. The monasteries of the early medieval period were supported by generous gifts. Their functions were not entirely those intended by Benedict. For one thing, out of the earlier (and largely monastic) practice of personal spiritual guidance by a "spiritual father," there had developed the legalistic medieval penitential system. This system required confessing sins to a priest, who proclaimed absolution conditional upon the performance of assigned acts of satisfaction, such as a specific time of fasting. Since this penance was regarded as a sort of legal debt, it could be performed by a paid agent as well, and often, in practice, had to be. The monks were entrusted with the task of making satisfaction for the sins of others. Furthermore, the younger children of landowning families were customarily sent to monasteries, to keep the estates from being divided among many heirs. Some monasteries accepted only novices of noble blood. In spite of these developments, so foreign to the original Benedictine conception, and in spite of the corruption of some monasteries, the reform movement had much success in restoring discipline and independence of feudal control in the monasteries.

The reforming monasteries cultivated lavish artistic adornment of their churches, and increased the number of "offices" (services) chanted by the monks. They worked to provide care for the poor and to curtail feudal warfare. They attacked simony (buying and selling ordinations and church offices) and the ordination of married men—the latter was widespread and in many places regarded as traditional and desirable, but Rome had preferred a celibate clergy for many centuries. There was a real danger that with married priests parish property might become hereditary, a practical point that strengthened the Roman case.

Christianity in Northern Europe. Christianity spread gradually into northern Europe. In the tenth century, the principalities of ancient Rus' (corresponding to present European Russia, Ukraine, and Byelorussia) accepted Christianity from Constantinople, and used the Slavonic translations of Cyril and Methodius. A single "metropolitan" (bishop of a capital city) at Kiev was the head of the bishops of all these principalities. In the west, the Vikings of Scandinavia gradually accepted Latin Christianity; the Viking threat to Europe was overcome by assimilating them to Christendom.

The pre-Christian religion of northern Europe was centered upon symbolizing cosmic powers of life and order; a highly developed tradition of visual arts gave it expression. This conception of the cosmos could not be without significance for Christianity, and in fact in these areas a culture developed

Stave Church at Borgund, Norway

somewhat like that of Celtic Christianity. As was the case with Greek myths and legends, those of Scandinavia were employed as Christian allegories, and scenes from them appear on Christian monuments. Perhaps the most remarkable products of this culture are the wooden stave churches of twelfth- and thirteenth-century Norway, about thirty of which still stand and are in use for worship. These comparatively small parish churches appear to have been built on pre-Christian cultic sites, carefully chosen to enhance the expression of sacred power that the architects achieved through proportion, and often through ornamentation such as dragon-heads projecting from the roof-ridges.

Stave Church at Urnes, Norway

The stave church at Urnes, Norway, includes a carved wooden panel, originally a portal frame, showing a vine-like tree, with a stylized animal and a serpent biting each other. This may be interpreted as a transposition of a motif found in ancient Christian baptistries, the deer eating the serpent, to the setting of northern mythology, in which the cosmic tree is said to have deer nibling on its leaves and the serpent of the underworld coiled at its roots.

The rite of human sacrifice had become an increasingly prominent element of the old religion. Especially grisly was the cult of the one-eyed god of the dead (Odin, in Scandinavia); human victims offered to this deity were hanged from the branches of sacred trees in the groves at cultic sites. It is under these circumstances that Christian missionaries encountered northern European religion. That they chopped down the sacred groves is perhaps due less to the missionaries' rejecting nature as a bearer of spirit than associations with human sacrifice.

The Recovery of Western Europe. During the ninth and tenth centuries, in England and France, the dark age conditions began to pass as national monarchies emerged. In Germany, a Saxon dynasty restored central rule (although they were unable to eliminate the rebellious tendencies of other German power groups), checked the Vikings and Magyars, and began to expand against the Slavs to the east. The imperial title and much of the Carolingian program were also restored; Otto I was crowned emperor by the pope in 962, and his successors customarily went to Rome for coronation. Under the influence of the monastic reform movement, they also struggled to reform the papacy, but the tenacity of the Roman nobles and the constant threat of rebellion in Germany frustrated them. (It was under imperial pressure that the Nicene Creed, with *filioque,* was inserted in the Mass at Rome in 1014). Finally, in the middle of the eleventh century, the emperor Henry III succeeded in placing the reform movement in control of the papacy. Like the Byzantine and Carolingian emperors, the Ottonians felt responsible for church affairs; they needed support from the bishops to govern, both in Italy and in Germany, and expected the right to choose and "invest" (induct into office by bestowing the symbols of the office, the ring and staff in the case of a bishop) "their" higher clergy in accordance with feudal custom.

10

The Later Middle Ages

The "Papal Revolution"

Lay control of church offices (that is, control by the rulers and nobles) was a major source of the corruption that the reformers were determined to eliminate. Henry III died young (1056), leaving a minor son and a weak administration; the reformers reorganized the method of choosing a new pope, placing it in the hands of the "cardinal" clergy of the pope's entourage. They worked tirelessly to establish papal control and leadership in church affairs everywhere. The imperial party resented what seemed to them ingratitude and disloyalty. The "papal revolution" was also opposed by many bishops who felt that centralization was undermining their traditional role. The issue came to a head in the conflict between the zealous and short-sighted Pope Gregory VII (Hildebrand; 1073–1085) and Emperor Henry IV over the appointing of bishops. The dramatic incident at Canossa (1076), where Henry stood barefoot in the snow for three days to obtain absolution, is popularly understood as proof of the papacy's total power. In fact, it was a successful maneuver of Henry's to break up a dangerous alliance between Gregory and German rebels, and to neutralize the papacy's most formidable weapon against rulers, the ban of excommunication and deposition. The "investiture controversy" was settled only in the 1150s, with a compromise: bishops were elected by the clergy and invested with ring and staff by another bishop; but the ruler could veto an unacceptable candidate, and retained the right to "invest" the new bishop with the symbols of his temporal power; a strong ruler could still effectively control elections.

The papacy built up a strong legal position for its claim to sovereignty over the Christian commonwealth (relying heavily on forged documents that everyone honestly believed to be authentic); simultaneously, an effective financial and administrative body developed, becoming the papal "curia" or court. A rival imperial legal theory was developed, but it never became as powerful a tool as the papal assertions. Councils dominated by the papacy were held in various parts of Europe, culminating in six councils, held between 1123 and 1274, that were recognized in the west as ecumenical councils. Under Innocent III (1198–1216), the papacy reached the height of its power, intervening successfully in the affairs of European states. Church positions with endowed livings (benefices), and legal matters involving the church, were disposed over by the papal court. European society, it seemed, was becoming a theocracy headed by the pope and the curia.

The Decline of Papal Power.

But it was not to be. The nation-states developing in France and England, outside the old "Roman Empire" model of sovereignty, proved stronger than the Empire in limiting papal power. When Boniface VIII (1294-1303) asserted the supreme power of the papacy in political as well as ecclesiastical affairs, it was already much less possible to realize these claims than it had been in Innocent's day; Boniface was arrested by an officer of the king of France in 1303. From 1309 to 1378, the papacy was moved to Avignon, on the border of the French kingdom, where the bureaucracy (especially the financial offices) flourished. An attempt to return the papacy to Rome led to a schism, with two rival popes, one at Avignon and one at Rome, supported by the kings of France and England respectively (1378-1409). The schism was disastrous for papal leadership. Confidence and respect declined everywhere; kings regained considerable control over the churches in their kingdoms; and earnest advocates of reform began to look to councils rather than to the papacy.

The "conciliar movement" failed to produce any real program, however. Its high point was the Council of Constance (1414-1417), which ended the schism in the papacy and attempted to institute regular councils as a center of reform and authority. The papacy soon rejected any such notion, and the Council of Basel (1431-1449) revealed such disunity and weakness that the leading reformers abandoned conciliarism. The Council of Ferrara-Florence (1437-45) marked the triumph of the papacy in the Church, but it never regained the moral leadership or the political power it had in the thirteenth century. Many of the fifteenth- and sixteenth-century popes were obviously politicians at heart, lovers of power, wealth, and pleasure.

The Papacy and the Christian East.   Beginning in the eleventh century, the "papal revolution" included a drive to extend papal authority to the eastern churches and to Muslim-controlled territories. An early result was a confrontation in Constantinople (1054) between zealous papal legates and the politically powerful Patriarch Michael Cerularius (Kerularios), ending in mutual excommunication. Better relations were restored by a more tactful reformer, Pope Urban II (1088-1099), but the papacy was now committed to the *filioque,* and no formal reunion was possible. The Normans conquered southern Italy from the Byzantines in the eleventh century (bringing the churches there under Roman jurisdiction); the Turks began the conquest of Asia Minor from the Byzantines about the same time (marking the beginning of the decline of the eastern Empire), and overran Palestine and Syria. Unlike the Arabs, they were intolerant and oppressive toward Christian pilgrims to the "Holy Land," the sites of biblical events in and around Jerusalem. A Muslim ruler of doubtful sanity had destroyed the Christian shrines in Jerusalem in 1009; they had been rebuilt, but another destruction was feared.

The Crusades

In Spain, a war raged between Muslims and Christians, assuming the character of a "holy war." Soldiers undertook religious vows, and combined military and religious training. The reformed papacy moved to establish control of the campaign against the Muslims, and over the churches in the reconquered territories. They met with some resistance from the Spaniards, who claimed independent apostolic authority (a legendary account attributed the origins of the Church in Spain to the apostle James).

But the papacy had more in view than the situation in Spain. Constantinople appealed for help against the Turks. Pope Urban II responded by proposing a war, based upon a combination of military-religious Spanish "holy war" institutions and the pilgrimage to Jerusalem, to restore Christian rule (under the papacy) to the Holy Land. The Crusader undertook a religious vow; if he died in battle, he attained the status of a martyr (an idea adapted from Islamic tradition).

The Crusades—a series of them lasting for several centuries—had only brief successes in "freeing" the Holy Land. They caused enormous destruction and achieved little good, even in terms of the original conception; but, even worse, the whole idea was soon perverted. Against the express orders of Pope Innocent III, the Crusaders in 1204 attacked and conquered the Byzantine empire, and attempted to impose Latin Christianity on the Greeks. A war of national liberation finally drove them out in 1261, but a double legacy was left: a permanently weakened eastern Empire, and an enduring distrust and hatred of the Latins. From this time on, the division between Roman Catholic and Eastern Orthodox Christians was deeply rooted in the consciousness of both communities; it ceased to be thought of as a temporary schism. The Armenians and Maronites had a better experience of the Crusades; some of the former, and all of the latter, accepted papal authority.

The "Crusade" in Northeastern Europe.   The (originally Muslim) idea of a military religious order appeared in Latin Christianity in connection with the Crusades. One such order, the Teutonic Knights, were driven out of Palestine by the Muslims. They settled in Prussia and began a "Crusade" against the pagan inhabitants of the Baltic coast; and, until they were badly defeated in 1242, fought also against the Russians, who as Eastern Orthodox Christians were regarded as heretics and as bad as pagans (at least by the Crusaders). Far removed from possible papal restraint, the Knights waged a savage war of conquest. When Lithuania accepted Latin Christianity, the Knights falsely claimed that the Lithuanians were about to revert to paganism, and redoubled their attacks. Their offensive power was finally destroyed by Lithuania in 1410, but Prussia, Latvia, and Estonia, "converted" at sword point, remained as conquered territories.

The "Second Foundation" Parish System

From Carolingian times on, population growth caused the old "first-foundation" parishes to be subdivided, by promoting chapels and oratories to the status of parish churches. Many of these were private estate chapels, owned by barons or knights. In these "second-foundation" parishes, the hierarchical structure of the community was largely lost. A priest or two, plus a lay clerk or reader, performed the necessary duties. The reformers' case for freedom from lay control was weaker where a church had been "proprietary" (privately owned) from its foundation. Communities and even whole orders of "canons," devoted to worship and pastoral service, could be established in cathedrals and first-foundation parish churches, but the second-foundation churches were much harder to reform. The tithes for their support were liable to misappropriation by baron or bishop, causing much demoralization.

Clericalization of Worship. The laity were increasingly reduced to the role of passive and uncomprehending spectators in worship. Private prayers to be said at specific points during the services were provided, as a substitute for real participation, for the devout. A new conception of services of worship brought new forms into existence: instead of a communal function, dividing several functions according to hierarchically defined roles, the services became essentially the individual responsibility of the priest. Beside the communal "High Mass" and "choral office," there appeared the "Low Mass" and "Breviary Office." In these, the priest recited in a low voice not only the prayers, but the readings from the Bible and, in abbreviated form, the psalmodic chants. The Mass was increasingly his duty and privilege, the old morning and evening services his private prayers. At best, the laity "heard Mass"; in larger churches, the altar was now far away from them. Except on the frontiers of Christendom, infant baptism replaced the communal, initiatory complex of the ancient Church. Private confession and "hearing Mass" largely replaced normal mysticism. The old apocalyptic imagery was still known through art and literature. Popular legends based on Jewish and Christian apocrypha circulated in Latin and vernacular languages. The legend of the Cross, for example, traced the "history" of the wood of the Cross from the Tree of Life in Paradise, through the Old and New Testaments, to the rediscovery of the Cross by Helen, the mother of the Emperor Constantine. Popular religion probably maintained contact with the themes of Cosmic Liturgy and (in a rudimentary way) History of Salvation through these sources, and through such preaching and instruction as were available; otherwise, it tended to become centered in a quasi-magical, or simply magical, reliance on sacraments and sacred objects.

Developments in Theological Thought

With the end of the Iconoclastic Controversy, Christian Hellenism had attained a state of maturity. No controversies arose equal in magnitude to those of antiquity. The result was not, as is often claimed, stagnation: rather, attention was now focused on some practical aspects. The teaching of Cyril and Methodius, for some reason not usually recognized as theological in character, is one example. Another is the work of the Byzantine abbot, Symeon the New Theologian (949–1022), who insisted that the true meaning of dogma is its practical realization in experience, in "deification" as participation in the cosmic victory of Christ and in the life of God. Like his Armenian contemporary Gregory of Narek, he wrote glowing devotional poetry.

The older western tradition was represented by Bernard of Clairvaux, whose particular concern was mystical theology and the spiritual life. He was influenced by Augustine and Origen, but also by the Cappadocians; his Augustinian Neo-Platonism was balanced by his emphasis on the Incarnation and the Virgin Mary, and including the emotions in spirituality.

The Rise of Dialectical Theology

Western theology took a new turn in the eleventh and twelfth centuries, when applied logic ("dialectic") began to be applied relentlessly to the accepted truths of faith, both to prove their reasonableness and to provide a clearer understanding of them. This was a new development of the Augustinian model, in which the data of faith are first accepted on the strength of the Church's authority, and then explored by reason to increase understanding. Anselm of Canterbury (1033–1109), a staunch supporter of papal reform in Norman England, proposed a proof of God's existence based entirely on analyzing concepts, without appeal to scriptural authority or experience (philosophers are still debating its validity). Anselm's confidence in dialectic provoked some opposition, although he kept it within modest limits: he always acknowledged the ultimate primacy of Scripture over dialectic, and held that dialectic can independently confirm only some and not all of the truths of faith.

Other practitioners of the "new dialectical theology" were suspected not only of misusing logic, but of doctrinal error.

Peter Abelard or Abailard (1079–1142) combined confidence in dialectic with a brash, abrasive style, and arrived at some rather erratic conclusions. Bernard of Clairvaux opposed him violently; from the viewpoint of the older western tradition, this new use of reason seemed presumptuous. Berengar of Tours (1010–88) denied that any material change takes place in the bread and wine at the Eucharist. The term "transubstantiation" came into use to oppose such views. Roscelin of Compiegne (1050–1125), an amateur dialectician, opposed the prevailing Augustinian view of the Trinity, and was accused of Tritheism (teaching that there are three Gods); he was an early forerunner of nominalism (see below, p. 114).

Dialectical Theology and Atonement. The new dialectical theology influenced the doctrine of the atonement. The traditional models of victory and deification were already understood in a limited and unsatisfactory way, and were being relegated to a minor role. Abelard located the work of atonement primarily in the exemplary moral influence of the Incarnation and Crucifixion, a somewhat moralistic reworking of the illumination model. But the dominant western medieval doctrine was essentially that of Anselm, who based his presentation on the "Christ the Victim" model, illustrated with ideas from contemporary feudalism. This doctrine reflects the medieval transition from a basically communal and initiatory experience to one basically individualistic and intro-spective. According to Anselm, humankind fell from "original righteousness" (giving God his due honor by total obedience) to an unrighteousness entailing indebtedness and liability, both for human nature as a whole ("original" or "natural" sin), and for each individual's disobedience ("actual" or "personal" sin). Since God's honor is infinite, finite mortals cannot make good this liability. But God does not abandon humankind to this plight: the incarnate God-man alone can and does offer due satisfaction by an obedience that goes beyond justice, the death of a wholly righteous one, which is raised to infinite value by his divinity. This restored righteousness is shared by the Christian. Original sin is removed by Baptism, actual sin through penance and progressive incorporation, in the Eucharist, into the righteous humanity of Christ and his obedient humility (both Anselm and Abelard followed Augustine in thinking of sin as a defect in the will).

Western theology has generally followed either Abelard (the "subjective" or "moral influence" theory) or Anselm (the "objective" or "substitutionary atonement" theory); the atonement is understood to overcome either a moral defect in an individual, or a requirement of God's righteousness that human beings be punished for sin. The eastern churches lacked the legally organized penitential system and the "low Mass"; they were averse to the new dialectical theology; they were not inclined to regard death as a punishment imposed on humankind by God as a result of original sin. They regarded sin, death, and corruption as an ontological and moral condition due to the satanic power of Death, and never developed a single "theory" of atonement, but retained the ancient models. The West chose logical consistency, the East retained an unorganized, and perhaps unorganizable, but richer complex of themes.

Persecutions

The papal revolution coincided with an increase in popular intolerance and fanaticism, which the bishops and the papacy opposed at first. They later had second thoughts, as the ideal of a uniform society gained ground. Following persecutions by the government in Spain and Byzantium in the sixth century, Jews in Christian countries had generally not been persecuted, although their social and economic position deteriorated. When Crusaders passing through the Rhineland attacked and plundered the German Jews, the bishops defended the Jews and denounced their enemies. But by the thirteenth century the papacy was demanding legal restrictions for Jews, and ignoring persecutions by the princes. Anti-Jewish propaganda represented the Jews as agents of the Muslim enemy, as well-poisoners, and as practitioners of ritual murder.

In the earlier Middle Ages, heretics were subject to fines; they were, of course, excommunicated and barred from sensitive positions, but that was usually the limit of penalty—unless the heresy was associated with politically dangerous activities. In eleventh-century Constantinople, some leaders of a neo-Manichean sect, the Bogomils, were executed; they rejected work, procreation, and civil obedience as demonic, which no medieval state (and few modern states) would tolerate. In the same century in the West, there occurred the first killings of heretics for many centuries; these were either lynchings or arbitrary executions by princes. In accord with tradition, the bishops did what they could to prevent such acts.

The Bogomil movement spread into southern France and northern Italy, where it became entrenched in the twelfth and thirteenth centuries. The Albigensians, or Cathari, as they were called in the West, rejected marriage and property, as well as Catholic doctrine. First bishops, and then the papacy, appointed courts of inquiry ("inquisitions") as an emergency measure to locate the centers of the movement. Theologians began to find justifications for remanding heretics to the government for imprisonment or death. This was done only in extreme cases, and the total number of heretics so treated by the papal Inquisition cannot have been large. Torture was used in interrogation, just as in other courts of the period. By imposing a degree of due procedure in place of lynchings and arbitrary sentences, the Inquisition may even have caused some improvement. The fact remains that ecclesiastical sanction was now given to torture and burning at the stake. Zeal for uniformity again triumphed over sound tradition. A "Crusade" called against the Albigensians in 1208 suppressed them, devastated southern France, and permanently destroyed its political autonomy.

The heresies attacked by the Inquisition had little in common with "classical" heresies such as Arianism. They were often radical and fanatical protests against both corruption and the papal variety of reform; their doctrinal aberrations often originated in moral indignation. Such movements could easily be labelled "Manichean" even when they were not in fact dualistic. In addition to movements of popular origin, there were troublesome theories arising in quite respectable circles. For example, Joachim of Flora (ca. 1145–1202) was a venerable abbot who divided history into three ages corresponding to the Trinity. Christ had ended the Age of the Father and begun that of the Son; the Age of the Spirit was to be established by a divine messenger in 1262, after which the institutional Church would wither away. Only in 1256 was this prophecy declared a heresy.

New Forms of Religious Life

The Benedictine reform movement was closely involved with feudal society, to the detriment, some felt, of personal spiritual growth. In the eleventh century, an attempt was made from within the Benedictine tradition to return to a less worldly monasticism; this resulted in the establishment in 1098 of a highly centralized order (a very non-Benedictine idea!), the Cistercians. The idea was too popular to succeed: after a period of very rapid growth, the Cistercians found themselves much involved in the world's troubles. Their greatest figure, Bernard of Clairvaux (1091-1153), was perhaps the most active and influential man of his age, both supporting and criticizing the papal reform. He opposed new tendencies in theology and the growing legalism of the papal reform. He supported the Crusades, and (unlike the peaceful Benedictine missionaries) wars of conversion against the pagan Slavs. He was the most important of the teachers of the Cistercian school of spirituality.

The centuries of Benedictine monopoly on western monasticism were over, and new orders appeared outside of the Benedictine framework. Some emphasized withdrawal from the world. The Carthusians, founded in 1084, followed a type of monasticism highly regarded in the Christian East, combining communal life with hermitage. The Carmelites, who claimed the Old Testament prophet Elijah as their founder, seem to have originated in Palestine during the Crusades.

Other orders, however, either combined traditional monastic activity with work in the world, or had such work as their constitutional purpose. The Premonstratensians (1120) were "canons," dedicated to pastoral and liturgical activity. Military-religious orders, orders dedicated to establishing hospitals for pilgrims, and orders dedicated to ransoming Christian captives from the Muslims appeared in connection with the Crusades. And there were many others. Eastern Christianity never adopted the innovation of specialized orders, especially not the idea of an order dedicated to some activity in the world, nor the other western innovation of ordaining all "religious" (those living a celibate life under a rule, whether monks or not) to the priesthood.

The Ideal of Poverty; Francis of Assisi. The papacy, while attacking the excessive interest in wealth and power of many of the clergy, inevitably became more and more concerned with these matters itself. In the twelfth and thirteenth centuries several movements, originating mainly among laymen, attempted without papal initiative to restore to the Church the poverty and simplicity of the life of the Apostles in Jerusalem. One such movement, founded by a merchant named Peter Valdes or Waldo in the 1170s, quickly ran afoul of authority and was suppressed as heretical by the Inquisition. A similar movement, founded by Francis of Assisi (1182-1226), allied itself to the papacy and generated a religious order dedicated to poverty and to preaching repentence. This order, the "Friars Minor," was to have no possessions even communally (monks had none individually, but monasteries owned property, often a great deal of it); the friars were "mendicants"—beggars. (This was an innovation: Christian monks had always rejected begging.) Originally full of laymen, the order was quickly clericalized. Rapid growth forced concessions on the point of communal property. A dissenting group of "Franciscans" rejected the concessions, and were soon in the same category as the "Waldensians." These "spiritual Franciscans" accepted the prophecies of Joachim of Flora, proclaimed themselves the spiritual church of the Third Age, and rejected and denounced the papacy. The "conventual Franciscans," who remained loyal to the papacy, became a major influence in medieval life.

Always renowned for his devotion to poverty, Francis has recently been recognized as the great Christian spokesman for the spiritual value of nature, independent of its usefulness for humanity, as a cosmic glorification of its creator. This is, of course, the traditional Cosmic Liturgy theme in one of its aspects. In the thirteenth century, Francis seems a unique figure in expressing it. Although it probably survived, in some areas at least, as a major factor in popular spirituality, the theme finds little expression in theological literature outside of the writings of followers of Francis, such as Bonaventure. The most likely explanation would seem to lie in the influence of Augustine's Platonizing idea that nature is to be used and not enjoyed.

The Dominicans. Another mendicant order, the Friars Preachers, was founded by Domingo de Guzman (ca. 1170–1221) to combat the Albigensian heresy. The "Dominicans" were to support Catholic doctrine by preaching, teaching, and practicing poverty. Together with the Franciscans, they prevented the poverty movement and popular reforming currents from rejecting the papacy. The two orders of Friars appeared just as the first European universities were being established, papally licensed institutions offering higher studies in medicine, law, and theology. Thus, for the first time, theology became a profession; and it was soon a profession dominated by Friars.

Scholasticism

The method used in philosophy and in theology at the universities was what is called "scholasticism." It was based on the study of authoritative writings (either original sources or anthologies), raising questions and applying dialectic to decide among alternative answers. Scholastic writings aim at maximum clarity: they are organized hierarchically into divisions and subdivisions, to exhibit the intelligible structure of an entire science or of a specific section of it. Their style is technical and nonliterary.

The Aristotelian Crisis. The scholastics faced a crisis caused by the appearance, during the course of the twelfth century, of Latin translations of Arabic translations of Nestorian Syriac translations of the works of Aristotle; previously, only some writings on elementary logic had been known. Aristotle denied the teaching of the Platonists that the soul can have an intuitive knowledge of eternal truths; all knowledge depends on sense experience, consequently on matter. The intellect abstracts form from the matter in which it is embodied. This doctrine of knowledge seemed to many to be superior to the Platonic view; at the same time, it threatened to undermine the Neo-Platonic Augustinian contemplation that was practically axiomatic in western Christianity. The strict Aristotelians taught the eternity of the world and denied God's knowledge of it and care for it.

Earlier Franciscan scholastics, of whom Bonaventure (1221-1274) was the most important, accepted some Aristotelian elements, but stayed close to the Augustinian-Platonic theory of knowledge. The Dominican Albert the Great (ca. 1200-1280) insisted that theologians should accept certain Aristotelian teachings as philosophically superior, although he still retained many Neo-Platonic elements (the Neo-Platonists had attempted to harmonize Plato and Aristotle, so the combination was not impossible.)

Thomas Aquinas. Albert's pupil Thomas Aquinas (1225-1274) coordinated such a philosophy with Christian theology in a grandly comprehensive way. By clearly distinguishing the realm of faith from that of reason, he avoided both the "rationalism" of an Anselm or Abelard, and the negative reaction of a Bernard. His approach has been characterized by the phrase "distinguish in order to unite." He employed to great advantage the distinction, established by the Arab philosopher Al-Fārābī (ca. 870-950), between essence and existence. Developing an idea first set forth by Anselm, he defined original sin primarily in terms of a lack of original righteousness. In the state of Adam before the Fall, Aquinas distinguished "pure" nature, conceived abstractly with only its own inherent powers, and the free, unowed gift of original righteousness or original justice, which enables human beings to keep their lower faculties under the control of reason. The Fall involved the loss of this divine gift, leaving the natural powers disordered but undestroyed. This is a much more optimistic view of fallen humanity than that of Augustine, and it came to be accepted by most later scholastics. Fallen nature is restored and renewed by another divine gift, that of grace. Pure nature is discontinuous with grace, which comes always as a gift from outside, never an internal development; yet in a sense grace is a special case of what nature contains in general; it does not destroy, but perfects nature. Grace is a created supernatural principle that allows human beings to be moved by God in a way that excludes any compulsion to an end that transcends nature. Nature has its own relative fulfillment; grace leads it to a supernatural, eternal fulfillment.

Aquinas represents the universe as consisting of hierarchically arranged orders of being, distinct from one another but exhibiting structural similarities. The mind can grasp this combination of like and unlike, sameness and difference, applying to the several orders common terms and concepts, the sense of which is neither identically the same from one case to the next, or wholly different. This relation is "analogy," the "analogy of being." The created universe, really distinct from God, mirrors something of him, for from him it receives both form and existence. This relation can be expressed by analogy. God's goodness is qualitatively, incommensurably different from humankind's, yet by knowing what goodness is in man and woman one can have a partial knowledge of God as good.

In this way, Aquinas can retain the essentials of Augustinian contemplation while accepting Aristotle's doctrine of knowledge. The intellect can move back from things to their source, as when it searches for a first cause or for an ultimate origin of motion. When gifted with the "light of nature," it knows God by analogy. Exceptionally, as with the prophets, it may receive the "prophetic light of grace" and attain a direct knowledge of eternal truths. And in the eternal life of heaven it shall receive the "light of glory" that makes possible the "beatific vision" of the divine essence. For Aquinas, no less than for Augustine, contemplation is an act of the intellect, but always of the intellect conditioned by love, *caritas,* which is a divine gift to humankind, and which transforms not only his intellect but his will.

The Condemnations of 1277; Duns Scotus. Some extreme Aristotelians among Aquinas's colleagues contended that philosophy must accept anti-providentialism, although by faith one knows better. They provoked a backlash leading to the condemnation, in 1277, of their position and also of some aspects of that of Aquinas. The Dominicans, some of whom had vigorously opposed Aquinas, now rallied to him and proclaimed him their official teacher (1278). In 1323, they secured his recognition as a saint. But his teachings were under a cloud, and the Franciscans recovered the dominant position.

The Franciscan Duns Scotus (1266–1308) followed something of a middle course between Aquinas and anti-Aristotelian Augustinians like Henry of Ghent (?–1293). He emphasized the freedom of God, and denied that necessary reasons can be found for God's actions in creation and redemption. This freedom he emphasized by distinguishing God's ordained power (what God actually does) from his absolute power (his ability to do quite otherwise).

Like Aquinas, Duns Scotus accepted the axiom that phenomenal being is a compound of matter and form. But whereas Aquinas held that it is matter that causes individual beings to exist (individuals of the same class have the same form), Duns Scotus held that the principle of individuation is conveyed through form, but is not to be equated with form. He designated it "thisness" (Latin: *haecitas*); his development of the principle of "thisness" as concrete individual existence anticipates a major element of contemporary existentialist philosophy.

Duns Scotus held that the Incarnation of Christ, although it is surely the remedy for the Fall, would have taken place even had the Fall never occurred, as the fulfillment of the creation. This idea had been briefly suggested by Maximus the Confessor, and fits well with the neo-Chalcedonian theology, but had never been developed before. Here Duns Scotus shows himself to be the heir of Francis of Assisi, who loved the created world and rejoiced in it. Aquinas had held that a *distinction* can be either "real" or "rational"—that is, either in the object itself, or only in the mind thinking about it. Duns Scotus made extensive use of an intermediate variety, the formal distinction, applied to the relation between different aspects or features of the same thing. How are the attributes of God—his goodness, wisdom, and so on—related to each other and to his essence? Aquinas held that it could not be a real distinction, for that would violate the "simplicity" of God and his "wholeness." It is a rational distinction, but of the sort that has a real basis in the object: a "virtual" distinction in God, actualized only in the mind thinking about him. Duns Scotus accepted the simplicity of God—a basic axiom important in all western medieval theology—but asserted here not merely a rational, nor yet a real, but a formal distinction. He earned the title "subtle doctor" from his fine distinctions. The word "dunce" (from "Duns") was coined to refer to later scholastics who engaged in endless hairsplitting for its own sake.

Scholasticism and the Mass. Scholasticism was not so remote from popular religion as it might seem. The Mass, with the associated penitential system, was central to ordinary religious experience at this time, and there was constant discussion of how Christ is present in the Mass, how penance removes sin, and so on. The doctrine of "transubstantiation" was officially endorsed by Rome in 1215, and ably defended by Aquinas: the substance of bread and wine is replaced by the substance of Christ's body and blood, the perceivable qualities ("accidents") remaining the same, when the priest, reciting the prayer of consecration, repeats Christ's words: "this is my body," and "this is my blood." To emphasize the definition of how and when the transformation takes place, a new ceremony was introduced: after the words "this is my body," a wafer ("host," from a Latin word for victim; since the early middle ages, western churches had used flat, round, unleavened wafers of bread instead of the bunlike loaves that remained usual in the east) was raised for the congregation to see. This rite, rather than actual communion by eating the bread (drinking the consecrated wine was restricted to the officiating clergy, for practical reasons, at about the same time), became the focal point of lay devotion at Mass.

For many centuries, the Eucharist had been celebrated in East and West alike not only as the center of the parish's communal worship, but also in connection with prayers for special concerns of persons or groups within the parish community; prominent among these were offerings for those of the parish who had died, usually requested by their families. The Eucharist had always been regarded as the center of the unity of the Church, a unity not broken by death. In the eastern churches, the Eucharist offered for the dead Christian was regarded as effecting for him the same Communion in the life-giving divine humanity of Christ as taking Communion had before death. In the West, the emphasis upon "satisfaction" for sin rendered to God somewhat complicated the matter: what degree of "satisfaction" was attained by a "requiem Mass" (a "votive Mass" for the dead)? Although Aquinas held that the Mass could not be limited in effect, Duns Scotus held that in the Mass the body and blood of Christ (already made present by transubstantiation) are offered by the Church through the priest, whose intention determines and thus limits the measure of satisfaction. Since the "private Mass," especially the requiem, was the duty involved in many endowed livings, and was the most common form of Mass in the later middle ages, the Scotist teaching, which became the usual view, had a profound effect on popular spirituality.

Nominalism.   Medieval Latin thought was much occupied with the problem of "universals" (categories like "man," in contrast to individuals), their ontological status and relation to individuals. The concern was not merely academic, for the universals were in some sense identified with the divine ideas; they are crucial to contemplation as the "intellectual cognition of things eternal."

Fourteenth-century scholasticism was dominated by disputes between Thomists (followers of Aquinas), Scotists (followers of Duns), and Augustinians. Dissatisfaction with this division led to the rise in Franciscan circles of a school that advocated sticking closer to the data of revelation. They followed Duns Scotus in applying the "ordained power/absolute power" distinction; they restricted reason in theology to showing that the data of revelation are reasonable (not that they are necessary); and they took a much more radical position on the universals than Scotus: they denied their existence as anything more than mental constructs or "names" (hence this school is called "nominalism"). They reacted against "dunces" by making a principle of restricting hypotheses to a minimum.

William of Ockham, or Occam, (1280–1349) and his nominalist followers have often been accused of destroying scholasticism by separating faith and reason, and of using "absolute power" to depict God as arbitrarily threatening the integrity of the created order; nature and grace are now opposed to one another, outside one another ("extrincicism"). But recent studies deny that they went much beyond the Scotists in insisting on God's absolute power, or in limiting the role of reason. They were upsetting because they undermined the basis of intellectual contemplation, but they had a compensation for it in a kind of "affective mysticism" that can be traced back to Bernard of Clairvaux, based on conformity not of human intellect with God's ideas, but of human will with God's will as known in revelation (ordained power). This affective mysticism operates on two levels: the infusion by the Holy Spirit of created grace, causing a "birth of Christ in the soul," is the condition of salvation for every Christian; the spiritual elite know a special, transforming, deifying union. In common with Augustinian and scholastic tradition, they reserve the beatific vision of the essence of God to eternal Life in heaven.

Augustinians attacked both Scotists and nominalists for reviving the heresy of Pelagius by teaching that man's salvation depends on his "doing his best." They replied that this is true only by God's ordained power; God did not have to so ordain, and salvation is still his doing. The Augustinians were not convinced. Popular piety in the later middle ages was marked by a growing anxiety about individual salvation: how can a man know that he has done his best?

Western Medieval Spirituality

Religious orders exercised decisive influence on medieval spirituality. Benedictine spirituality was a continuation of ancient tradition, biblical, liturgical, and communal. During the "Benedictine centuries," there was still much similarity between eastern and western forms of spirituality. But the successive changes introduced into worship in the West made this tradition increasingly harder to maintain, at least outside the monasteries.

The Cistercian school of spirituality was influenced by Origen and Augustine, and by the Cappadocian Fathers. It cultivated Augustinian contemplation, but also emphasized the humanity of Christ, and a response of the will and emotions as well as of the intellect.

With the appearance of the Friars, these two tendencies became specialized without ever being entirely divorced. Aquinas had a strongly "intellectualist" view of contemplation that became characteristic of the "Dominicans." The Franciscans further developed the devotion to the humanity of Christ, concentrating on the Nativity (they invented the Christmas creche) and especially on the Passion. They cultivated "affective mysticism," stressing the will and feelings. Special devotions to the Wounds of Christ, to the Sacred Heart of Jesus, to the Heart of Mary, and the like, began to multiply. But Dominicans also accepted these devotions. Intellectual mysticism allowed a role for will, and affective mysticism a role for intellect.

The Dominican Meister Eckhart (ca. 1260–1327) cultivated a mysticism of intellectual contemplation based on what appears to be a gnosticizing view of the soul as containing a "spark" of divine intellect that is prevented from reuniting with God—more accurately, with Godhead, the simple intellectual essence beyond the trinity of persons—by time, matter, and plurality. Thus creation itself is the condition to be overcome. Accused of heresy, Eckhart insisted that his expressions are Catholic in meaning, and must not be interpreted amiss.

In the later middle ages, both intellectual and affective mysticism flourished, sometimes in combination, sometimes in sharply defined form. Both could be included in the definition by the nominalist mystic Jean Gerson (1363–1424): "Mystical theology is the knowledge of God by experience, attained through the embrace of unifying love." Neither variety led, as has sometimes been thought, to social irresponsibility and apathy. Practical works of charity abounded in the same milieu in which mysticism flourished.

Architecture and Art

The Eastern Orthodox churches achieved a thorough integration of architecture, painting, and worship after the end of the iconoclastic controversy. The "monophysite" churches did not carry the process so far, but achieved something similar; the Assyrians rejected icons completely. Byzantine churches were typically built on a centralized plan, with a central dome and surrounding smaller domes. Scenes and figures painted in the domes and on the walls followed specific plans. During the middle ages, the low railing that separated the altar area from the "nave" (the central area, where the congregation stands)

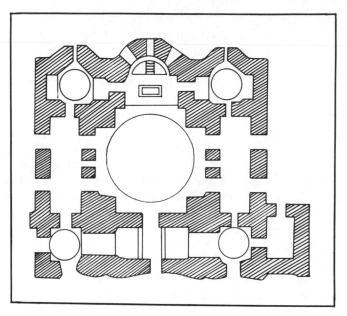

Floor plan of a Byzantine church (Church of the Dormition, Nicea), showing position of the altar.

was enlarged into a wall, pierced with doors for processions, covered with panel icons—again according to a fixed plan. This "iconostasion" formed and forms a partial visual barrier between the laity and the altar, but the characteristic centralized floor plan minimizes the distance between altar and congregation.

In the West, the Carolingian attitude toward iconography prevented the kind of integration of art and worship found in the East, except perhaps in certain Italian churches with essentially Byzantine decoration. But in the Ottonian period "romanesque" art and architecture flourished (including sculpture, which was not used in the East). The remarkable Catalan mural paintings of the eleventh to thirteenth centuries deserve special mention. Much of the art of this period was in keeping with Benedictine spirituality: biblical, liturgical, and communal. On the other hand, the use of an elongated floor plan, widely separating the laity from the altar, and the introduction of numerous small altars for the "low Mass," also date from this period.

In keeping with the anti-iconoclast emphasis on a concrete depiction of the History of Salvation, Byzantine icons of the death of Christ upon the Cross appeared by the eleventh century. The older type of crucifix had depicted Christ alive and reigning as king from the Cross. The papal legates to Constantinople in 1054 protested against the Byzantine innovation. But the growing emphasis in western spirituality on the humanity of Christ soon led to acceptance of the

The Byzantine icon of the Nativity, after the Stroganovsky *Podlinnik*. Earlier medieval representations in the West were similar.

idea, and even to a further development: the realistic depiction of the death-agonies of Christ, in three dimensions. A similar emphasis may perhaps be detected in thirteenth-century Byzantine icons, but only in a stylistic use of softer modeling for human features, somewhat mitigating the ascetic linearity of the previous style.

"Gothic" Art. Technical architectural advances in the west enabled the weight of church roofs to be transferred from the walls to an ingenious system of buttresses, giving rise to the Gothic style, with its towering cathedrals and vast expanses of stained glass. The articulation of divisions and subdivisions of the Gothic cathedral has aptly been compared to the form of the scholastic treatise, a product of the same age. The altar, now far distant from the congregation, was often hidden behind an elaborately carved screen. Carefully situated, the cathedral of this period dominated the skyline of the western European town. Size was increased until the limits of the technique were reached, yet proportion and order were not drowned in mere bigness. Different Gothic styles arose in France, England, and Germany; the style never took root in the Mediterranean countries.

Mural painting was much restricted, and Gothic art reflects the more individualistic spirituality of the later middle ages. Visions and "private revelations" began to have a major impact. For example, the visions of St. Birgitta of Sweden completely altered the western iconography of the Birth of Christ.

The Church as "Institution"

By the fifteenth century, a crisis was developing in western Christianity. The Church was experienced no longer as a community, but as an institution, an authoritative, expensive institution with its own political and economic interests. Hierarchy no longer functioned to integrate the local community; it now appeared to be a bureaucratic, clericalistic administrative system. A legalistic emphasis on authority and obedience was prevalent. And complementing the institutionalism of the Church, individualism in spirituality and religious experience largely supplanted the sense of community. Reform movements were not lacking, but the history of the medieval ages shows how easy it is for a reform movement to fail by succeeding too well. Apocalyptic consciousness was strong in the late middle ages, but it tended to find outlets outside the official structures, and even opposed to them. If a majority still looked to the Gospel and the sacraments as the true inner core of the visible Church, there were not lacking those like the Augustinian John Wycliffe (ca. 1320–1384), who in the name of the Gospel attacked the papacy, canon law, transubstantiation, sacramental confession, and the Church's holding property or political power. He at least questioned the sacramental priesthood. If few were yet willing to go so far, at least the question of what in Christianity is temporary and dispensable, and what true and essential, was increasingly troubling many of the best hearts and minds in western Christendom.

The later medieval depiction of the Crucifixion: the body of Christ is contorted by pain, blood flows from the wounds, the feet are crossed, the arms are at a considerable angle rather than perpendicular to the body, and the head is crowned with thorns.

A crucifix of the earlier medieval type, the "Holy Face" (*Volto* Santo) of Lucca, Italy. It dates from the late eleventh century, but local legend claims that it was carved by Nicodemus (see John 3.1, 19.39) and was washed up on a beach in Italy in 783.

Eastern Christians

Although a few of the same problems that plagued the West (those associated with outside lay ownership of monastic properties, for example) occasionally appeared in the eastern churches, neither the extent of corruption necessary to give rise to a western-style reform movement, nor an independent focus of

After Rembrandt's *Nativity* of 1646, which follows the iconography of the
vision of St. Birgitta of Sweden.

power like the Roman papacy, existed there. The churches under Muslim rule
were increasingly restricted and persecuted. The vast Mongol empire, established in the thirteenth century, was originally tolerant of all religions. The
rulers were mostly shamanists, and some Mongol tribes were in fact Christian
(Nestorian); many subjects of the Khan in Russia, Central Asia, and the
Middle East were eastern Christians, Chalcedonian, "monophysite," or Nestorian; and papal envoys journeyed to Mongolia. The failure of Christians in the
thirteenth century to exert sufficient effort to convert the Mongol court to
Christianity is regarded by some recent writers as a lost opportunity of prime
historical importance. The conversion of the eastern Mongol rulers to Buddhism, and more especially of the western Mongols to Islam, began for many
eastern Christian communities their "dark ages," which have lasted until the
present. After the conquests of Timur the Lame (1336–1404), the once-flourish-
ing Central Asian Christianity vanished.

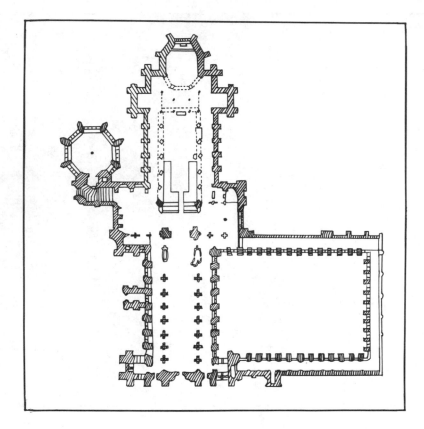

Floor plan of the Cathedral of Wells, England, showing the typical elongated arrangement.

The Byzantine Church.   The Byzantine empire's greater degree of political and cultural stability, compared to the West, creates an appearance of stagnation, which modern historians have thoroughly dispelled. Tension between an involved, activist monasticism and a charismatic, eschatological, and counter-cultural monasticism was felt here, just as in the West. Lay literacy and learning remained at a high level; the hierarchical structure of the community was somewhat obscured, but not to the same extent as in the West. No controversies comparable to those of antiquity occurred, and theologians were occupied in drawing out the implications of the neo-Chalcedonian synthesis for social and cultural life (Cyril and Methodius) and for spirituality. Simeon the New Theologian, the abbot of a small monastery, insisted that the "knowledge of God by experience" is not an unattainable goal, but is precisely the content of normal Christian life, which the life, death, and resurrection of Christ have made possible for humankind.

In the later centuries of the Byzantine empire, a sort of limited feudalism developed. The emperors struggled unsuccessfully to oppose its growth, for ethical as well as political and economic reasons. But as the empire dwindled before the onslaughts of Turks and Crusaders, the humanitarian legacy of its earlier period was greatly compromised, social services declined, and the government tended increasingly toward a police state. Even in the last centuries, however, art and learning flourished.

After the Latin invaders had been driven out, the emperors were anxious for western help against the Turks, and sometimes willing to accept Roman primacy in the Orthodox Church as the price for it. Such a reunion was officially negotiated by Greek bishops at the Council of Lyons (1274); it fell through when the Angevin rulers of Sicily secured the papal throne for a friend, who approved their scheme—ultimately unsuccessful—for a second conquest of Constantinople. Church union was a dead issue for a time. The second negotiated union was signed in 1439 at the Council of Florence; it failed when the Turkish conquest of Constantinople put an end to the Byzantine Empire (1453). In neither case, however, was the union really effective: a majority of bishops supported it, but the populace would not follow them, or accept Roman primacy as the papal party understood it.

Hesychasm. The intimate connection between dogma and spirituality is evident in some events of the fourteenth century. Some Armenian Christians seeking union with Rome were discovered to hold beliefs regarded by Latin theologians as unheard-of errors, which were duly condemned by Pope Benedict XII in 1341. Among the "Armenian errors" was the conviction that there is simply no such thing as a vision of the essence of God for created beings, not even in the eternal life of heaven. The basis of disagreement is hard to understand in this case; it is clarified in connection with a controversy of the same period in Greece.

A method of spiritual training known as "hesychasm" (from a Greek word for "tranquility") was cultivated by monks in the Byzantine empire. It involved control of breathing and posture, concentration of the mind upon the heart and bowels, and use of a brief prayer (usually: "Lord Jesus Christ, Son of God, have mercy on me a sinner"—*cf.* Luke 18.13—or "Lord Jesus Christ, have mercy on me") as a sort of *mantra*. The object of this method was to unite mind and heart in prayer, to attain the gift of ceaseless prayer (I Thess. 5.17), a prayer that continues even during sleep and is undisturbed by bodily and intellectual activities, while influencing both. Unceasing prayer may culminate in a vision of God. This is not regarded as a vision by the intellect; the divine illumination itself produces the "divine eye" that sees it, enabling mind and body alike to behold God by participating in his being.

A controversy broke out when an Italian-trained Greek-speaking monk attacked the hesychasts; a number of differences in the presuppositions of eastern and western Christian thought came to light. All schools of theology in the West stressed the *simplicity* of God and denied real distinctions in his being. The East emphasized rather the *infinity* of God, and interpreted the traditional distinction of essence and energies or attributes as a real distinction (the Scotists, who emphasized the infinity of God more than other western schools, allowed a *formal* distinction here). The vision of God, in the eastern tradition, is a vision of God not in his essence, but in his uncreated energies, alike for the prophets of the Old Testament, Christian saints, angels, and the blessed in heaven. As the Armenians held, there is no vision of God's essence, for vision is participation, and the creation is "deified" in its own essence.

Further, the vision of God is *not* an *intellectual* cognition of eternal truths. Neither by discursive reasoning nor by intuition can the intellect grasp the infinity of God. No concepts, ideas, forms, or definitions apply (including "simplicity"). Theological concern with "universals" was minimal in the East. The nominalist mysticism, based on a conformity of human will to God's, would probably have been almost as unattractive to the hesychasts as Augustinian wisdom; it sounds very much like Nestorianism. It is no accident that the nominalists were accused by western Augustinians of Pelagianism.

The western notion of "created grace" was equally foreign to the eastern tradition. In the East, "grace" is identified with the uncreated divine energies, the creative powers of God. "Created grace" and "created supernatural" are regarded as self-contradictory expressions, acceptance of which is equated with superstition.

Defended by the monk and bishop Gregory Palamas (1296–1359), the hesychast teachings were affirmed by councils in Constantinople in 1341, 1351, and 1368. The theologian Nicolas Cabasilas (ca. 1300–ca. 1370), a layman and civil servant associated with the hesychasts, wrote pregnant treatises on sacramental spirituality, intended mainly for laymen.

Although Aquinas was translated into Greek in the fourteenth century and attained a certain following among Byzantine intellectuals, it was the hesychasts who represented the native eastern tradition and were the spiritual guides of later generations. "Distinguish in order to unite" describes what is probably a basic aspect of all human knowledge; for the eastern Christian tradition, however, the "synthetic distinction" is that between God in his essence, utterly transcending all knowledge, and God in his uncreated energies, immanent in the creation and knowable by supra-intellectual experience, but still beyond all rational knowledge.

IV

RENAISSANCE AND REFORMATION

11

The Age of Reformation

The end of the western middle ages was an exceedingly complex period. Only one aspect of this time of ferment will be considered: the growing dissatisfaction of the laity with the clericalized church structure.

Lay Religious Movements

We have already seen this dissatisfaction as it was expressed in the later medieval heresies. For several centuries, the friars succeeded in heading off this danger. But the poverty movement, too successful for its own good, eventually lost much of its force. Apocalyptic fervor, always a threat to established institutions, produced bizarre penitential movements in reaction to the plagues of the fourteenth century. During the same century, in parts of northern Europe, women (called "beguines") and men (called "beghards") adopted a lifestyle similar to that of the recognized religious orders, but outside their formal structure. The lay movements were often associated with houses of friars, but they reverted to the older monastic tradition of earning their own living. Their appearance stirred up a controversy, and by 1400 they had been required to regularize their status.

But in the meantime a similar movement had appeared in the Netherlands under the leadership of one Gerhard, called Gerhard Groote (1340–1384), a merchant's son who was ordained a deacon, but never became a priest. He founded small communities with no recognized rule (these were usually called "Brethren of the Common Life"), as well as some that adopted the officially approved Rule of Augustine. Like the beghards and beguines, most Brethren of the Common Life at first remained laymen and supported themselves by their own work; but, unlike their predecessors, they were a learned, rather elite group who could defend themselves against the attacks of the regular orders. Even the Brethren of the Common Life finally became largely clericalized; their work was increasingly limited to keeping school and producing books. But their practical spirituality, the so-called *"devotio moderna,"* which stressed affective mysticism, and their emphasis on simplicity and inwardness (embodied in a well-known book, *The Imitation of Christ,* written by one of the Brethren on the basis of Gerhard Groote's teachings), were widely influential, and provide a good index to the desires of many laymen at the close of the middle ages.

Humanism.   A movement originating among the faculties of the "humanities" (Latin grammar, rhetoric, and poetry; history; and moral philosophy) of four-teenth- and fifteenth-century Italian universities, and consequently called "Hu-manism," sought to revive classical Latin literary culture, and soon embraced Greek culture as well. The humanists insisted on studying original sources, not the anthologies often used by the scholastics. They rejected the utilitarian style, and often also the method, of the scholastics. Not essentially a philo-sophical movement, humanism contributed both to a revival of Platonism and to a renewal of Aristotelianism. Especially after Greek scholars arrived in Italy as refugees from the Turks, Greek learning advanced rapidly. Hebrew and other near-eastern languages were soon being studied as well.

In a broader sense, humanism often is understood as a central interest in humankind and its potentialities. Some interpreters go farther, seeing in it an emphasis on individual greatness or possible greatness that is ultimately incom-patible with Christianity, at least as the middle ages understood Christianity. Humanists used traditional Christian language, according to this view, but meant by it something totally different from its traditional content.*

Many humanists did have an individualistic and moralistic approach to religion. However, many were Christian reformers, sometimes with a critical and satirical spirit, but in the tradition of such figures of late medieval Chris-tianity as the poet Dante (1265–1321). Humanists often criticized scholasticism, but some also rose to its defense.

"Renaissance Religion."   The renaissance culture, of which humanism was a prominent part, was fascinated by the rediscovery of ancient learning and wisdom not only in literature but in philosophy and religion. How is such knowledge related to Christianity? Renaissance thinkers faced the problem with confidence: did not Augustine of Hippo himself assert that Platonism and Christianity agree? So there arose what we may call "renaissance religion," a bipolar phenomenon, combining traditional Christianity (in its late medieval Western form) with a variety of elements understood to be secret religious teachings from antiquity, which we may designate "occult wisdom."

"Occult Wisdom."   What was this "occult wisdom"? We may define it roughly in terms of three elements: Neo-Platonism (see above, p. 84ff.), *kabbalah,* and *Hermeticism.*

Kabbalah is a mystical-esoteric movement in medieval and postmedieval Judaism, including elements from both rabbinic Judaism and gnosticism.

---

*Outside of the context of the Renaissance period, the word "humanism" has acquired a bewildering variety of meanings that need not be considered here.

Kabbalists were interested in esoteric methods of interpreting Torah, and in speculations on God's unity and attributes, and on creation and eschatology. Some were quite orthodox, while others accepted pantheistic or gnostic-dualistic ideas (or a combination of both), and the doctrine of the reincarnation of souls.

The Hermetic writings are a pre-Christian Egyptian Hellenistic collection of syncretistic texts on philosophical and religious topics, magic, astrology, and alchemy.

"Occult wisdom" was thus a vast, unsystematized reservoir of teachings, not always well understood and not equally accessible. Which elements of "occult wisdom" were accepted, and how they were combined with traditional Christianity, varied from individual to individual; the conviction that they could and should be harmonized was the common denominator of "renaissance" religion. Even those figures who appear to be only superficially Christian, such as the Neo-Platonist George Gemisthos Plethon (ca. 1135–1450), doubtless honestly thought that they were rediscovering a truer, more profound understanding of Christianity. It is easy to see that renaissance religion, in some of its manifestations, was compatible with another common feature of renaissance culture: a boundless thirst for personal greatness and reputation.

Among the most widespread convictions of "renaissance religion" was the belief that each individual is a microcosm, whose composition and proportions correspond to those of the universe; and, similarly, that physical reality is a manifestation of spiritual reality, and can reveal truths of a spiritual order. This attitude toward matter is much more positive than that of Augustinian Neo-Platonism. The correspondences between human beings and cosmos, and spirit and matter, were to be expressed mathematically—the individual is "the measure of all things" in a very real sense. Here we have returned to the broader understanding of the term "humanism."

Science and Art

An important root of modern science lies embedded in renaissance religion. Many great figures of renaissance science shared the conviction that numerical and geometrical proportions were the key to understanding the cosmos; some of them were much involved in cosmological speculations, alchemical symbolism, and the like.

Italian Renaissance Art.   Italian renaissance art reflects the ambivalence of renaissance culture and society. It originated not as a revolt against Byzantine iconography but as a development of it, attaining an independent direction under the impact of Franciscan spirituality, and cultivating a naturalistic portrayal of an idealized reality. Traditional Christian themes continued to occupy artists, but inevitably classical, "pagan" themes became equally popular. These latter, however, were generally understood as allegories of Christian truths; they do *not* express a new "secular" spirit. But, equally, Christian themes might be understood in terms of "occult wisdom"; and any subject matter could be merely an occasion for displaying the artist's technical skill. Many renaissance paintings combine tender emotionality with an atmosphere of harmony and self-assurance (see, for example, Giotto's *Lamentation* of ca. 1305, Fra Angelico's S. Marco frescoes of ca. 1440, or Leonardo da Vinci's *Virgin and Child and St. Anne* of ca. 1510). Architecture and music were cultivated in connection with the widespread idea that interest in mathematics and geometry reveal cosmic and spiritual truths.

Northern Renaissance Art. Some of these tendencies also mark northern European renaissance art. But here there was less idealization (ugliness and imperfection were portrayed more freely), and on the whole probably less harmony. The violence of the later middle ages and the religious dynamism of the sixteenth century are reflected in the paintings of Hieronymos Bosch (1450–1516), Matthias Gruenwald (1460–1528), and Albrecht Duerer (1471–1528).

Jan Hus

Among the late medieval and renaissance reformers who zealously combatted moral abuses in the Church, some challenged papal authority, and of these several were burned at the stake as heretics. Jan Hus (1369–1415) of Prague was influenced by the Augustinianism of Wyclif. He held that the true Church consists of the predestined alone; and although he was not so radical as Wyclif, he allowed only a qualified value to the institutional structures of the Church, taking Scripture and tradition consonant with Scripture as the true authority.

Hus was also influenced by a native Bohemian (Czech) reform movement, and by the teachings of Cyril and Methodius. He appealed to the tradition of the five patriarchates against papal absolutism. He supported a movement, inspired by eastern Christian practice, to restore communion of wine—the chalice—to the laity in the Mass. And he devised a form of the Latin alphabet, adapted to the sounds of the Czech language, that is the basis of the alphabets of modern Czech, Slovak, Slovene, Croatian, Lithuanian, and Latvian. Hussite circles supported a movement in favor of a vernacular liturgy rather than Latin.

Hus was condemned to death at the Council of Constance, and his followers split into rival groups. One group, the Taborites, raised a revolution, rejecting the papacy and the established government; they were suppressed only in 1435. The other, the Calixtines or Utraquists, accepted Roman authority on condition of receiving the chalice at Mass, and were tolerated by Rome, having their own bishops, for about two centuries until the Thirty Years' War. A third group, the Unity of Brethren, split from the Calixtines and from Rome and survived as an illegal sect.

While many reformers concentrated on corruption and moral abuse in the Church, Hus and others raised some basic doctrinal issues. In Germany, however, the laity showed their fervor primarily in approved or at least tolerated religious practices. There was resentment at the flow of money to the papal coffers in Rome, but national consciousness was not centered on a unified nation-state (as in France and England), nor aligned with radical theological reforms as in Bohemia. Yet it was in Germany that the alienation of reformers from the papacy first became a struggle that destroyed the unity of the western Church.

Martin Luther

Martin Luther (1483–1546) joined the mendicant order of the Hermits of St. Augustine in 1505. His training was not humanistic, but primarily in the nominalist tradition of later scholasticism, with its Franciscan voluntarist heritage; theologically, he was deeply influenced by Augustine. Like others of his time, Luther was profoundly troubled by the idea that his individual salvation depended on his "doing his best." He engaged fervently in numerous devotional and penitential activities, without ever gaining confidence that he was in fact doing what was required; he was unable to love God, or to believe that God loved him.

In 1512, Luther became a professor of biblical studies at Wittenberg University. His intensive study of the Bible led to a new vision of God's righteousness: it is not a demand for perfection, or even for doing one's best (which, for a person as intent as Luther, amounted to the same thing), but a gift of righteousness to the uprighteousness. He became convinced that this was the teaching of the Old and New Testaments; his conscience, for so long oppressed by the endless demand to make himself as righteous as possible, was at last liberated.

The medieval penitential system required satisfaction for sins, by penance before death or by a condition of temporal punishment, called purgatory, after death. This requirement could be remitted, wholly or partially, by an "indulgence" granted by church authorities; indulgences could be applied to the living or to souls in purgatory. In Luther's day, such indulgences were sold for the benefit of the "princes of the church," the higher ecclesiastical authorities. An especially blatant case of unscrupulous indulgence-huckstering in 1517 drove Luther to public protest, in which he set forth what he firmly believed to be the biblical teaching on repentence and forgiveness. The ensuing controversy revealed extensive popular support for Luther, who was protected from his enemies by the Elector (prince) of Wittenberg. When papal authority was applied to silence him, he studied the histories of the papacy and canon law, and concluded that it was a mere human institution, and full of abuses at that, not a necessary basic feature of Christianity. In a debate in 1519, he rejected papal authority and the infallible authority of councils, and approved some condemned teachings of Hus. A papal decree condemning Luther's teachings and threatening excommunication was issued in 1520; Luther burned a copy of it, along with other papal documents, in a public demonstration. In 1521, the emperor summoned him and asked if he would recant; he did not, and was shortly declared an outlaw. But it was too late. Some for good reasons and some for bad, many German princes introduced reform according to Luther's teaching in their territorial churches.

Priests were permitted to marry; monks and nuns were permitted to leave monasteries and to marry; the number of sacraments was reckoned at two (Baptism and Eucharist; confession and absolution was regarded as an extension of Baptism, usually not as a third sacrament, although it was valued as sacramental in character). Requiem and private masses and masses without communion were discontinued. Communion was given "in both kinds"—bread and wine. Preaching was improved: German hymns began to be used more extensively; rites and ceremonies held to be incompatible with scripture, and those that were unintelligible, were abolished. The orders of clergy were reduced in Lutheran doctrine to a single office, a "ministry of word and sacrament," the bishops being regarded as administrative functionaries only. (This view was, in fact, not far from the beliefs of many later medieval theologians.) Most bishops refused to go along with these measures, but the princes and city councils instituted them regardless.

Luther translated the Bible into German, composed hymns, and continued to write books and pamphlets in great number. He married a former nun and reared a family. Plagued by painful diseases, he died in 1546.

Luther was inevitably controversial; he has had bitter enemies from his own day to the present. His approval of a bigamous marriage on the part of a powerful prince was scandalous in his own time. Later ages have found his colorful, earthy language shocking (the sixteenth century was not a prudish period). More seriously, the venomous attacks on the Jews that he uttered in his later life are an embarrassment to his modern followers. Many now regard Luther as excessively subservient to political authority in matters of social justice, particularly in his behavior during the Peasant Rebellion of 1524. Luther had been sharply critical of the princes for exploiting and oppressing the peasants, but when the peasants resorted to confrontation, he urged them to bear their condition patiently, and not oppose legitimate authority; and when they resorted to violent rebellion, he urged the princes to suppress the revolt ruthlessly—which they did. Lutherans have often urged a patient acceptance of acknowledged wrongs as preferable to rebellion and anarchy, giving color to the criticism of Marxists and others that Christianity is a tool of ruling elites to keep the oppressed from doing anything effective about their condition.

Nevertheless, few would now deny that Luther, who certainly had his failings, was among the great religious geniuses of history, a prophetic figure of great moral power, vision, and courage.

Luther's Teaching. Perhaps the best way to understand Luther's teaching is to begin with Adam and Eve. Luther understood the creation account in Genesis to mean that they were placed in paradise in order to live by faith, that is, to trust God for their life and well being; and, on the other hand, to exercise a loving and peaceful dominion over the earth and the natural world. Inherently neither mortal nor immortal, Adam and Eve had no anxiety as long as they lived by faith. By trying to seize divine knowledge, they "fell" from living by faith. Subsequently, man has tried to find a substitute, to establish for himself an adequate ultimate basis for his life and destiny—to "justify" himself. He cannot do so. But he cannot admit his fault, either: he makes excuses, he "conceals his transgressions like Adam, hiding his iniquity in his bosom" (Job 31.33); and so he cannot be restored simply by God's forgiveness. Yet he knows that something is terribly wrong; no matter how hard he tries, he cannot be sure that he has "done his best" so that nothing further is required. The quest for self-justification fails; only absolute perfection could quiet the anxiety that is constantly reawakened by social norms, by any sort of failure, by the thought of death, always by something. This accusing voice is "law"; its sharpest and clearest form is the law of God, the divine commandments that Luther had tried so hard to fulfill. Before the demands of the "law," all human powers and achievements are shown to be empty (Luther had no use for the relatively optimistic view of fallen man set forth by Aquinas and the scholastics.) Its purpose is to drive man to see that no way of excusing or justifying himself can ever work.

At this point, however, he becomes open to the "gospel," the message that whatever evil he may bring on himself has already been absorbed by God himself in the suffering and death of Christ; that Christ has overthrown the power of sin, death, and Satan; and that man and woman can again live by faith, regardless of their lack of the perfection demanded by the law—Christ having fulfilled this demand and silenced the law.

Here we see that "faith" is not just the acknowledgment (under the guidance of the Holy Spirit) of divine truths, as it is for Aquinas; in Lutheran usage, faith involves knowledge and assent, but what is essential is trust, living ultimately by trust in God, in Christ, not in self-excuse or self-justification.

Traditional Lutheran theology explains "justification" as a "forensic" (courtroom) term. It states that Christ's righteousness is *imputed* or *reckoned* to the Christian, who remains in himself sinful: Luther spoke of him as being "at the same time just and a sinner." This has often led to the understanding that nothing changes in man objectively, but that God accepts a legal fiction to the effect that man is just, because his demands have been bought off by Christ. This is not correct. For one thing, the "second stage" of sin, the "concealing like Adam," is gone. Even more strongly, Luther insists that the self who was determined by the need for self-justification, the "old Adam," is put to death (in the legal terminology of Luther's day, "justification" could be employed to mean either an acquittal in court or the execution of the death sentence on a convicted criminal!); it is a new, reborn being who lives by faith. The "forensic" context of justification does bring out one aspect of Luther's teaching, but is not able to encompass all of it. Luther has often been understood exclusively in terms of "objective atonement"; in fact, he employed this approach, to some extent also the "subjective" theory, and integrated them by a striking emphasis on the "Christ the Victor" model which medieval western theology had largely lost.

"Justification by faith" is a shorthand expression, a fuller form of which is "justification by grace through faith" (or even "justification by grace alone, through faith alone, on account of Christ alone, on the basis of scripture alone"). "Faith alone" does not mean that good works are ignored; they are necessary, but as the necessary result of faith, not as necessary precondition for justification. Nor does Luther think that persons can do no good works before justification. They can, and some in fact do heroic acts of righteousness, what Luther calls "civil righteousness." But nothing of this sort is of any value for justification, in the sense of an adequate ultimate basis for life. Only perfection will do for "spiritual righteousness"—but that Christ has already taken care of, so the Christian can concentrate on caring for the world, and perhaps even do a better job of it.

Lutheran theology always stresses the sharp distinction between law and gospel, between the "old" self-justifying state and jujstification by faith, between anything that human beings can attain to by "works" and the new being that is theirs by grace, and by grace alone.

In an effort to overcome a widespread ignorance of Christian doctrine among common people in many parts of Germany, Luther composed a "Large Catechism" (a handbook for the clergy) and a "Small Catechism" (for use in the households of ordinary people). These were published in 1529. The following year, the emperor summoned a diet (official assembly of the empire) at Augsburg, to deal with the threat of a Turkish invasion and with the religious conflict in Germany. Supporters of the papacy had tried to associate the Lutheran movement with ancient and medieval heresies. The Lutheran princes wanted to present a statement defending the churches of their territories from such charges and explaining the doctrines taught, and the changes in practice that had been introduced, in those churches. This statement (based on several earlier documents) was prepared by Luther's chief assistant, Philip Melanchthon (1497–1560), a humanist scholar; it came to be called the "Augsburg Confession." The ancient "Nicene" and "Apostles'" creeds, the "Athanasian Creed," Luther's two catechisms, and the Augsburg Confession were adopted as official statements of faith and doctrine by all Lutheran churches; some territorial churches added several other documents during the course of the century (largely as a result of intra-Lutheran theological disputes), the complete collection being called the *Book of Concord.* These documents provided a formal basis of unity for what came to be called the Lutheran church.

The Swiss Reformation

Other advocates of church reform, encouraged by Luther's example, broke with the papacy. In the independent free cities of the empire, the ideal of a

Christian commonwealth was still very much alive. In German-speaking Switzerland, several such cities, with neighboring rural cantons, introduced a drastic church reform under the leadership of another humanist, Huldreich Zwingli (1484–1531).

The Swiss reformers generally agreed with Luther about "justification by faith." Like Luther, they appealed to scripture as the standard for reforms, but in a much more restrictive way. The Lutherans eliminated all practices that they judged to be contrary to scripture; the Swiss Reformed usually demanded direct biblical warrant for all religious pracices. For example: especially in cities, where organized choirs existed, Lutheran services for a century after the Reformation continued to be partly in Latin, largely because the text of the choral music was in Latin. Zwingli not only abolished the use of Latin, but eliminated all music, even congregational singing, from worship, because he found no express biblical warrant—in spite of the fact that Zwingli loved music no less than Luther, and had even better training in it!

Efforts were made to unite the two movements, but Luther and Zwingli could not agree on a number of issues. The most controversial was the nature of the Christian's participation in the being of Christ in the eucharist. Zwingli held that the words of Christ, "This is my body" (I Cor. 11.24) are a figure of speech. Christ, having ascended into heaven in his humanity, and being seated at the right hand of the Father, cannot be present in his humanity in the eucharistic bread and wine on earth. The bread and wine *signify* the body and blood, they are a vivid reminder that make Christ "present to the contemplation of faith."

The Eucharistic Controversy. Luther was horrified at Zwingli's interpretation. For him, faith included trust in the promises of God, and among the greatest of these was Christ's promise to be truly present, in his divine humanity, for the participation and nourishment of the Christian. Luther rather disliked the scholastic doctrine of transubstantiation, but he regarded the bread and wine as the vehicle or medium by which Christ is present in a quite realistic way. Once the consecrating words "This is my body" and "This is my blood" had been spoken over them, the bread and wine were to be regarded as the true body and blood of Christ. Luther allowed that a figure of speech was involved: a woman may say, "This is my child," pointing to the cradle in which the child does in fact lie, and this is one of the figures (synecdoche) of rhetorical theory; but the child is truly there. On the other hand, the "sitting on the right hand of God" is surely a figure of speech denoting Christ's sharing, in his humanity, in God's power—including his omnipresence, and his ability to be specially present to his people.

So Luther and Zwingli, when they met in 1529, remained unable to agree, and the two movements never merged. Both knew that their differences on this one issue implied significantly different understandings of basic elements of Christianity. Lutherans spoke of the body and blood of Christ as being present "in, with, and under" the consecrated bread and wine; the Reformed held that Christ was truly present "to the contemplation of faith," in the midst of the congregation, but denied the bread and wind any special role as the vessel of that presence.

John Calvin.   Zwingli died in battle in 1531. In 1534, a young French humanist with a doctorate in law, John Calvin (1509–1564), definitively renounced the papal church and embraced the Reformation movement and the teaching of justification by faith. France was not a hospitable country for the Reformation. Unlike the imperial German territories, it was already a unified, centralized nation-state; and the "Concordat of Bologna" of 1516 had given the kings of France extensive power over church affairs, at the expense of the papacy. In practice, a *national catholic* church existed in France from 1516 to 1789, and the kings disliked any sort of reform that would upset this arrangement. So Calvin went to Switzerland, and settled in Geneva, where he became the organizer of the reformed church. Calvin sought for the consistory of pastors a greater degree of independence from the city council, and more control over the moral life of citizens. He was only partly successful, but in the end he was able to accomplish much of his program. The city council continued to intervene in church affairs, but, then, so did the consistory continually intervene in civic matters. The "Christian commonwealth" idea had a dynamism in Calvin that was largely lacking in the more individualistic Luther.

Calvin, unlike Luther, rejected the late medieval idea of a single ministerial office, supplemented by an administrative bishopric; he wanted to renew the corporate, differentiated ministry of the early church, somewhat disguised as a fourfold ministry of pastors, teachers, ruling elders, and deacons (in practice, in Geneva, the latter two classes were appointed by the city council, and were largely its agents). Much more inclined than Luther to do away with pre-Reformation forms of worship, he did not accept the jejune forms of Zwingli. Rather, he retained the basic structural outline of the medieval mass in simplified form, although everything within this order was thoroughly revised; and he added congregational singing, although only in unison, and only of metrical paraphrases of psalms and other biblical texts. Such a service, with sermon and communion, was Calvin's model for Sunday worship every week. But in Geneva, the city council allowed the celebration of communion only four times a year.

Calvin was in many ways closer to Luther than to Zwingli, but in the controversy about Christ's presence in the communion he did not quite agree with either. Philosophically a Platonist, at least in part, he regarded sacraments as visible signs of a spiritual reality. Christ is indeed at God's right hand in heaven, not in the bread and wine; but in the communion the congregation is mystically elevated to participation in the heavenly reality of Christ, whose body and blood are for Calvin given "with"—although not "in and under"—the body and blood. A similar position had already been defended by Martin Bucer (1491–1551), a would-be reconciler of Luther and Zwingli who influenced Calvin deeply. Melanchthon found it acceptable, and published a version of the Augsburg Confession revised to accommodate it (1540). But most Lutherans were not satisfied, and the Book of Concord rejects this understanding, along with Zwingli's.

Calvin's *Institutes of the Christian Religion* (first edition, 1536; final edition, 1559) is a comprehensive expression of his teaching, more systematic than Luther's writings and distinguished by an admirable clarity of arrangement and style (not, as is often supposed, by a rigidly consistent scheme of logical deduction). Its central concerns include exclusive dedication to God, Scripture as the sole norm of life and doctrine, and the conviction that God is the only adequate and proper witness to himself. The papal church had become idolatrous, in Calvin's view, by claiming to be an adequate witness to God. It had attempted to domesticate God and dispense his power on its own conditions. It had turned attention away from God's word, toward human inventions.

The best known aspect of Calvin's teaching is the doctrine of "double predestination." Some people come to faith and some do not, and Calvin, like Luther and many prominent medieval theologians, was convinced that the reason in both cases must lie wholly in the mysterious depth of God's will, which is ever just, and is, in fact, the ultimate criterion of justice. The division of the human race into the elect, who will glorify God and enjoy him forever, and the reprobate, whose inevitable destiny is separation from God (for Calvin, the traditional, graphic descriptions of hell are metaphors for that separation)— this division is rooted in God's will, which is not determined by outside factors. This doctrine looms large in the *Institutes* because it was much debated just at that time; elsewhere in Calvin's writings, it is much less prominent. And it appears that Calvin did *not* teach the "limited atonement," the idea that Christ died not for all humankind but only for the elect. Christ died for all, but only the faithful can receive his benefits, and according to God's secret will only some are chosen to be the faithful. Calvin would not try to reconcile the apparent contradiction between universal atonement and limited election: God's will transcends reason and logic. But it does not appear that Calvin or his followers dwelt morbidly upon the mystery of negative predestination.

The English Reformation

A break with the papacy came in England largely, in the first instance, for political reasons: to preserve the dynasty, King Henry the Eighth needed to have a marriage annulled; largely also for political reasons, Pope Clement the Seventh could not grant the annulment. So Henry, who wanted only a national catholic system like that of France, renounced the papacy and had himself declared supreme head of the Church of England. Those who publicly rejected royal supremacy were subject to the death penalty. Henry also disbanded all of the monasteries, an act that aroused some open resistance, but not a great deal. Otherwise, church institutions remained much as before, and harsh laws were passed against denying transubstantiation or the value of private masses, and the like.

But the influence of the continental Reformation was growing, and after Henry's death (1547) reforms similar to those in Lutheran Germany took place. In 1549, a Book of Common Prayer was isued, containing church services reformed in the Lutheran manner and translated by the Archbishop of Canterbury, Thomas Cranmer (1489-1586), into majestically beautiful English. However, Zwingli's influence soon came to dominate the English reformers, and in 1552 a new Book of Common Prayer, revised by Cranmer in the direction of the Swiss reformed services (although still much closer than the latter to the medieval form) was issued. It was required by law to follow the Book of Common Prayer in the churches; in connection with the 1552 book, images were removed from churches and the interior arrangement of the buildings was altered to approximate the Swiss Reformed practice more closely. The 1552 Prayer Book also reflected a Zwinglian view of the Eucharist. Even so, the Zwinglians and Calvinists were not satisfied, and pressed for more radical change, while the majority of the laity probably regretted the dissolution of the monasteries and resented the alterations in their worship.

An attempt to reimpose the papacy in England during Queen Mary's reign (1553-1558), in which a number of former leading men were burnt at the stake, brought the reformers into greater favor with public opinion. Among those who fled abroad to escape persecution (the "Marian exiles"), many came to accept the doctrines and practices of the continental Reformed churches. Others continued to favor a more moderate reform, in which the office of bishop and the 1552 Prayer Book would be retained; and, after Mary's death, Queen Elizabeth imposed a settlement along these lines.

Those who insisted on a direct biblical warrant for all aspects of worship and church polity came to be called "Puritans"; they disliked the Prayer Book and government by bishops; they preferred Calvin's theology, and his system of government by elders or *presbyters*. A Presbyterian Calvinist church was established in Scotland, under the leadership of John Knox (?-1572). Those Puritans who agitated against the Elizabethan settlement were liable to persecution; so were the "Recusants," who remained loyal to Rome and participated in illegal masses offered by fugitive priests.

The "Magisterial Reformation."   Thus, there arose three varieties of Reformation that rejected the papacy and espoused justification by faith and church reform on the basis of scripture, while retaining, where possible, establishment as official state churches: Lutheran, Reformed, and Anglican. Collectively, these movements are called the "Magisterial Reformation."

The "Radical Reformation"

Others, however, were more conscious of the negative effects of establishment, and more optimistic about the possibility of overcoming them, on one condition:

true Christians must abandon the idea of a Christian state, a society or culture or civilization generally Christian. The world is always against Christ and against his true followers, and a state church is only a part of the world. In contrast to the "Magisterial Reformation," the movement that rejected any alliance of church and government is called the "Radical Reformation."

The largest number of these Radicals were termed "Anabaptists" ("re-baptizers"), because they rejected infant baptism and practiced only a voluntary believer's baptism, even for those who had been baptized into a state church as infants. (In their eyes, of course, this was not a "re-baptism" or "second baptism," but the only real baptism.) Most of the Anabaptists came to be grouped into regional, organized communities of the sort often called "sectarian," practicing a strict internal discipline enforced by total exclusion ("the ban" or "shunning") for serious offenders. They attempted to live according to the pattern of the New Testament Christian community, and believed that real, empirical holiness could be achieved in such a life—in contrast to the skeptical attitude of people like Luther toward such claims. Otherwise, the Anabaptists, most of them, were peaceful—indeed, pacifist—and many of their groups shared theological doctrines of the Trinity and Incarnation with the state churches.

Yet the Anabaptists were persecuted by Inquisition methods by all the state churches, in part because they were not distinguished from other, violent varieties of radical Reformation. Most prominent among the latter were the followers of Thomas Muenzer (1489–1525), an apocalyptic prophet who led the unsuccessful rebellion of German peasants in 1524; and another band of apocalyptic revolutionaries who seized the city of Muenster-in-Westfal (Germany) and instituted a fanatical tyranny in 1534–1535, only to be stamped out when the city was taken by an army raised by its Roman Catholic bishop. Thereafter, all Anabaptists were generally regarded as dangerous, revolutionary fanatics.

Another tendency in the Radical Reformation was Spiritualism, a development of late medieval mysticism that emphasized direct divine inspiration and rejected institutional forms, sometimes openly and completely, sometimes only by relegating them to the rank of indifferent human conventions, to which the spiritual person conforms outwardly. Perhaps the spiritual Radicals were connected with underground survivals of the Spiritual Franciscans.

A third tendency, Rationalism, led in its extreme form to rejection of both the divine nature of Christ and the Trinity ("Unitarianism").

These three tendencies interacted in complex ways, making it difficult to briefly characterize the Radical Reformation. Among its most common features were intense apocalypticism, rejection of the state church, rejection of infant baptism, the doctrine that the souls of the dead sleep until the Resurrection ("psychopannychism"—a doctrine especially disliked by Calvin); and an intense missionary zeal that the Radicals regarded as imperative for all true Christians.

"Protestantism"

2nd Diet of Speyer At an imperial diet of 1529, pro-Lutheran German princes delivered a formal "Protestatio," stating their position and complaining of the policies of the emperor and the anti-Lutheran princes (in Latin, "protestatio" can mean either a statement of one's own position or a protest against something). From this minor document, the pro-Lutheran princes came to be called "Protestants." The term then spread as a designation that came to include the entire Magisterial Reformation, and finally even the Radical Reformation. All "Protestants" rejected the papacy, and the majority of them shared certain broad beliefs and emphases, but the term is a historical accident, justified more by convenience than by any identifiable unity in the total ensemble of Magisterial and Radical Reformations. Those who remained with the papacy came to be called "Catholics," in contrast to the "Protestants"; more specifically, "Roman Catholics."

"Protestantism" was thus never a unified movement, although some general convictions were shared by the vast majority of those who rejected the papacy. Many important features of late-medieval piety, including the specialized cults of saints and the high popular regard for miraculous events, relics, and images as foci of devotion, were replaced in all varieties of Protestant devotion, usually by private and family Bible-reading (newly possible because of printing and increased literacy), supplemented by books of prayers and sermons, and catechisms. With Luther, Protestants generally rejected the specific sacrificial function, and often the sacramental character, of the ordained clergy, together with the notion that the "religious" life, in the sense of celibate life under a rule, is holier than "secular" life (life in the "world"), and superior to it. They followed Luther's innovation of extending the notion of "vocation" or "calling" to any honest occupation: the Christian as a butcher or nurse can serve God as truly as can the priest, nun, or monk. Except for certain survivals among the Lutherans (some monasteries and convents continued to exist within Lutheran territorial churches for a century after the Reformation), monasticism vanished among them.

Worship in the Reformation.   In their communal worship, as we have seen, the various reforming movements adopted quite different and conflicting principles of reform, but all attempted, with some success, to restore participation in what we have called "normal mysticism," and to eliminate the medieval clericalism. The ancient morning and evening services, simplified and emphasizing scripture and psalmody; a simplified cycle of annual feasts and special seasons; a church centered upon an altar, and a reformed Mass or Communion service emphasizing communion rather than sacrifice, were retained by most Lutherans and (with several important concessions to Zwingli!) Anglicans, while the Reformed and the Radicals introduced much more drastic changes; but scripture and preaching were emphasized by almost all. The metrical hymns, called "chorales," that constituted the major Lutheran contribution to communal worship, include many fine texts happily set to equally excellent melodies; the metrical paraphrases of biblical texts favored by the Reformed, if usually homier and less exalted, include texts and tunes that rival the best Lutheran productions. Luther could compose liturgical prayers in the best classical style:

> Almighty God,
> who by the death of thy Son
> > hast brought to naught sin and death,
> and by his resurrection
> > hast brought again innocence and everlasting life
> so that, delivered from the devil's power,
> > we may live in thy kingdom:
> Grant us that we may believe this with all our heart
> > and, steadfast in this faith, praise and thank thee always;
> > through the same thy Son Jesus Christ our Lord.

So could Cranmer:

> Almighty God,
> give us grace that we may cast away the works of darkness
> > and put upon us the armor of light,
> now in the time of this mortal life,
> in which thy Son Jesus Christ came to visit us
> > in great humility;
> that in the last day,
> when he shall come again in his glorious majesty
> > to judge both the quick and the dead,
> we may rise to the life immortal;
> through him who liveth and reigneth with thee and the Holy Ghost.

And Calvin:

> Heavenly Father, full of goodness and grace,
> as thou art pleased to declare thy holy will unto thy poor servants,
> and to instruct them in the righteousness of thy law,
> grant that it may also be inscribed and impressed upon our hearts,
> in such wise, that in all our life
> > we may endeavor to serve and obey none beside thee;
> neither impute to us all the transgressions
> > that we have committed against thy law;
> that, perceiving thy manifold grace upon us in such abundance,
> we may have cause to praise and glorify thee
> through Jesus Christ, thy Son, our Lord.

Some sections of the Radical Reformation preferred extemporaneous prayer. Others devised services on the basis of Scripture, usually with little reference to traditional norms. At its worst, the worship of the churches of the Reformation could bog down in tedious didacticism and introspection.

The Catholic Reformation

The classical medieval alliance between reformers and papacy collapsed in the sixteenth century, but not entirely and not everywhere. Many Christians continued to hope and work for a reformation under papal auspices, that would bring the "Protestants" back into union with Rome. In fact, the "Catholic Reformation" was continuous with earlier reform efforts; but these had failed time and again to prevail against the entrenched bureaucrats and money grubbers. Not even the shock of the Magisterial Reformation produced much action at first; those in power used it as an excuse to attack Catholic reformers like the humanist Erasmus (1466–1536), claiming that "Erasmus laid the egg that Luther hatched."

But the reformers gained strength under Paul III (pope 1534–1549), and in 1537 a commission of proreform cardinals issued a report calling for drastic institutional reform. On these issues, Protestants and Catholic reformers largely agreed. The report failed to deal with the crucial doctrine of justification, but the chairman of the commission, the humanist Cardinal Contarini (1483–1542), hoped that agreement could be reached. In 1541, he succeeded in obtaining agreement at a conference between moderate Catholic theologians and conciliatory Protestants, including Bucer and Melanchthon; but the conference failed to produce agreement on transubstantiation, and even the agreement on justification was largely rejected by both sides.

The "Counter-Reformation."   A hard line was now adopted. In Italy, a new Inquisition was organized, and the Catholic Reformation became not only zealous, but also rigoristic, prudish, and intolerant. The more speculative aspects of renaissance religion became risky: the Dominican philosopher Giordan Bruno (1548–1600), who taught a sort of pantheism, was burnt at the stake. Even the comparatively nonspeculative astronomer Galileo (1564–1642) was imprisoned; he supported the new theory of Copernicus, that the earth and the planets revolve around the sun; advocates of the Aristotelian theory (in which the sun revolves around the earth) represented the quarrel as a theological issue, and in an historic blunder Roman Catholic Church authorities sided with them and attempted to silence Galileo. The Inquisition returned to prominence. (The Spanish Inquisition, the worst of all inquisitions, was in fact an instrument of the Spanish monarchy, operating from 1479 to 1808, and should be distinguished from the papal Inquisition.) From its defensive, anti-Protestant aspect, the Catholic Reformation is often called the "Counter-Reformation."

The Council of Trent.   A reforming council was finally convoked at Trent (Trento, northern Italy) and met in three sessions (1545–47; 1551–52; 1562–63).

The council avoided questions disputed among Catholic theologians, but re-affirmed the general Catholic position against Protestant attacks, and provided for educating the clergy, for better preaching and instruction, and so on—reforms that were only slowly implemented. It also commissioned the preparation of a standard printed edition of the Roman service books, a measure that led in the end to an unprecedented degree of uniformity in Roman Catholic worship; and it gave official approval to the restrained style of choral polyphony named for Giovanni Palestrina (ca. 1525-1594), while condemning extravagance or theatricality in liturgical music.

The Jesuits. The Counter-Reformation benefited from the services of a new religious order, the Society of Jesus (Jesuits). It was founded by a somewhat disreputable Spanish soldier, Ignatius Loyola (1491-1556), who, disabled by a wound, was converted to the religious life. He composed a set of *Spiritual Exercises,* designed to instill the soldierly virtue of total obedience in the service of Christ and the Church. Unlike the older, "contemplative" orders, the Jesuits were engaged in social and educational activities, and did not practice communal prayer. The order grew rapidly, and had to adopt a military form of organization. Jesuit schools, following a uniform and effective plan of education, appeared in far-flung parts of the world. It was the Jesuits who led the ultimately successful struggle to prevent Poland and Hungary from becoming Protestant countries.

Spanish Mysticism. Descriptions of progressive stages of prayer, incorporating the western developments of the doctrine of grace from Augustine on, began to appear in the later middle ages. The Jesuits, who abandoned the traditional worship and devotions of the religious life, typified one kind of development: a systematic method of meditation was cultivated, combined with an "active" life in (but not of) the "world," in contrast to the withdrawn, "contemplative" life of the older orders, and even to the "mixed" active-contemplative practices of the friars. Similar methods were also devised by others, and became popular among Catholics.

Among the older orders, however, there was a new wave of "contemplative" mysticism, best embodied in the writings of two Spanish Carmelites, Teresa of Avila (1515-1582) and John of the Cross (1542-1591). Their influence has since largely dominated Roman Catholic mystical theology. In it a distinction is made between prayer requiring deliberate acts of the will and discursive reason ("ascetical," "acquired," "active," or "meditative" prayer), and prayer in which such acts are replaced by special divine gifts of love and vision ("mystical," "infused," "supernatural," or "contemplative" prayer); each is subdivided into various grades. Different writers and schools disagree in terminology, and partly in substance, so that there has been constant controversy down to the present about whether it is proper or useful to speak of "acquired contemplation," whether all Catholics or only a spiritual elite can legitimately aspire to the prayer of contemplation which leads to union with God, and so on. When this mystical movement fell under the suspicion of the notorious Spanish Inquisition, its center shifted to France.

Catholic Worship and Spirituality. While introducing reforms parallel to those of the Protestants, Roman Catholics retained and developed those aspects of late medieval spirituality that the Protestants rejected, including devotions to the Sacred Heart of Jesus—although the English Calvinist Thomas Goodwin (1600–1680) developed something similar in his *The Heart of Christ*—and to the Blessed Sacrament (a consecrated wafer of bread from the Mass, exhibited for adoration in a crystal container on a metal stand), and the Stations of the Cross (meditations before a series of pictures illustrating events of the Passion of Christ). Liturgical services proper continued to be increasingly laden with secondary features and treated as spectacles. More reverent behavior and attitudes in church were encouraged, but on the whole there was little effort to renew active lay participation and "normal mysticism" except in the seventeenth-century France, where translations and explanations of the Latin services were provided and the services were conducted so as to encourage participation.

Distribution of the Churches. During the century following 1517, the geography of religion gradually stabilized itself in Europe. England had its own national state church. Much of Germany, the national Scandinavian monarchies, and the Baltic areas dominated by Germans and Scandinavians, were officially Lutheran. Reformed churches were established in much of Switzerland and Holland, in Scotland, and in parts of Germany; there were strong Reformed minorities in France and elsewhere. Southern and east-central Europe, Flanders, Ireland, and large parts of Germany were Roman Catholic; in France and Spain, the Roman Catholic national monarchies controlled church affairs tightly.

The Beginnings of Tolerance

Tolerance appeared early in some areas, such as the ethnically pluralistic province of Transylvania. The Counter-Reformation succeeded in restoring most Hungarians to the Roman Catholic Church, but in Transylvania the Hungarian Reformed church succeeded in withstanding it; a Unitarian church separated from the Reformed and became a major element in the religious composition of the province. The Saxon German populace remained predominantly Lutheran. Toleration was finally extended to Roman Catholics, Reformed, Unitarians, and Lutherans; the Orthodox Rumanians of the province continued to suffer legal disadvantages until the introduction of the Unia (see page 150), around 1700.

Inquisition methods did not vanish, however (they worsened in Spain), and few governments as yet dared tolerate religious pluralism. But Protestant governments, though unready to grant freedom of worship to Roman Catholics,

would not persecute them as heretics—only "Arians" (Unitarians) and other
extreme deviants were so treated. Freedom of conscience thus began to win
acceptance in politics. The Radical Reformation, by inspiring passive resistance
to all state-church systems, if necessary to the death, contributed heavily to the
ultimate victory of religious freedom. Those Radicals who espoused armed
rebellion and the Calvinist minorities of sixteenth-century France ("Huguenots") and seventeenth-century England, made the major contribution to radical politics in an age of absolutism, while Lutherans, in particular, contributed
to the growth of absolutism. In France, the bloody wars of the period 1562-1598
(the St. Bartholemew's Day Massacre of thousands of Huguenots in 1572 was
one of many such acts by both sides) ended only with the Edict of Nantes (1598),
which granted limited toleration of Huguenots. The aristocratic Catholic essay-
ist Montaigne (1533-1592) opposed such slaughter on the basis of skepticism:
none of the contending beliefs can be proved conclusively, so it would be better
if no changes were made that would bring turmoil or violence.

The destructive sixteenth-century wars of religion unleashed by the Reformation were followed by the horrors of the Thirty Years' War (1618-1648) in
Germany. At first, it seemed to be a "crusade," Catholics and Lutherans
battling each other for religion; but opportunistic political motives became
increasingly dominant and evident. The end result was a negotiated recognition
of religious pluralism, including now the Reformed, in Germany (over the bitter
protests of the papacy). The material culture and the worship of the Lutheran
Churches suffered a blow from which they never recovered.

Puritans and Anglicans. In England, the adherents of the Reformed movement became increasingly alienated from the monarchy and from the state
church, with its bishops and Book of Common Prayer. After 1580, these "Puritans" were divided between Presbyterians, who preferred Calvin's system of
church governmment and worship, and "Independents" (or Congregationalists)
who wanted neither bishop nor a presbytery to exercise authority over local
congregations, and preferred extemporaneous prayers to any order of worship.

The Puritans, like the Pharisees, came to be popularly identified with the
worst excesses of their movement. "Puritanism" came to mean "the haunting
fear that someone, somewhere, may be happy" (Mencken). But the ranks of
the Puritans included the humanist Peter Sterry (1613-1672), whose joyous
spirituality was a sort of Calvinist version of Origen's; Francis Rous (1579-
1669), a disciple of medieval mystics, and Richard Baxter (1615-1691), who
combined a method of meditation similar to Loyola's with a reminder that
"justification by faith" is a message not of anxiety but of peace and confidence.

Unlike the continental Reformations, the Anglican Reformation originally
had no particular theological vision motivating it. But the Puritans issued a
torent of sharp criticism against bishops, the Book of Common Prayer, and
the Constantinian idea of a Christian society in which the "body politic" and
the Church, the body of Christ, are coterminous. However, a defender of these
aspects of Anglicanism appeared in the person of Richard Hooker (1554-1600),

a very learned and eloquent country priest. Hooker's many followers came to be called "High Churchmen."

The English Roman Catholic minority were associated in the public mind with England's archenemy, Spain, and with the treasonous Gunpowder Plot (1605); the Puritans regarded "prelacy" (government by bishops) as only a short step from "popery," while the rulers felt that it was so bound to the monarchy that the two institutions stood or fell together. Charles I (king 1625-1640) and the Anglican Archbishop of Canterbury, William Laud (1573-1645), used high-handed methods to bring the Puritans into line. A very destructive civil war ensued; both Charles and Laud were deposed and beheaded, and a republican government and a presbyterian church were established—only to result in more political repression and more religious dissension. Monarchy and episcopacy were restored (1660), but the Roman Catholic inclinations of the Stuart kings led to a bloodless revolution (1689) that placed a Dutch Calvinist, William of Orange, on the throne, and at last allowed limited religious toleration for everyone except Romanists, Unitarians, and Jews.

Tolerance and religious liberty thus appeared and gained in northern Europe, slowly and with setbacks. In France, the Edict of Nantes was revoked in 1685, and the Huguenots were again repressed. The result of religious coercion in England and France was not religious uniformity, but the beginnings of non-Christian, and even anti-Christian, movements that denied providence ("deism") or even God ("atheism"), hidden under a cloak of outward conformity.

Scholasticism Again.   It is perhaps not surprising that Aristotelian philosophy and the scholastic method enjoyed a revival among Roman Catholics; the Jesuit Francisco Suarez (1548-1617) combined humanism and Thomist scholasticism in a profound and influential synthesis. But this revival also included Lutheran and Calvinist schools and universities, although Luther had strongly opposed Aristotelianism and scholasticism in theology, and almost all the other important Reformers had been antischolastic, and often Platonizing, humanists.

Luther and Melanchthon had distinguished between theoretical, academic theology, which endeavors to ascertain the objective meaning of Scripture, and "true" theology, which involves the apprehension of being concretely addressed by the word of God. The one requires only scholarly competence, and results in "historical faith"; the other requires the gift of true, saving faith. But "true" theology requires a factual, objective basis of knowledge; and so academic theology flourished in Lutheran and Calvinist universities. In spite of the attitudes of the reformers, and the efforts of the Huguenot humanist Peter Ramus (1515-1572) to provide a non-Aristotelian logical basis for philosophy, Aristotelian scholasticism dominated in the seventeenth century, the age of "Protestant orthodoxy" or "Baroque dogmatics."

Lutheran scholastics emphasized "forensic justification." To avoid making salvation wholly formal and external, they developed the idea of sanctification as a distinct, subsequent stage, and arrived at a schematic "order of salvation":

call to faith, illumination, repentance and conversion, sanctification, and mystical union. The common idea that this theology was narrowly intellectualistic and spiritually arid is probably based on the assumption that all scholastics are "dunces," and on a failure to recognize the objective purpose of academic theology. Johann Gerhard (1582-1637), perhaps the greatest of the Lutheran scholastics, was a friend and disciple of Johann Arndt (1555-1621), the translator and editor of medieval devotional classics and himself the author of the greatest of all Lutheran books on spirituality, *True Christianity.* In these circles, doctrine was inseparable from burning devotion.

Reformed scholasticism emphasized the doctrine of double predestination, leading to the position that predestination precedes the fall, or even the creation, of humankind, and that Christ died only for the elect. (Transposed into philosophy, this extreme predestination produced the idea that all apparently human acts are really performed by God: A. Geulincx, 1624-1669.) These developments were resisted by the followers of Jacob Arminius (1560-1609) in Holland, and, in a more moderate way, by humanist Huguenot followers of John Cameron (1579-1673) and Moses Amyraldus (ca. 1620-1664) in France.

"Renaissance Religion" Again. "Renaissance religion" did not vanish in the age of Baroque dogmatics; it flourished in northern Europe. Interest in alchemy, plans to reform society embodied in fanciful utopias, and apocalyptic hopes mingled in the writings of John Dee (1527-1608) and Robert Fludd (1574-1637) in England, and in the Naometrician and Rosicrucian movements, and the writings of Valentin Weigel (1533-1588) and Jacob Boehme (1575-1624) in Lutheran Germany.

Jacob Boehme. Boehme, a cobbler and merchant, wrote a number of works, in an often obscure but movingly poetic style, on "theosophy"—a vision embracing all of reality and aiming a mystical rebirth to salvation. He combined the now familiar parallelism of spirit and matter, and of humankind and cosmos, with the conviction that all life, including God's, depends on the interaction of opposing forces. God is pure, undetermined, active will (Abyss or "Ungrund"), but he also possesses a passive structure of order (the "Virgin Sophia," or wisdom) that causes the will to reflect on itself, thus becoming two; their interaction produces a third, and thus God is a Trinity. The Trinity possesses a positive and a negative energy, which cause the internal dynamic to achieve outward expression in creation. The two opposing forces in creation set up a turmoil, but these are harmonized and brought into conformity with Sophia.

Like Origen, Boehme envisions a precosmic fall into time and matter. Originally androgynous, Adam is divided into male and female and enslaved to self-will, until Christ reunites humanity with Sophia and subordinates self-will to love. Boehme is not precisely a pantheist: the world is a reflection of God's inner life, but it is really distinct from God. Nor is he precisely a dualist: the negative energy is not evil in God, and its counterpart in the world is evil only when not yet subjugated to the positive energy—and each needs the other. Discursive reason (*Vernunft*) sees evil in God, but the higher understanding (*Verstand*) established by selfless love sees that God is wholly good.

Boehme was suspected of heresy by the Lutherans of his own day, and modern interpreters differ, some regarding the traditional Christian elements of his thought as an artificial accommodation to established views, while others see him as an eccentric but profoundly original heir to medieval German mysticism and to Luther; he resembles Origen in being ever controversial. His notion of a "dialectical" relationship (opposing forces requiring unity in a higher synthesis) between God and the world underlies much of later German philosophy; his influence was also considerable in England and Russia.

The Reformations and Culture: Science.   The energies released by the several reformations had a great social and cultural impact. In addition to the revolutionary proclivities of some Radicals and Calvinists, almost all the other reform movements involved or generated support for social and economic reform. The reformers strongly opposed the exploitation that accompanied the growth of a money economy. They instituted major improvements in education. Interest in the study of history increased enormously as an outgrowth of reformation polemics. If the period saw the ill-advised effort of church authorities to restrict Galileo's freedom of scientific inquiry (1633), it also witnessed a partial recovery of the old "cosmic liturgy" motif that stimulated research. Luther's emphasis on the universal presence of the incarnate Christ, and his broadening of "vocation" to include research in natural science, permitted both methodological autonomy and theologically motivated support. Many Lutheran theologians were amateur astronomers or chemists and strong supporters of the professionals, who in turn were amateur theologians. Among the latter was John Kepler (1571-1630), who ended his *Harmony of the World* with the following prayer:

> I thank thee, O Lord, our Creator,
> > that thou hast permitted me to look at the beauty
> > > in thy work of creation;
> I exult in the works of thy hands.
> See, I have here completed the work to which I felt called;
> I have earned interest from the talent that thou hast given me,
> I have proclaimed the glory of thy works
> > to the people who will read these demonstrations,
> to the extent that the limitations of my spirit would allow.

Calvin shared this perspective, although not the Lutheran view of the Incarnation. He contributed a methodological reform, emphasizing both empirical data and (with the Renaissance Platonists) mathematics. It is probably no accident that the telescope and the microscope were invented by Dutch Calvinists. Followers of the German Spiritual Radical Caspar Schwenckfeld

(1490–1561) had a speculative interest in science. In England, the destruction of monastic libraries had a regrettable effect on scientific and mathematical learning, and the Puritans, who tended to be suspicious of the speculative uses to which mathematics was put, were of some importance in spreading the non-speculative, empirical view of science propounded by Francis Bacon (1561–1626); the Platonizing aspects of Calvinism were developed in the seventeenth century by the "Cambridge Platonists." On the continent, the Jesuits cultivated mathematics, and educated René Descartes (1596–1650), who attempted to bring all knowledge into conformity with the abstract certainty of mathematics.

The Reformations and Culture: Language. The heritage of Cyril and Methodius was conveyed through the Hussites to the Lutherans, and a number of languages achieved literary status as a result, not only those of then-colonized Lutheran peoples (Finns, Estonians, Latvians). Several predominantly Roman Catholic peoples trace their national literatures to Lutheran founders: Primoš Trubar (1508–1586) in Slovenia, Jonas Rēza (1576–1629) and Kristijonas Donelaitis (1714–1780) in Lithuania, L'udovit Štúr (1815–1856) in Slovakia.

The Reformations and Culture: Fine Arts. After the upheavals of the Reformation, the art of Catholic southern Europe lost its calm aura and developed into the exuberant, dynamic, and often grandiose *baroque* (approx. 1600–1750). The passionate ecstasy of the Carmelite mystics was embodied in such works as Bernini's sculpture, *The Transverberation of St. Theresa* (1647), and in an entirely different way in the strangely dematerialized figures painted by El Greco (ca. 1548–ca. 1614). Counter-Reformation polemics influenced painters' subject matter: the Virgin, the throne of St. Peter, and Catholic sacraments and saints were favorite topics.

A more restrained baroque was cultivated by German and Scandinavian Lutherans. A sober intensity of personal faith, rather than Carmelite ecstasy, is expressed in the works of Rembrandt (1606–1669), a Dutch Calvinist influenced by the Anabaptists. The Anglican "metaphysical" poets embodied baroque spirituality in violent literary images. The greatest contribution of the Lutherans was their massive patronage of baroque music, which culminated in the works of J. S. Bach (1685–1750).

The Reformation and Eastern Christians. Although the Reformation regarded itself as a (universally valid) rediscovery of the Gospel, it was essentially a western answer to a western problem, both determined by the Augustinian framework of individual salvation with its emphasis on predestination and justification. A number of informal attempts, first by Hussites and then by Lutherans, to discuss union with the Orthodox all failed. Melanchthon, a good scholar in Greek patristics, translated the Augsburg Confession into Greek, and, as far as possible, into non-Augustinian and nonscholastic terms, playing down "forensic justification." But even in this form the Confession was not satisfactory to the Orthodox, on the one hand; on the other, Melanchthon's

After Bernini's *The Transverberation of St. Theresa* (1647).

bold, experimental translation had no official status among Lutherans. Other Protestant efforts in the same direction met the same fate.

Catholic Missions.   The Renaissance and early modern period was a "golden age" of Roman Catholic missionary activity. Catholic Spain and Portugal became world sea powers and explored far-distant lands. France also sent explorers to North America. In the Americas, Catholic missions were often associated with military conquest (see chapter 14).

In Africa and Asia, however, Catholic explorers searched for the legendary Christian empire of "Prester John," and in fact encountered Eastern Christians in Ethiopia and India. It must be acknowledged that these contacts already exhibit Western cultural imperialism toward Eastern Christians.

On the other hand, the Jesuits initiated remarkable missionary efforts in India and China, based on the opposite principle: Christianity was to be adapted, as far as possible, to the highly developed cultures of these areas, and in such a way as to appeal especially to the leaders of the society: Jesuits became first-class Confucian scholars in China. The rivals of the Jesuits accused them (not without justification in some instances) of going too far and compromising Christianity. The remarkable Chinese mission collapsed because of anti-Jesuit intrigues in Rome, after considerable initial success; another successful mission was destroyed in Japan by the Japanese government; but the Vietnamese Catholic church, originating at the same time, survives to the present.

Christians in the Turkish Empire

The Christians of the Balkans and the Near East were ruled by the Ottoman Turkish empire, which recognized non-Muslim nationalities on the basis of religion, rather than language or territory, and permitted them a degree of internal self-administration; they were thus able to survive and preserve a sense of identity. But the Turks exploited them by charging large fees for permission to consecrate bishops, and by deposing (or even killing) bishops frequently. This led to considerable demoralization. The Slavic and Rumanian Orthodox under Turkish rule were Hellenized culturally; later, they came to resent Greek influences. Conversion to Islam was encouraged; reversion to Christianity carried an automatic death sentence, and produced the Orthodox "New Martyrs." The Turks removed boys from Christian families and raised them as Muslim soldiers, the "Janissaries"; Christians who rose in revolt knew that they were fighting the sons of their own people.

Moscow and Lithuania

The Orthodox of what had formerly been the Kievan Rus' state were free of Turkish rule. After the thirteenth-century Mongol conquest, the Grand Duchy of Moscow gradually imposed centralized, autocratic rule over the northern and eastern Rus' principalities, while the Grand Duchy of Lithuania absorbed those of the south and west. Moscow was Orthodox; Lithuania was converted from the indigenous pre-Christian religion to Latin Catholicism, under strong Polish influence, but the rulers granted full equality to the Orthodox under its rule ("Ruthenians"). Each duchy claimed its Orthodox metropolitan to be the successor to the earlier metropolitans of Kiev. The metropolitans were chosen in Constantinople, and were usually Greek.

The Muscovites rejected the Union of Florence and reluctantly began to consecrate their own metropolitans in 1448; the Ruthenians also rejected the Union, but continued to recognize the jurisdiction of Constantinople; after the Turkish conquest of 1453, the Union was abolished, but the Ruthenians had to bear indirectly the burden of Turkish economic exploitation.

A Monastic Conflict. Two monastic reform movements collided in Muscovy. The "Possessors," led by Joseph of Volokolamsk (1439–1515), had large monasteries that owned much property. They were socially and politically active, sponsoring educational and welfare institutions. Their monastic rule covered details of external behavior, and stressed correct, decorous performance of worship services. When a widespread, underground heresy was discovered (the "Judaisers"—probably based on Kabbalistic "occult wisdom"), the Possessors reacted with panic and called for methods copied from the Inquisition.

The Non-Possessors, led by Nil of Sora (ca. 1433–1508), had small, isolated monasteries with a minimum of property. They avoided social and political activism; they did not elaborate regulations on all aspects of life, but stressed prayer in the hesychast tradition. They rejected torture and death for heretics as incompatible with the Gospel.

The Possessors prevailed; when a controversy arose over minor differences in liturgical practice between Greeks and Russians, they defended the old Russian practices, and their position was upheld in the "Hundred Chapters' Council" of 1551 (*Stoglav*). The Non-Possessors withdrew into remote northern forests, unwittingly causing Russian colonization of the north: peasants eager for spiritual guidance followed them and settled nearby. Many monasteries absorbed and maintained the spirituality of the Non-Possessors; but the Possessors had already won in Moscow when the metropolitanate was raised to patriarchal rank in 1589, restoring the number of the Orthodox pentarchy. The church played a major role in Muscovy's recovery from the "Time of Troubles" (1584–1613), when Poland attempted to take advantage of a dynastic crisis and seize control.

The "Unia." Most of the "Ruthenians" were transferred from Lithuanian to Polish rule in 1569. In 1596, a majority of Ruthenian bishops accepted papal authority and Roman Catholic doctrine, while retaining their own customs and forms of worship. This arrangement, called the "unia," eliminated Turkish exploitation, but it encountered strong opposition. Brotherhoods of Orthodox laymen formed to resist it; rival "Uniat" Brotherhoods and a monastic order, the Basilians (founded 1604), arose to protect it. Violent confrontations occurred. Finally the government, which had recognized only Uniat bishops, gave legal recognition to Orthodox bishops as well.

The "Old Believers." In the middle of the seventeenth century, the Muscovite rulers reversed their previous policy, rejected the Stoglav Council as heretical, and insisted that Russians "correct" their Slavonic service books and worship

A northern Russian church built in 1714: the Cathedral of the Dormition, Kem, on the White Sea.

practices to conform to the supposed original (in fact, along with some inaccurate translations the Russian versions preserved more original forms than the post-Byzantine Greek books). The leader of this reform was the powerful Nikon (patriarch 1652–1667). A large part of the Russian church (predominantly those who followed the tradition of the Possessors) refused, even under vicious persecution, to accept it. These "Old Ritualists" or "Old Believers" have survived and preserved the older Russian customs, texts, and chant to the present day;

but even after Nikon was deposed for his high-handed tactics, the government continued his reform.

A number of sectarian movements, influenced by aspects of Reformation doctrines and "occult wisdom" that filtered into Muscovy, and by indigenous apocalyptic tendencies, diverged more or less radically from both the established Orthodox church and the conservative Old Believers.

The Invasion of Western Theology.   The Russian government, wanting no more powerful patriarchs, increasingly dominated and exploited the church from the late 17th century on. Byzantine theological scholarship, which had been of the highest quality, began to decline under the Turks; the Russians had always been weak in scholarship. Orthodox Ruthenians, in fierce competition with Uniats and Latins, were forced to establish their own schools on the Jesuit model, and transmitted the system to the Muscovites. So western scholasticism, which had always found some Orthodox admirers, was copied wholesale—including western views on the atonement. The native eastern tradition, to the extent that it did not fit into a scholastic framework, was not rejected, but simply neglected. The result was a separation of theological study from traditional spirituality (preserved largely in monasteries) and the "normal mysticism" of worship.

Russian Church Art.   The Russians developed their own architectural style for churches, derived from Byzantine models but with greater emphasis on verticality, and employing the well-known onion-shaped domes and other characteristic features. In addition to the city churches, the smaller wooden churches built in the seventeenth and eighteenth centuries in rural northern Russia deserve attention: they are often as strikingly expressive as the medieval stave churches. Several major schools of icon-painting arose in Russia. The older liturgical chant ("znamennyj" chant) flourished among both Muscovites and Ruthenians; from the later sixteenth century, the Ruthenians supplemented it with several other varieties of monodic chant and with Renaissance polyphony, developments resisted by the Muscovites until the later seventeenth century.

V

THE MODERN WORLD

12

The Age of Reason and Piety

Several aspects of the sixteenth- and seventeenth-century Christian establishment in western Europe produced strong reactions, both intra-Christian and anti-Christian.

The Witch Hunts.   The most notorious of these was the wave of trials and executions of alleged witches. According to a late theory of some scholastic theologians, witches are Christians who apostisize, become worshippers of the Devil, and, in consort with demons, work evil against their neighbors by magic and perform nefarious acts in the obscene worship of Satan. This theory was accepted in civil and ecclesiastical law courts in both Roman Catholic and Protestant countries of western Europe and in their colonies. Persons accused of witchcraft might be of any age or sex. They were deprived of normal rights to due legal procedure, and had almost no chance of acquittal. Confessions were extracted by torture, and the "witches" were burnt or (in English-ruled territories) hanged. Over a period of several centuries, probably several hundred thousand died in this way.

Some modern historians have believed that the "witches" were in fact practitioners of a pre-Christian religion, perhaps involving human sacrifice, that had continued to exist in secret. Others have attempted to connect them with the Cathari. In the borderlands of western Europe, where Christianity was imposed at a late date as the religion of a foreign conqueror, the theory of a pre-Christian religion may be partly valid. But in the vast majority of cases those historians are probably right who regard the accused witches as innocent persons, accused because of fanaticism, personal enmity, or the greed of the magistrates, who confiscated the property of condemned "witches" (it is no accident that many "witches" were wealthy).

Although it is rather a historical accident that a bizarre and unfounded bit of speculation by some scholastics thus provided the basis for extensive judicial torture and murder, some theological writers contributed books detailing the "menace" and calling for more vigorous witch hunts. It was not so well remembered, later on, that other Christian theologians courageously wrote books denouncing the cruel hysteria.

War and Persecution. The destructive wars of the sixteenth century and the first half of the seventeenth were fought ostensibly for "religious" reasons; and religious toleration spread unevenly, and with serious setbacks, even after 1648. The result was a reaction against wars and coercion motivated or excused by doctrinal conflict. The period 1648–1787 was one of realism about war, in that it was acknowledged to be fought for the self-interest of governments; ideological causes were avoided; wars were fought by professional or mercenary personnel, actual combat was avoided when possible, and civilians were subject to less destruction than before.

Philosophy and Scientific Methods

Science made enormous progress in the Renaissance and early modern periods. Many conceptions that had been accepted since antiquity were overthrown. Two kinds of intellectual procedure were dominant in the early modern period. Descartes employed a deductive process of reasoning from established principles, which produced important results especially in mathematics. The influence of this rationalistic method was increasingly qualified, however, by an emphasis on experimentation and factual observation, and by a theory of knowledge that denied the existence of "innate ideas" and relied on experience acquired through the physical senses (empiricism). Through experimentation, important new knowledge of the world was acquired; and as the empiricist philosophy Francis Bacon of Verulam (1561–1626) said, "Knowledge is power." Attempts to intervene in this proceess by coercion (as with Galileo) proved utterly futile.

Isaac Newton (1642–1727) revolutionized the study of physics and astronomy; his universe was a great mechanism, subject to strict laws of cause and effect. Newton was convinced that only a supremely wise, transcendent God could have brought this marvelous system into being. But his discoveries raised questions: what does God have to do with the universe, once it is set running? And how are man and woman free, if an impersonal, mechanistic order governs all things? No longer could the old conviction that man the microcosm mirrors the great universe serve to make sense of his place in it; something like Descartes's sharp dualism of mind and body seemed necessary to make the human being more than an elegant machine.

The "Enlightenment"

The dominant European intellectual movement of the seventeenth and eighteenth centuries is known as the "Enlightenment." The name indicates an appreciation of and confidence in new knowledge, in contrast to a prior period of comparative "darkness." It marks the beginning of modern "avant-gard-ism," the notion of an "enlightened" elite overcoming old prejudices and superstitions, and fighting for the liberation of humankind at large from the "dead hand of the past."

"The Reasonableness of Christianity." The common denominator of Enlightenment thought was an acceptance of "reason" (understood broadly enough to encompass both deductive rationalism and empiricism) as a standard by which ideas are to be judged; and a corresponding abhorrence of fanaticism, or, as it was called in the English usage of that time, "enthusiasm." Scientists and theologians alike thought of science as contributing to the rational knowledge of God. Christian writers of the Enlightenment tended to regard biblical revelation as mostly a confirmation of what is known by Reason; and to reduce dogmas to a few simple teachings. They minimized more involved dogmatic statements (such as the traditional teachings about Trinity and Incarnation), hierarchical structures, and elaborate rites and ceremonies in worship. They emphasized ethics (sometimes on the basis of promised rewards or punishments after death), the "subjective" theory of atonement, and toleration.

In the Church of England, the Enlightenment attitude was known as "latitudinarianism." Among the English Presbyterians, it went further, linked up with the "rationalist" branch of the Radical Reformation, and led to the rise of a Unitarian Church, which rejected Trinity and Incarnation and emphasized the immortality of the soul. A few theologians attempted to support the traditional dogmas with Reason (not unlike the medieval dialectical theologians), but most played them down.

A well-known representative of Enlightenment Christianity was the English empiricist philosopher John Locke (1653–1704); his book *The Reasonableness of Christianity* was quite influential in its time, and its ideas and spirit still have currency. Carried to its extreme, Locke's preference for a minimum of simple dogma and an emphasis on moral action contributed to the rise of the Deist movement.

Deism. A more rigorous attempt to ground religion in Reason alone, separate from the authority of scripture or tradition, was the Deist movement. Deists accepted God as creator, but rejected divine providence in the world. They differed among themselves on such issues as the special value of Christ's teachings and the immortality of the soul. Some (especially in England) continued to think of themselves as Christians. Others did not, and attacked the Christian scriptures, both for being unbelievable (by the standards of Reason) and for being immoral (the Old Testament, and to some extent the New, seemed to them to depict God as an arbitrary tyrant).

The "latitudinarian" sort of Christianity was moderate, tolerant, respectable, sensible, and reasonable; it was also too uninspired and commonplace to respond effectively to Deism. But a devastating critique, from which British

Deism did not recover, was launched by the mystical writer William Law (1686–1761), and by two Anglican bishops, the idealist philosopher George Berkeley (1685–1753) and the theologian Joseph Butler (1692–1752). Law is best known as the author of a devotional classic, *A Serious Call to a Devout and Holy Life.* In his later years, Law fell under the influence of Boehme, an influence regretted by many of his admirers, including the Wesleys.

A Christian Hymn of the Enlightenment Period.   The "Reasonableness Christianity" of the Enlightenment period is exemplified by a hymn text, based on Psalm 19, written by the English poet Joseph Addison. Set to an elegant classical melody by Franz Joseph Haydn, it is still sung today in English-speaking Protestant churches:

> The spacious firmament on high
> With all the blue ethereal sky,
> And spangled heavens, a shining frame,
> Their great original proclaim,
> > The unwearied sun from day to day
> > Does his Creator's power display;
> > And publishes to every land
> > The work of an almighty hand.
>
> Soon as the evening shades prevail,
> The moon takes up the wondrous tale,
> And nightly to the listening earth
> Repeats the story of her birth:
> > Whilst all the stars that round her burn,
> > And all the planets in their turn,
> > Confirm the tidings as they roll
> > And spread the truth from pole to pole.
>
> What though in solemn silence all
> Move round the dark terrestrial ball?
> What though no real voice or sound
> Amid their radiant orbs be found?
> > In reason's ear they all rejoice,
> > And utter forth a glorious voice;
> > For ever singing as they shine,
> > "The hand that made us is divine."

Here we have the traditional "Cosmic Liturgy" theme, developed from a scriptural passage: characteristically for the period, it is Reason that apprehends the testimony of the heavens to their creator. In its positive content, the hymn hardly goes beyond Deism, although a real Deist would not be likely to take his theme from the Old Testament.

The Enlightenment and the French Catholics.   The mathematician and scientist Blaise Pascal (1623–1662) early detected a weak point in Enlightenment thought: its reliance on the goodness and rationality of human nature. Pascal was involved with the controversial "Jansenist" movement, which wanted to restore in the French Catholic church Augustine's teachings on grace and predestination, and to overcome the lax moral attitude cultivated by some prominent Jesuits. Unlike most Enlightenment thinkers, the Jansenists believed that human motivations are much more complex, less reasonable, and often less noble than they appear on the surface. They rejected Aquinas's views on the Fall and original sin. Pascal denied the power of Reason to satisfy human needs. A human being is rational, but is much more besides, and cannot live by Reason alone. Reason can be used to rationalize evil (it seemed to Pascal that the Jesuits were inviting this abuse). Pascal died early, leaving only fragmentary notes (known as the *Pensées*) for what might have been, had he lived to complete it, a comprehensive and classic Christian critique of the Enlightenment.

Other religious thinkers were more optimistic about Descartes' rationalism. The Jewish philosopher Baruch Spinoza (1632-1677) of Amsterdam combined Cartesianism and pantheism into a system that has been described as a "frozen volcano of Jewish mysticism" (Tillich). The Augustinian and Neo-Platonic elements of Cartesianism were developed by the Christian philosopher Nicolas Malabranche (1638-1715).

A mystical movement known as "Quietism" resembled Jansenism in opposing thorough rationalism and easy optimism about human nature. The Quietists advocated a cessation of all human activity, including the meditations of the Jesuit school, and a passive waiting for God's initiative, for a flooding of the soul with divine love that brings with it indifference to the earthly forms of the church and to one's individual destiny.

A promising "French school of spirituality" had been established by Cardinal de Bérulle (1575-1629) and others. Two bishops, Bossuet (1627-1704) and Fénélon (1651-1715) likewise attempted to further a spiritual renewal in France. But the controversies that surrounded the Jansenist and Quietist movements, and led to their condemnation by the Catholic church, set the two bishops against one another, undermined their efforts, and hampered attempts to reintegrate Bible, liturgical worship, and spirituality. However, the French bishops, taking advantage of their administrative freedom from Rome, continued to issue thoroughly revised forms of the Breviary and Missal, designed to emphasize Scripture and to facilitate popular understanding and participation (although the texts remained in Latin, excellent translations with scholarly notes were provided). A disadvantage of this movement was that the lack of coordination among the editions issued by the various dioceses caused a confusing degree of variation.

The Decline of Papal Authority. The power and influence of the papacy waned drastically after 1648. The Jesuits, long the champions of the papacy, had many enemies among sincere Catholics who regarded them as clever, immoral opportunists. They also had enemies in the absolutist governments of the eighteenth century, where papal control of church affairs was not appreciated. From about 1750, the absolutists in Portugal, Spain, and France began to strike crippling blows against the Jesuits; so great was absolutist power, and so weak the papacy, that in 1773 Pope Clement XIV was forced to proclaim the Society of Jesus totally dissolved. (It continued to exist in Protestant Prussia and Ortho- dox Russia, where the governments did not enforce the papal order.) Papal power remained at a low ebb until the end of the Napoleonic wars in the early nineteenth century.

Anti-Christian Aspects of the French Enlightenment. The constant harass- ment of Huguenots, even when the Edict of Nantes was in effect, and their persecution after it was revoked led to defections, not to Catholicism, but to a corrosive and bitter antiecclesiastical rationalism. The most vigorous of the Huguenot dissidents moved to Protestant countries, especially Holland, where they enjoyed more liberty; but they disliked the Protestant churches almost as much as they did the Catholic church. Pierre Bayle (1647–1706) set the style for scathingly sarcastic assaults on superstition and oppression. The French Enlightenment, under this sort of influence, took on a marked anti-Christian character, and no figures of the stature of a Pascal appeared to neutralize the attack.

In Enlightenment circles, it was believed the Reason would bring about a perfect, or at least a much better, human society, when prejudice, superstition, and privilege were eliminated. The witch hunts (they became rare in the eigh- teenth century, but isolated executions occurred as late as 1750 or 1775) de- pended on the theory of a pact with the Devil; not just the pact, but the whole notion of a personal devil and demonic spirits was denounced as sheer super- stition. Wars and persecutions had been caused, or excused, by disputes about dogma; away with all dogma! (The word "dogma" began to have a pejorative sense at this time.) Only Reason provides valid knowledge.

Even enlightened thinkers were not sure that a doctrine of reward or punishment in an afterlife was not needed to keep the unenlightened majority in line. But most of them believed that Reason could discover the basic prin- ciples of morality as surely as it was discovering those of the physical sciences. Many efforts were made to construct a rational science of ethics (the results were meager and sometimes silly).

The "Philosophers" (the writers of the later French Enlightenment; their importance as philosophers as such is slight) continued Bayle's assault on Christianity, using the same methods of sarcasm and polemics disguised as objective inquiry. They gave an anti-Christian twist to the widespread confi- dence in a better world based on reason; some historians see here a secularized version of Augustine's "City of God." Their devotion, confidence, and sense of urgency mark this movement as the first of the modern anti-Christian quasi- religions.

The Enlightenment in Germany. The philosophy of toleration was more wide- spread in Germany than in France, and the outstanding figures of the German

Enlightenment were mostly rationalistic Christians, like the philosopher Leibniz (1646–1716), and not anti-Christian polemicists. Here, as in England, the Enlightenment critique of social evils was accepted by many Christians. Whereas Christians had generally regarded torture and slavery as ineradicable evils, efforts to eliminate them began to meet with increasing success in those areas where the relation between Christianity and Enlightenment was most positive.

Bayle and his disciples in France (the "Philosophers") and England (for example, the historian Edward Gibbon, 1737–1794) employed history in their campaign to discredit Christianity; more important, however, was the work of the German scholar Hermann Reimarus (1694–1768), who applied to the Gospels the same critical standards of historical scholarship that were being used in the study of other ancient texts. These studies were published posthumously by the writer, philosopher, and librarian Gotthold Ephraim Lessing (1729–1781), an advocate of nondogmatic, relativistic sort of Christianity. Lessing believed in a progressive education of the human race through history, and insisted that Christians had nothing to fear from an open historical examination of the origins of their religion, even though the literal truth of various scriptural accounts should prove untenable.

The historical-critical method accepted by Lessing and others treats the Christian scripture and tradition as products of human culture, comparable to those of other religions. Previously, the sacramental life of the church and the Christian Scriptures had been self-authenticating witnesses to the truth of the Christian message. Now, it was becoming possible to view them as mere human phenomena, products of history like any other. Christianity has largely succeeded in assimilating critical-historical scholarship in respect of its own origins, and the idea of a historical development of its own tradition, because of the wide acceptance of Lessing's principles (even by many who find his understanding of Christianity inadequate). But a large portion of educated people refuse to regard it as more than a product of human history (whether they approve or disapprove of it); and, on the other hand, a considerable number of Christians retain a suspicious or hostile attitude toward the historical-critical method, at least as applied to the foundations of their religion.

Pietism: Spener

In the Lutheran and Reformed state churches of continental Europe, dissatisfaction with both Baroque dogmatics and Enlightenment rationalism led to the rise of a new movement, *Pietism*, whose roots can be traced to the classical Lutheran spirituality of Arndt, to Jakob Boehme, to English Puritanism, to the Radical Reformation, to French Quietism, and even, in some forms, to the Hussite movement.

Philip Jakob Spener (1635–1705), the founder of Pietism, was a German Lutheran pastor who believed that academic theology was being overemphasized at the expense of "true" theology. Theologians expended their energies on doctrinal polemics against other churches, while the Christianity of much of the population remained superficial, a matter of convention rather than conviction. Spener wanted Christians to be able to experience directly a rebirth to a new life as children of God. He established small, voluntary associations of church members who met privately for prayer, Bible-reading, and discussion of the application of Scripture to their lives. He reinstated the practice of "confirmation," not as a sacrament, but as personal, voluntary reaffirmation of the vows of infant baptism, following an intensive period of catechetical instruction and preceding the first reception of Holy Communion. This practice had existed in some areas in the sixteenth century, but through Pietist influence it spread widely and became a common puberty rite (often erroneously called "joining the church") among Lutheran and Reformed.

Pietism: Francke and Arnold.   A pupil of Spener's, August Hermann Francke (1663–1727), underwent a dramatic conversion experience, and insisted on such an experience as the mark of the true, "reborn" Christian. Francke and his disciples pushed their conviction to such lengths that they appeared to reduce the practice of Christianity to a datable, once-for-all conversion experience. Francke came into conflict with outstanding representatives of both the Enlightenment and Lutheran orthodoxy: he clashed with the philosopher Christian Wolff (1679–1754), a follower of Leibniz, and had him driven from the University of Halle; he also quarrelled with Valentin Ernst Loescher (1673–1749), one of the outstanding representatives of "Baroque dogmatics," and a critic of Wolff's rationalism. Loescher wrote a thorough, perceptive critique of Pietism; he did not wholly reject the movement, but regarded Francke's variety as excessive and unbalanced.

Another extremist exponent of Pietism was Gottfried Arnold (1666–1714), a follower of Boehme and of the Quietists. Rather than attempting to harmonize their views with Lutheran doctrine, he attacked all Christian doctrine as a perversion of true Christianity, and praised heretics in general for opposing the doctrines of the major churches. Although Arnold disliked the orthodox Church Fathers as teachers of doctrine, he approved of early Christian devotionalism, and translated writings of Makarios of Egypt (ca. 300–ca. 390) into German, thus releasing into Pietism the influence of the spirituality of the early Christian hermits.

Zinzendorf and the Moravians.   A German nobleman, Nikolaus von Zinzendorf (1700–1760), gave his estate at Herrnhut for a settlement of a community of Hussites. He became the bishop of these "Bohemian Brethren" or "Moravian Brethren." Under pressure from the school of Francke, he tried to induce a conversion experience, but soon realized it was futile and broke with that variety of Pietism. The "Brethren," living under a quasi-monastic rule, had some legal difficulties because their relation to the Lutheran state church was ambiguous; as yet, only Roman Catholics, Lutherans, and Reformed were tolerated in Germany. They formed a sort of church of their own, but hoped for a reunion of all Christians, and did not compete with established churches.

Although Zinzendorf was somewhat eccentric and liable to excessive sentimentality, he succeeded in organizing a widely influential movement. "Moravian" missionaries were soon travelling to far places. Zinzendorf himself went with a party to the British colony of Georgia in America; a Moravian settlement in Bethlehem, Pennsylvania, introduced German baroque musical culture to the New World. Other Moravians went to Livonia on the Baltic coast (annexed by the Russian Empire in 1721) and worked among the Estonians and Latvians, nominally Lutheran since Luther's day but largely untouched by the German state church. The Moravians, continuing the traditions of Hus (and ultimately of Cyril and Methodius), emphasized the indigenous languages; the movement acquired so strong a national coloring that it was illegal between 1743 and 1764, and existed underground.

Effects of Pietism. Although in many ways they appear to be opposites, Enlightenment rationalism and the more extravagant forms of Pietism both contributed to the erosion of traditional norms of doctrine and worship. Pietism, especially the exclusivist variety taught by Francke, sometimes led to formal or de facto ruptures in the unity of the established churches; the bishops and theologians who opposed Pietism were not all as appreciative of its constructive potential as the perceptive Loescher.

The more moderate pietists, however, worked to revitalize the state churches. Pietists founded orphanages and hospitals, sent foreign missions to colonial and "primitive" societies, and founded "inner missions" to bring the message of spiritual rebirth to nominally Christian northern Europeans. The outstanding representatives of Lutheran Pietism include the great German New Testament scholar Johann Albrecht Bengel (1687–1752), and Scandinavian teachers of spirituality such as the Norwegian Hans Nielsen Hauge (1771–1824) and the Swedes Henric Schartau (1757–1825) and Carl Olof Rosenius (1816–1868).

Gerhard Tersteegen. A great exponent of Pietism in the Reformed church was Gerhard Tersteegen (1697–1769), a learned weaver who lived on the Dutch-German border. Tersteegen developed Pietism into a mystical theology, thoroughly grounded in Scripture and Reformation doctrine. His devotional poetry is the source of several well-known hymn texts. One of these is based on Isaiah 6 and traditionally associated with a vigorous tune by Joachim Neander:

> God himself is present, let us now adore him
> And with awe appear before him.
> God is in his temple, all within keep silence,
> Prostrate lie with deepest reverence.
> Him alone God we own
> Him, our God and Savior; praise his name for ever.
>
> God himself is present, hear the harps resounding,
> See the hosts the throne surrounding.

"Holy, holy, holy"—hear the hymn ascending,
Songs of saints and angels blending.
Bow thine ear to us here;
Hear, O Christ, the praises that thy Church now raises.

O thou fount of blessings, purify my spirit,
Trusting only in thy merit.
Like the holy angels who behold thy glory
May I ceaselessly adore thee.
Let thy will ever still
Rule thy Church terrestrial as the hosts celestial.

Although the nineteenth-century translation is incomplete and somewhat stilted, it does convey something of the spirit of the original. Like Addison in the hymn quoted above (page 156), Tersteegen develops the "Cosmic Liturgy" motif, but he differs from Addison in expressing an immediate presence of God to the worshippers, both communally and individually. Unlike many Pietist texts, this one does not fall into an introspective, sentimental individualism.

Influenced by Makarios of Egypt, Tersteegen adopted a hermitlike life style and withdrew from active participation in the Reformed church, but his followers spread his influence in the church.

British Spiritual and Devotional Movements: The Quakers. An obscure English tradesman, George Fox (1624-1691), renounced all concern with the doctrines and modes of worship about which Roman Catholics, high Anglicans, Puritans, and Baptists fought so bitterly. He became a solitary wanderer in search of spiritual understanding. Meditating on the Bible, Fox received a series of insights that brought him to the conviction that God addresses each woman and man exclusively by an "inner light." Relying on this inner testimony of the Spirit, the Christian can dispense with hierarchy, dogmas, and sacraments; even Scripture assumes a second place. Remarkably, Fox did not fall into total individualism, but insisted that the inner conviction be verified by the testimony of others in a community united by its participation in God's love. The Religious Society of Friends (popularly called "Quakers") was formed on this basis; its members adopted a lifestyle of deliberately cultivated simplicity and nonviolence.

British Spiritual and Devotional Movements: The Methodists and Evangelicals. John Wesley (1703-1791) and his brother Charles (1707-1788) were well-educated Anglicans who, at Oxford, gathered together a small group of fellow students, nicknamed the "Holy Club" or the "Methodists," who kept strictly to the fasts and other observances of the Church of England, attended worship regularly, and received Holy Communion weekly.

As missionaries to the American colony of Georgia, the Wesleys met some Moravian missionaries, learned the message of Pietism, and themselves underwent a conversion experience. In league with George Whitefield (1714-1770), a powerful preacher, the Wesleys set out to spread the message of the immediate experience of salvation in the Church of England, and particularly to the poor, who had become increasingly alienated from the Church.

The Anglican bishops disapproved of this "enthusiasm," and the Wesleys and Whitefield had to preach in houses, barns, and open field. Hunger, poverty, and the dislocations of the early Industrial Revolution had created a nasty mood, and they were often hooted down or even beaten. But they never allowed themselves to be cowed or discouraged. For those who had known only the dry Reasonable Christianity of the Enlightenment, a spiritual way that offered direct personal experience and provided for emotional expression was a new thing. It was certainly a new thing for the industrial working class, which was already producing a generation that had simply lost contact with the established church.

John Wesley founded tightly organized, highly disciplined associations of followers, still called "Methodists." He wanted them to be private societies within the Church of England, dedicated to strengthening one or another aspect of church culture, like many other societies that had flourished since the later seventeenth century. But after he died the inevitable break came. Many of his followers formed a Methodist church; others remained in the Church of England, where they were called "Evangelicals." The Methodists mostly followed the Wesleys in accepting the "Arminian" teaching, that God wills universal salvation and that man and woman have free will in responding to God. Most of the Anglican Evangelicals, and (especially in Wales) the "Calvinist Methodists," followed Whitefield in affirming a limited saving will and strict predestination.

The Wesleys wrote many hymn texts; Charles was the more prolific hymnist, but John found some of his texts too sentimental. The Evangelical movement (broadly defined to include Methodists) is the British equivalent of Pietism, and, like Pietism, made much use of hymns from its very beginning.

Eastern Christianity

The Ottoman Turkish empire embraced the Balkan peninsula, Asia Minor, and the Near East, where a very large number of Byzantine, "Monophysite," and Nestorian Christians had their homelands. The Christians were tolerated; they lived in internally self-governing communities (*millet* is the Turkish term for such a community), based on religion rather than language. They could and did rise to important posts. But the Turks imposed conditions that encouraged quarrels among the several Christian communities, and corruption and demoralization within them.

The entire Maronite Syriac Christian community in Lebanon had been united with Rome since the Crusades, and a line of Uniate bishops from the

Nestorians had come into existence already in 1533, and another from among the Syriac Monophysites in 1667. As the power of the Turkish Empire declined, France became influential and used her diplomatic resources to protect and promote Roman Catholicism. The Eastern churches, unable to maintain satisfactory schools under the Turks, had to send their more promising young men to be trained in the West. Thus, theological thought came to be forced into an alien mold, as in Russia. Furthermore, some of these students were recruited for the cause of union with Rome. Some prominent bishops recognized papal authority, but this was often secretly, and for some years did not result in a "Unia" like that of the Ruthenians.

But in 1724 a pro-Roman faction of the Orthodox Patriarchate of Antioch elected their own patriarch, who proclaimed allegiance to Rome; an Armenian Catholic patriarch was established in Lebanon in 1740; and the Syrian Catholics of Monophysite origin, who had appeared to be on the verge of extinction, were strengthened by the conversion of five Monophysite bishops, one of whom became their patriarch, in 1783.

The non-Uniat eastern churches therefore came to regard their contacts with Roman Catholics as a danger; they adopted a more reserved, and sometimes hostile, attitude.

The Eastern Christian theologians of that period often knew western theology well enough, and they were, in varying degrees, both influenced by it and hostile to it. A Greek monk from the mountain peninsula of Athos, Nicodemus the Agiorite (1748-1809), sponsored a renewal of Orthodox church life. He edited a collection of canon law; he translated several Roman Catholic spiritual works into Greek, even ingeniously adapting a manual of Jesuit meditation to the eastern perspective; he wrote devotional books; and with his friend Makarios of Corinth (1731-1805) he supported a movement for more frequent Communion. (Out of respect for the penitential discipline involved, eastern Christians have tended, at least in recent centuries, to take Communion infrequently.)

Nicodemus and Makarios edited the *Philokalia,* a large anthology of passages on prayer from the Church Fathers, designed to reveal the sources of the spirituality of Palamas and his associates.

The spiritual tradition of Nil of Sora was rediscovered by a monk from Poltava (Ukraine), Paissy Velichkovsky (1722-1794). He settled in Rumania, where he translated into Slavonic Greek writings on spirituality, including a somewhat abridged version of the *Philokalia.* In this way, the resources necessary for a renewal of Byzantine spirituality were made available to much of the Orthodox world. The Russian government, during the eighteenth century, controlled the Orthodox church tightly, and favored a wholesale importation of Enlightenment culture from the West, so the movement was as timely there as in the Ottoman Empire—otherwise, it was a bleak age for Orthodoxy. Among the "Ruthenians" under Polish, Austrian, or Hungarian rule, the Unia progressed steadily, and by the end of the eighteenth century had almost completely supplanted Orthodoxy there.

The Ethiopian church, although free of Turkish rule, was largely isolated during this period. Attempts to establish an Ethiopian Unia had begun in the sixteenth century, but were not very successful.

The French Revolution

The French Revolution was initially supported by most of the Catholic clergy and laity, except for members of the threatened privileged classes. The Civil Constitution of the Clergy (1790) that reorganized church administration to conform to civil administration, and reduced the pope's role in France to that of a figurehead, was a drastic reform measure. But it stayed within the limits of the former national Catholicism or "Gallicanism." Most of the Bishops rejected it and left the country; the rest of the clergy were about evenly split.

But as radical elements seized control of the Revolution, it became explicitly anti-Christian. During the Reign of Terror, the cult of the Goddess of Reason was enforced, and Christians—especially members of religious orders and clergy—were massacred or sentenced to death. When Napoleon came to power, the French Catholic church was weak and divided. Napoleon scarcely bothered to conceal his view that the value of Catholicism lay in its usefulness as a means of sublimating potentially dangerous grievances against the social and political order—what would later be called "the opium of the people." He forced the pope to approve a thorough reorganization of the French church; the Napoleonic wars occasioned drastic reorganization elsewhere. As a result, the previous tendency toward administratively independent national Catholic churches was reversed, and papal centralism ("Ultramontanism") began to gain ground.

The French Revolution had destroyed the old social and political order as thoroughly as the most radical "Philosopher" could have wished. But the result was not the rational society for which the Enlightenment had confidently hoped, but the beginnings of modern mass terror, and a return to ruthless ideological warfare. These developments, in turn, helped to discredit Enlightenment rationalism, although historians still debate the extent of its responsibility for terror and fanaticism.

Hume and Kant

The age of Enlightenment was ending, in any case. The Scottish philosopher David Hume (1711-1776) developed empiricism into a radical attack on the rational foundations of metaphysical and theological knowledge. He did not directly criticize religious beliefs, practices, or institutions, but he did undercut the philosophical basis of "rational religion," Christian or Deist. In Germany, Immanuel Kant (1724-1804) realized that Hume had made untenable the confidence of the Enlightenment in rational religious knowledge. Kant's critical philosophy denied the possibility of knowing "things in themselves," or of

Reason's ability to attain to a knowledge of God. Instead, he sought to ground
religion in "Practical Reason," based on the experience of an unconditional
claim of morality upon human life (the "Categorical Imperative"). Kant intended to "limit knowledge to make room for faith," faith in God, immortality,
and freedom as postulates of Practical Reason. He was more openly critical
of religious beliefs, practices, and institutions than was Hume, and the effect
of Kant's writings on educated Germans was to destroy the religious ideas of
the Enlightenment, without providing a satisfactory alternative.

13
The Age of Romanticism and Industrialism

Romanticism

A new appreciation of aspects of the human personality that had been slighted by the Enlightenment marks the movement, or movements, called "Romanticism." Although they did not reject discursive reason, the Romantics characteristically subordinated it to intuition and imagination. They believed that the infinite and eternal is indeed manifest in human life but at a level deeper than that of Reason; the infinite and eternal comes to expression in the human imagination. In part, Romanticism is a reappearance and a new development of Renaissance Religion and, like Renaissance "occult wisdom," it could be combined in various ways with traditional Christianity or with a sort of neo-gnosticism.

In contrast to the Enlightenment, Romanticism refused to dismiss past historical ages as "dark ages" of superstition and barbarism. The result was sometimes an uncritical and unrealistic admiration of other periods ("romanticizing" them, one would now say); but on a broader scale Romanticism opened perspectives on culture and society in a dimension largely inaccessible to the Enlightenment. The new perspective provided contrasts necessary for a critique of capitalist industrialism; it encouraged historical research, and it led to a new respect for, and interest in, ancient and medieval Christianity.

Schleiermacher.   In response to the post-Kantian situation, Friedrich Schleiermacher (1768–1834), a theologian with a Moravian Pietist background, aimed at vindicating religion, not by restoring Enlightenment rationalism, but by showing that religion is universal in human experience. He held that along with man's prereflective awareness of his own being, there is an immediate, intuitive awareness of a power on which he depends for his very being, and for the meaning of his existence. Unfortunately, Schleiermacher called this awareness "the *feeling* of absolute dependence"; and so he has often been misinterpreted as holding that religion is a matter of arbitrary, subjective emotions. His intention was quite different; it was to show that humanity's primal self-consciousness is bound up with God-consciousness.

For the Enlightenment, God was an object of rational knowledge, the "Supreme Being." For Kant, God was a postulate of the moral Practical Reason. In neither case is there any immediate contact between human being and God. But for Schleiermacher the contact is so intimate that self-consciousness and God-consciousness can never be separated; God cannot become an "object" of knowledge at all.

Thus religion is seen as a universal human experience. Christian religion is a special instance of that experience, in which Jesus Christ, the bearer of a perfect God-consciousness (this, according to Schleiermacher, is the meaning of his "divine nature") and the perfect revelation of God, becomes the savior of humanity by transforming the limited human consciousness into his own perfect consciousness. Schleiermacher has been called both "the Theologian of Romanticism" and "the father of modern Protestant theology."

Hegel.   Schleiermacher's rival, the philosopher Georg Hegel (1770–1831), did try to restore a rational knowledge of God. For Hegel, as for the ancient gnostics, creation and fall are one. Nature is the product of a "tragedy in the Absolute"; it is a manifestation of the divine spirit, but spirit alienated from itself. In the development of the self-conscious human spirit, however, a reconciliation takes place, the alienation is overcome, as the divine breaks forth into consciousness and "God-manhood" is attained.

For Hegel, the fulfillment of the divine idea takes place not on the level of the human individual (only in Jesus Christ is the essential unity of God and human being realized on this plane), but in the course of world history, in which individuals and lesser nations are crushed with no apparent sense or purpose, but the divine life continues to actualize itself, dynamically and progressively, in the social and cultural life of great nations, in "the state," and in the understanding expressed in philosophy itself.

Schleiermacher attempted to go beyond any particular object of faith, while allowing for all of them, by going back to a primal consciousness in which self and God are "given" together. Hegel attempted to encompass "God-manhood" and overcome the alienation of existence in a universal philosophical synthesis. Some writers have aptly seen in both a response to the fact that the traditional loci of sacredness in Western society, Church and Bible, were for an increasing number no longer self-authenticating; it was possible to regard them as mere products of human culture. But both Schleiermacher and Hegel had bitten off more than they could chew.

New Cultural Forces

The nineteenth and twentieth centuries have been marked by nationalism, imperialism, progress in scientific and historical knowledge, industrialism, and what is called "secularism," all of which have had a profound effect on Christianity.

Nationalism.   An agressive French nationalism came to dominate the French Revolution. In reaction, nationalism was strengthened in already unified countries (England and Russia, in particular), and a struggle for national unification began in Germany and Italy. Nationalism spread through Europe and the Western Hemisphere in the nineteenth century and to non-Western peoples in the twentieth, becoming the most potent political force of modern times. Often attaining the status of a quasi-religion, it was sometimes associated with hatred of neighboring peoples. At the same time, it worked for the liberation of subjugated and oppressed nationalities, and made possible an appreciation of their cultural achievements.

Nationality and religion have often been closely associated, and the rise of modern nationalism inevitably impinged upon the churches. The problem of the relation between Christianity and national consciousness proved to be a thorny one, and is still largely unresolved.

Imperialism and Missions. British rule in India began in the eighteenth century, but the nineteenth and twentieth centuries were the real age of European imperialism in Asia and Africa. They have also been the age of Christian missions to those continents. All too often, the colonialized peoples could experience the missionaries only as the religious representatives of imperialism. Often enough, the missionaries had no understanding or appreciation of the cultures of colonial peoples, which ranged from "primitive" to highly developed, literate, and philosophically sophisticated societies. In earlier periods, Christian missions had commonly appealed to the leaders of the societies to which they were addressed. The modern missionaries, aiming at individual conversions and often concentrating on the least influential elements in the society, have often split tribal societies into hostile factions, and had only marginal success in more complex and developed societies. Where churches have been established among colonial peoples, western missionaries have often been reluctant to grant them autonomy, even after several generations.

Protestant missionaries, experiencing almost total resistance from Muslims, turned their efforts to the ancient eastern Christian churches that had suffered under centuries of Muslim rule, and began to proselytize among them. Western Protestants of this period were often extremely hostile toward the older Christian cultures of the east.

There were enough exceptions to the above generalizations to make them a bit unfair as an overall characterization. The Lutheran mission to the Bataks of Indonesia, to take one example, avoided most of these pitfalls, produced a strong, independent Batak church, and enabled the Bataks to deal successfully with twentieth-century pressures and to take a major role in Indonesian affairs. In this and many other cases, solidly based Christian communities did appear. And many writers have pointed out that it was mission schools that educated many of the postcolonial leaders of Asia and Africa.

Science and History. Controversies over the relation of scientific knowledge to religion became much sharper and more widespread in the nineteenth century, as geology and paleontology arrived at visions of the history of the earth and human life that were incompatible with older views based upon a literal understanding of Scripture. Creation and Fall, as recounted in Genesis, could no longer be regarded as true in a literal sense by those who accepted the results of scientific enquiry.

Equally controversial were the critical historical methods that came to be employed on ancient texts. When applied to the Bible, they undercut belief in Moses' authorship of the first five books of the Old Testament, in the Gospel writers having been eyewitnesses of the life of Jesus, and so on.

Some Christians simply rejected scientific and historical knowledge as false whenever it conflicted with a literal understanding of the Bible. But there had always been a current that preferred nonliteral interpretations, and other Christians readily accepted the results of scientific historical study. This polarization has continued to the present day.

Over and above controversies about specific issues (literal inerrancy of Scripture, evolution by natural selection and so on), there was a feeling abroad that scientific knowledge was the only valid knowledge, the only reliable way of getting information about reality.

Both modern natural science and the historical-critical method arose within a Christian society, and were first developed in large part by theologically aware Christians. They correspond to the two major themes of Christian normal mysticism, Cosmic Liturgy and History of Salvation. Yet both have succeeded only by establishing methodological independence. Scientific method regards the universe as subject throughout to the same principles and "laws" (although developments in atomic physics have complicated and qualified this conviction); historical method likewise treats all of history as subject to the same basic motive forces; and neither permits resort to God to account for anything in its purview. (The historian is aware, of course, of human religious beliefs, but that is another matter!) The person employing these methods may be an atheist or a devout Christian (or Jew, or Buddhist)—the same knowledge is accessible to all, given equal technical competence.

The conviction that all knowledge must be subject to testing and verification by logical or empirical methods is referred to as "positivism." Positivists generally reject any form of traditional religion, although some efforts have been made to reinterpret religions (including Christianity) so radically as to fit them within a positivist framework.

At the other extreme are those who reject scientific and critical methods wherever they impinge upon centers of religious authority—the doctrine of the literal truth and inerrancy of Scripture current among a major segment of Protestants often functions in this way.

Many Christians, however, accept fully the modern natural scientific and historical-critical methods, including their applications to Scripture and to the question of Christian origins. Among these, some hold it necessary to recast religious beliefs into new forms, replacing historically conditioned traditional formulations with what they regard as new expressions of the perennial *substance* of Christianity. And others defend the enduring validity of the traditional formulations while interpreting them, in the light of historical studies, in contemporary terms. The former approach is particularly the task addressed by constructive theology, or philosophical theology. The latter approach has been associated with renewal movements, which have benefited greatly from research in biblical and church history.

The Industrial Society.   The triumph of industrialism was accompanied by the appearance of a new class of urban industrial workers. It is generally agreed that the reaction of the churches to this development was woefully inadequate. The established state churches mostly ignored the workers, and the workers lost contact with the churches, resorting to them only for the life-cycle rites of baptism, marriage, and burial.

The workers had to struggle against the industrial owners and managers to secure their rights; the churches came to be regarded as the domain of the upper and middle classes. The Methodists, who originally worked among the lower classes, were so successful at instilling inner discipline and encouraging education that they became mostly a middle-class church, although the Primitive Methodists retained a working-class character. A direct and original mission to the urban poor appeared in the form of the Salvation Army (founded in 1865, reorganized 1878), operating mostly in English-speaking countries and independent of church organizations. On the whole, the churches' response to the industrial order was not impressive. Disagreement about what churches and individual Christians can or should do about the social and political problems of industrialism continue to the present.

Secularism.   Where anti-Christian influences such as the French Enlightenment or Marxism-Leninism have been strong, "secularism" has meant the seizure of social and political institutions by anti-Christian forces. Where such influences were not strong, the growing acceptance of toleration has entailed an agreement that government shall either be formally neutral in religion (separation of church and state), or, if there is a state church, that government shall not impose it upon citizens who do not adhere to it—meaning that government becomes religiously neutral in most of its practical functions. A similar neutrality came to exist in commerce, industry, and education, with the result that it is possible to function in Western society without reference to the religious traditions of that (or another) society. This situation is called "secularism." It may be symbolized by the observation that in medieval Europe the cathedral church often dominated the skyline of a city, whereas in modern cities the skyscrapers tower over churches.

The "marginalization" of churches also appears in the fact that they had earlier been the major patrons of the arts, and that a very large portion of art was ecclesiastical, or at least derived its theme from Christian tradition. This becomes increasingly less so from the Enlightenment on, while mass-produced sentimental Kitsch became common (the "plastic Jesus" and its forerunners).

Nineteenth-Century Protestant Theology.   Continental Protestant theology after Hegel and Schleiermacher was to a large extent concerned with the question of how much of either (or both) of their syntheses could be successfully maintained. Søren Kierkegaard (1813-1855), a Danish writer with a pietist background, attacked the Hegelians of his day in a series of brilliant, complex books, denying that Christianity could be encompassed in a philosophical synthesis. The Christian must take a "leap over fifty thousand fathoms"; he must embrace, in passionate subjectivity, a paradox that reason and philosophy must regard as absurd: that the eternal is infinitely, qualitatively distinct from time, and yet has come into time. In his emphasis on passionate subjectivity, on having to choose beyond the limits of rational thought, Kierkegaard was a founder of "existentialist" philosophy. At the end of his life, he bitterly attacked the Danish Lutheran state church as a betrayal of Christianity.

Other theologians (the "theologians of mediation") still hoped for a synthesis along the lines of Schleiermacher and of Hegel, or alternatively of Kant. The "liberals" retained much of the attitude of the Enlightenment and of Kant: they valued reason, but chiefly as "Practical Reason"; they distrusted metaphysics, "Pure Reason," and "dogma"; and they regarded ethics as the core of religion. An outstanding representative of this school was the great church historian Adolf von Harnack (1851-1930). His *History of Dogma* followed the lead of the Hegelian historian Ferdinand Christian Baur (1792-1860) in regarding dogma as a hellenization of Christianity; but, unlike Baur, Harnack considered dogma a wholly illegitimate distortion of an original ethical teaching. In his very popular and influential *What Is Christianity?* (1900), he distinguished sharply between the dogmatic "religion *about* Jesus," and the "religion *of* Jesus," the threefold teaching of the fatherhood of God, the brotherhood of man, and the infinite value of the human soul.

Among a number of nineteenth-century writers, God was more or less equivalent to humanity-at-its-best. Ludwig Feuerbach (1804-1872) and Emile Durkheim (1858-1917) regarded religion as a projection of human life, Durkheim emphasizing the social aspect more strongly. For Karl Marx (1818-1883), religion was a function of economic class in society, and would disappear when a classless society is attained; for Sigmund Freud (1856-1939), it was a neurotic illusion. Most of these writers are regarded as antireligious, but "religious" writers of this period were sometimes not far removed from them in their emphasis on continuity between human beings and God. A further characteristic of the nineteenth century was the widespread belief in Progress, leading to a perfect (or more nearly perfect) society, which some religious writers equated with the Kingdom of God. Only exceptional figures like Kierkegaard did not share the optimistic belief in progress. Auguste Comte (1798-1857) tried to found an organized religion based on belief in human divinty and Progress.

Renewal Movements.   The new attitude toward the Christian past initiated by Romanticism, together with the growth of historical scholarship, gave rise to what we may broadly call "renewal movements," that is, movements to make accessible those resources of the Christian tradition that had been forgotten or rejected during the preceding several centuries. In England, where Samuel

Taylor Coleridge (1772–1834) had done for the Anglicans something comparable to Schleiermacher's work in Lutheran Germany, the "Oxford Movement" aimed at restoring appreciation of catholic doctrine, and of a catholic view of the episcopacy, among Anglicans. A violent reaction against some publications of the movement drove its greatest figure, John Henry Newman (1801–1890) to become a Roman Catholic; he was made a cardinal in 1871. But the movement grew into an "Anglo-Catholic" party in the Church of England. The "Cambridge Movement" promoted a revival of pre-Reformation traditions in liturgy and architecture; its major figure was John Mason Neale (1818–1866), who wrote on church history, liturgy, and spirituality, composed many hymn texts, and translated medieval hymns from Greek and Latin.

In continental Protestantism, renewal movements were more oriented toward Reformation teaching, and led to new interest in Luther and Calvin, although they also valued pre-Reformation traditions. Wilhelm Loehe (1808–1872) in Germany and Nicolai Gruntvig (1783–1872) in Denmark are representatives of the "Lutheran Awakening," or renewal. Less successful were the "theologians of repristination," who attempted a wholesale restoration of Baroque dogmatics, to the point of rejecting critical biblical and historical scholarship.

The renewal movements often clashed both with liberalism and with the Pietist-Evangelical parties in the Protestant and Anglican churches.

In the Roman Catholic church, several renewal movements flourished under papal approval: a renewal of Thomism dominated Roman Catholic philosophical thinking until the 1960s (oddly enough, Aquinas's *theology* proper was comparatively neglected); and a movement to restore Gregorian chant led to a wider movement for liturgical renewal. This, in turn, led to a major attempt to recover worship as normal mysticism. One leader of the movement, the Benedictine Odo Casel (1886–1948), held that Christian worship is a mystery in which the saving act of God in Christ is continually reactualized. Casel rather overstressed the Hellenistic mystery religions as a clue to the meaning of the Christian mystery, but his work has proved fruitful in recovering the dynamism and depth of the early Christian worship.

In the Eastern Orthodox church, where the spiritual movement associated with the *Philokalia* had prepared the way for a renewal movement, Alexis Khomiakov (1804–1860), a retired Russian captain of cavalry and theologian, initiated a movement back to the eastern theological tradition, after a long period of subservience to western models.

Christian Social Movements. As we observed above, the churches reacted feebly to the plight of industrial workers. However, there were a number of prominent figures within the churches who realized that traditional, mostly private forms of charity were not adequate to the new situation. They advocated institutional changes in the political and social order. It was mainly the steadfast opposition of the Evangelical-Methodist movement that caused black slavery and the slave trade to be abolished in the British Empire in 1807.

Activism on behalf of the working class distinguished such figures as the Scottish Presbyterian minister Thomas Chalmers (1780-1847); the Anglican Christian Socialists John Malcolm Ludlow (1821-1911), Frederick Denison Maurice (1805-1872), and Charles Kingsley (1819-1875); and, on the continent, the supporters of "Social Catholic" movements, such as Wilhelm Emmanuel von Ketteler (1811-1877) in Germany.

Christian social movements contributed significantly to the passing of laws against child labor and other flagrant abuses in a number of countries. The Religious Socialist movement in Germany after World War I, and the movement associated with the newspaper *Catholic Worker* (founded 1933) in America, exemplify the diverse twentieth-century descendents of these earlier movements. Not infrequently, Christian social movements have been linked to renewal movements; the connection is especially strong in such a figure as Eric Gill (1882-1940), the English Catholic craftsman and social philosopher.

The Roman Catholic Church

The "Ultramontanist" movement succeeded, during the course of the ninetennth century, in securing a large measure of centralized papal authority in the Roman Catholic church, at the expense of tendencies toward national autonomy. The Jesuit order was restored to official existence in 1814, in line with this program. In opposing nationalism (at least in respect of church administration), the papacy found itself also at odds with nineteenth-century liberalism, which was closely connected with nationalism. In Italy, the conflict was especially sharp; the papacy clung to the centuries-old conviction that it had to rule at least central Italy politically, to avoid exploitation by lay rulers. The nationalist movement (*risorgimento*) aimed at unifying Italy politically under a liberal monarchy. Attempts to forge an alliance between Rome and political liberalism failed; the greatest figure of this movement, the Frenchman Félicité de Lamennais (1784-1854), finally left the church. In 1864, Pope Pius IX (pope 1846-1878) issued the *Syllabus of Errors*, which appeared to condemn "progress, liberalism, and modern civilization" wholesale.

Although the nationalists won the struggle for central Italy, leaving the papacy in political control of Vatican City only, Ultramontanism succeeded in church affairs: at the First Vatican Council (1869-1870), it was declared that when the pope speaks in his office as head of the Church, on a question of faith or morals, his decrees are divinely guaranteed against error, and cannot be rejected or corrected. This is the doctrine of papal infallibility. (Those who would not accept it joined with the Dutch Jansenists to form the Old Catholic church.)

The conflict between Ultramontanism and nationalism (continued in the "Kulturkampf" in Germany in the 1870s) had made the Roman church appear politically reactionary; but nineteenth-century liberalism was closely allied to industrialist capitalism, whereas the Roman church held to older ideas of corporate social responsibility that were incompatible with gross exploitation of workers. In 1891, the encyclical issued by Pope Leo XII, *Rerum novarum,* while rejecting a socialism that would abolish all private property, gave official approval to the goals of "Social Catholic" movements in support of worker's rights.

In respect of scientific and historical knowledge, Roman Catholic authorities adopted a defensive attitude wherever the question of biblical inspiration was involved. There was no lack of minds capable of constructively assimilating the new knowledge. The implications of a historical understanding of the development of doctrine were worked out by Johan Adam Moehler (1796-1838) in Germany, and by John Henry Newman in England. But public statements on many topics were strictly censored, and the "Catholic Modernist" movement of the early twentieth century was condemned; Roman Catholic scholarship—at least, that which reached publication—flourished, often at a very high level, mostly in less sensitive areas of research. And to many the Roman Catholic church continued to appear monolithically intransigent toward other Christian communities and suspicious of human freedom in social relations, personal life, and scholarship.

Russian Orthodoxy

In Russia, state control of Orthodox church affairs increased. Many in the church wanted more freedom, but little could be done. Movements for social justice often came to regard the church as a mere tool of an oppressive government.

The spiritual movement associated with the *Philokalia* continued to spread; it was popularized in Russia in the anonymous *Way of A Pilgrim* (first printed in 1884). After Khomiakov, there was a new era of scholarship in theology and church history, part of a brilliant "golden age" of Russian scholarship that lasted until 1917. There was also a striking recovery of the linguistic traditions of Cyril and Methodus in the Orthodox missions among the peoples of the Russian empire, a tradition carried to North America by the great missionary bishop and spiritual teacher, Innokenti Veniaminov (1797-1879).

Western influence on Russian religious thought remained strong, however; especially the influence of Jakob Boehme, who had been known in Russia since the seventeenth century. The theologian and philosopher Vladimir Solovyov (1853-1900) was heavily influenced by both Boehme and Schelling, and in turn influenced theologians, especially Pavel Florensky (1882-?1946; Florensky died in a Soviet concentration camp) and Sergei Bulgakov (1871-1944). Ideas of these three writers that often strike Western readers as peculiarly characteristic of "Eastern mysticism" turn out to be derived from Boehme.

Barth and "Neo-Orthodoxy"

The political and social order of the nineteenth century, with its optimistic progressivism, was shattered in Europe by World War I. The "liberal" view of

Jesus had already been shaken by Albert Schweizer (1875–1965), whose book *The Quest of the Historical Jesus* (1906) presented apocalyptic, and not progress and morality, as the key to understanding. Theology continued for a decade to be dominated by a combination of "liberal" motifs coming from the Enlightenment and from Kant, and the tendency to stress continuity between human religious consciousness and God's being, inherited from Schleiermacher. All of this was challenged by the Swiss Reformed theologian Karl Barth (1886–1968). Barth applied to liberalism and romanticism Kierkegaard's corrective, the "infinite qualitative distinction" between humanity and God. He denied that religion, understood as a function of human God-consciousness, provides any real knowledge of God, who is always "wholly other" than people's notions of him.

Certainly, as Schleiermacher had held, God is not an object of rational knowledge among many other such objects; certainly revelation is not a set of true propositions about God that become themselves an object of faith. (Protestant theologians still customarily characterize almost all theology before Schleiermacher in such terms, along with later approaches based on the principle of literal inerrancy of Scripture. Barth agreed, but his basis was in the "wholly other" character of God, and in the distortion of the human mind by sin. But he also came to hold that God can and does graciously permit himself to become the object of a real, rational, and even objective knowledge, which is the mark of a mature faith. In his later work, Barth resorted to a doctrine of the Incarnation derived from the Council of Chalcedon as the determining factor in his theology, including his view of creation—he endorsed the Scotist view that, even apart from consideration of the Fall, the end to which creation is ordered is the Incarnation.

Barth's theology is usually called by the somewhat unsatisfactory name of "neo-orthodoxy"; more loosely, this term is applied to all the postliberal theologians influenced by Barth, who dominated Protestant theology until the 1960s.

Nazism and Fascism

The rise of Nazism in Germany and of Fascist and quasi-Fascist movements elsewhere caught the churches quite unprepared. The Nazis never developed a unified policy toward the churches; against a background of bureaucratic regulation, Nazi agencies simultaneously employed sporadic and unpredictable acts of repression, rabid anti-Christian agitation, and declarations that Hitler was the savior of the churches. Prominent church leaders, like many others, accepted Nazism (at least at first) as a return to discipline, heroism, self-sacrifice, and national dignity; even in the face of increasingly harsh policies, they did not protest publicly or officially. In general, the church leadership protested only when the interests of the churches were threatened, a pattern analogous to the policy of appeasement adopted by the leading European governments. Leaders of the opposition, including a number of prominent theologians, left Germany: Barth returned to Switzerland, Paul Tillich (1886–1965) settled in America. Dietrich Bonhoeffer (1906–1945), who was becoming recognized as a major theologian, remained as an underground opposition leader, and was hanged by the Nazis. Sermons from both Catholic and Protestant pulpits condemned Nazi atrocities even when the official church leadership was silent; and the active German opposition to Hitler, small though it was numerically, was composed largely of Christians acting in accordance with their faith.

The assessment of the church's response to the Nazis is still highly controversial. For example, it is hotly debated whether Pope Pius XII should have publicly condemned the Nazi extermination of the Jews, or whether the course he actually did follow, of intervening quietly in particular cases (he undeniably succeeded in saving many Jews from death), was the most effective available to him.

The New Martyrdom in the East

The eastern churches in the Turkish Empire suffered from the political turmoil attending its breakdown. In some areas, they subsequently enjoyed more freedom, but in Turkey the Armenians and Nestorians were persecuted and massacred; this policy came to a climax in 1914–15, in mass deportations and the murder of over a million Armenians.

In Russia, the Orthodox church had a broad base of faithful members (especially among the peasants), a large number of clergy who desired reform, and the support of an able minority of intellectuals (some of whom, however, were primarily nationalists). When the old regime collapsed in 1917, a council of clergy and laity met to begin the process of reform, and for the first time in two centuries a patriarch was elected, Tikhon (d. 1925). Thus the church had already taken the initiative for substantial reforms when the Bolsheviks seized power. But Lenin, an anti-Christian fanatic, immediately instituted a policy designed to eradicate all traditional religion in Russia proper and in the Russian empire, most of which was recaptured by the Red Army and renamed the "Union of Soviet Socialist Republics."

The situation worsened as Stalinist terror grew. The number of those who have died because they were Christians under the Soviet government is, of course, unknown, but it has been reasonably estimated at three million—many times the total of the classical "age of martyrs." And the persecution involves not only the former state church (of the Orthodox bishops alone, over 130 were killed), but the Baptists and others who had been persecuted under the tsars.

The brilliant flowering of scholarship in the Russian church was cut off quickly by these events, but it was partly perpetuated, and also made known to Western readers, by émigrés in the West. And it has been succeeded by the rise of scholarship in Greece, so far little known or appreciated elsewhere.

14

Christianity in the New World

The European powers began to colonize the Western Hemisphere in the sixteenth century. It was mostly a process of military conquest; in the centers of colonization, the indigenous peoples ("Indians") were either destroyed, or totally subjugated, and replaced by European settlers.

Early European contacts with Native American cultures were often not of a sort to impress the Europeans favorably: the Aztecs offered a steady stream of human sacrifices to the sacred sun, and the Iroquois delighted in subjecting prisoners of war to refined tortures. This element of savage cruelty in a few of the native peoples obscured to most Europeans the depth of spiritual insight reached by the American cultures; it also served as an excuse for the atrocities so often committed against the Indians.

The wholesale destruction of preliterate cultures by violent or nonviolent means is only now beginning to be recognized as a serious moral issue, although particular examples have drawn protest from time to time. The loss to the peoples whose cultures have been destroyed is obvious; Christianity has also suffered by being associated in many minds with this sort of destruction. And one may speculate about what Christianity might have gained if it had penetrated humbly and peacefully into cultures which possessed a genius for ceremonial form and sacred art, in which Native Americans excelled (compare early medieval Ireland).

But the Christian role in the colonial Americas was by no means as disreputable as some now claim. The Spanish and Portuguese religious orders struggled heroically and successfully to outlaw the enslavement of Indians (unfortunately, a substitute was found: black slaves from Africa). In Paraguay, the Jesuits established the "Reductions," a system of colonies, admittedly highly paternalistic, but designed to shield the Indians from exploitation and the greedy pressures of European civilization. When it became known that Paraguay was prosperous enough to enrich the Jesuit order, the governments involved began to eye it; and when the Jesuit order was suppressed in Spain (1767), the entire system collapsed.

Varieties of Christianity in the New World

Only Roman Catholicism was tolerated in French, Spanish, and Portuguese colonies. Elsewhere, a more pluralistic pattern prevailed. Some colonies were composed of members of European state churches—Anglican, Swedish Lutheran, and Dutch Reformed communities appeared along the Atlantic coast of North America. But the New World appealed to many as the wilderness in which a new Exodus could occur, a place of refuge and purification to those who were persecuted as heretics (French Huguenots, English Roman Catholics), or who were dissatisfied with the Government and worship of the state church (English Puritans), or who experienced persecution or discrimination because they rejected the state church system in principle (Quakers, English and Continental Baptists, Amish, Hutterites, and others).

New England Puritanism.   In Puritan Massachusetts, only members of the Calvinist congregations had full citizenship. Every effort was made to secure the "rule of the saints," and to establish a model English community with a thoroughly reformed state church, free of "prelacy" and "popish superstition." Dissenters were banished. But the stringent requirements of covenanted church membership proved too severe. In spite of a thorough educational system (including Harvard College), fewer and fewer colonists became enfranchised citizens. Finally, the authorities were forced to accept a "half-way covenant" as sufficient for citizenship. Social stability was secured, and the rule of the saints was ended.

Quakers.   In the colony of Pennsylvania, founded by Quakers, toleration was practiced on a wide scale, and a precedent was established for religious pluralism. The Quakers did not quite attain their goal of a society free from violence and coercion, but Pennsylvania became a haven for many religious communities, including many of Anabaptist origin, mostly speaking German dialects and called the "Pennsylvania Dutch" ("Dutch," cognate with German *deutsch,* dialect *deitsch,* meaning "German," originally meant in English the language and people of both the Netherlands and Germany, and still does in colloquial usage in Pennsylvania).

The "Great Awakening."   Both continental Pietism and British Evangelicalism had arrived in America by 1725. George Whitefield made seven visits to New England, and died in Massachusetts. Between 1725 and 1775, the "Great Awakening" swept through the colonies, establishing the characteristic form of American Protestant revivalism. Itinerant preachers addressed large crowds, who responded with outbursts of emotional expression, rising gradually to an ecstatic pitch of excitement. The goal was to reach the nominally Christian population and to win each individual to the Gospel as understood by revivalism: conviction of sin, repentence, and a conversion experience involving the inner conviction of indefectible personal salvation.

Prayer Book Anglicans (who came to be called "Episcopalians" in America); the stricter Scottish Presbyterians; those of the New England Congregationalists who preferred the "Reasonable Christianity" of the Enlightenment; these all resisted the "Awakening." But it spread through the Protestant churches of the colonies, giving many of them a common culture and facilitating the political unification of the colonies. Preachers and converts alike were often uneducated, but the greatest theologian of colonial America, Jonathan Edwards

(1703–1758), supported the Awakening, hoping that it would halt the decline of New England Calvinism.

Denominationalism. In post-Revolutionary America, the existence of established churches in some states was a vestige of no great importance. The state-church system was replaced by religious toleration on the part of the government, and by the "denominational" principle on the part of the Protestants, who were in the great majority. Fragmentation into "denominations" was accepted at the organizational level, putting "magisterial" denominations (Episcopalians, Congregationalists, Presbyterians, Lutherans) on the same footing as Methodists, Baptists, and others. All renounced any ambition for legal establishment. But there was a widespread conviction that the Protestant denominations agreed on the fundamentals of true Christianity, and that they could and should join forces to reform society and to construct a Christian American civilization. Instead of a single politically established church, there was to be a socially and culturally established interdenominational Protestantism.

Revivalism. A "Second Great Awakening" began about 1800 and dominated American Protestantism until the middle of the century. Revival techniques developed greatly. "Camp meetings" were held during the summer in wild frontier areas: vast throngs of people, camping for days in tents, gathered to hear the revivalist preachers and, in many cases, to experience conversion, in an atmosphere of intense emotional excitement marked by ecstatic outbursts and seizures. In more settled areas, revival campaigns, with nightly meetings, might last for several weeks.

Revivalism was often connected with apocalypticism. There were controversies over whether the thousand-year reign of Christ on earth, the "millennium" (Rev. 20), would be a period *before* the Second Coming of Christ, during which the world would be converted to the Gospel ("Postmillennialism"), or a period *after* the Second Advent, which in turn would follow an almost universal *rejection* of the Gospel ("Premillennialism"). The pre-Christian belief that the Messiah would come either when Torah was followed faithfully in all parts of the world, or when it was followed only by a tiny remnant, continues to the present in some forms of Christianity. Attempts were made to predict the date of the Second Coming; "Adventist" denominations were formed, emphasizing the belief in a "soon coming of Christ."

Voluntary interdenominational societies were formed to support a number of causes. Sabbath observance was enforced by "blue laws," although Seventh Day denominations rejected the common English-speaking Protestant identification, going back to the Puritans, of Sunday as the Sabbath. "Temperance" (meaning total abstinence from alcoholic beverages, and legal prohibition wherever possible); the abolition of slavery (strongly supported in the North and opposed in the South; the largest Protestant denominations divided over this issue in the 1840s and '50s); feminism (which came to be associated with "temperance"); Sunday schools, and foreign missions were among the causes supported. Followers of Alexander Campbell (1788–1866) rejected the denominational principle and advocated Christian union on the basis of the New Testament alone, but they too became a de facto "denomination." They and many predestinarian Baptists disliked the interdenominational societies and the causes they promoted, but the "anti-effort" Protestants could only abstain from activism, which went on without them.

After the Civil War, under the influence of Wesley's teachings on holiness as an attainable and necessary goal for Christians, the "Holiness Movement" carried revivalism a step further. The movement emphasized a postbaptismal gift of holiness, bestowed by the Holy Spirit; healing as a gift of the Spirit; and millennialism (the "four-square Gospel": Jesus as savior, sanctifier, healer, and coming Lord). "Holiness" denominations formed as a result. At the beginning of the twentieth century, heightened emphasis on particular gifts of the Spirit, especially speaking in unknown tongues (glossolalia), developed into the Pentecostal movement, and Pentecostal denominations appeared.

Romanticism and Renewal Movements in America. America had no Schleiermacher or Coleridge, and an astute European-born observer has claimed that "America never had a real period of Romanticism. . . . very little of Romanticism influenced the whole life of the educated people."*

Renewal movements were not as strong as Revivalism, but they did exist. The "Mercersburg Theology" that flourished in the German Reformed Church (ca. 1835–ca. 1860) was an important alternative to Revivalism. Among the Lutherans, Renewal movements succeeded in minimizing the influence of both Rationalism and Revivalism, although the legacy of European Pietism remained strong. In the realm of religious philosophy, the New England Transcendentalist movement, contemporary with the Mercersburg theology, was strongly influenced by Romanticism; both Transcendentalism and Enlightenment rationalism influenced the New England Unitarians, who broke away from the Congregationalists in 1825. German Idealist philosophy was a major source for the Personalist movement of the late nineteenth and early twentieth centuries, to which Josiah Royce (1855–1916), regarded by many as America's greatest philosopher, belonged. Royce's friend and colleague, William James (1842–1910), stressed the practical function of religion, defending evidence of religious belief drawn from emotional experience.

Liberals and Conservatives. Disputes over the challenge of new scientific and historical knowledge increasingly split Protestants, in America as in Britain, into rival "liberal" and "conservative" camps. In 1910–1912, an interdenominational "conservative" group published a series of 12 booklets entitled *The Fundamentals,* which set forth five doctrines as "fundamentals" of Christianity: the Virgin birth of Christ; his physical resurrection; the total literal

*Paul Tillich, *Perspectives on 19th and 20th Century Protestant Theology* (New York: Harper, 1967), p. 81.

inerrancy of Scripture; substitutionary atonement (the "objective theory"); and the imminant and literal second coming. The term "fundamentalism" has since been used loosely used to describe any Protestant position involving the literal inerrancy of the Bible.

Both camps were socially activist, although weakness in the social program of American Protestants had been revealed by the denominational splits over slavery, by the later acquiescence of northern Protestants to segregationism, and by the fact that blacks had to form their own denominations to escape the second-class status they had to endure even in progressive northern congregations.

Among the denominations that had supported abolition, however, some of the more "sectarian" continued to insist on racial equality.

The "liberal" Protestants mostly avoided the racial issue, but, unlike the "conservatives," they did turn their attention to the urban poor, rejecting the common opinion that the poor had only themselves to blame. "Social Gospel" leaders like Walter Rauschenbusch (1861-1918) were imbued with faith in Progress and in the "Kingdom of God" as an attainable social order. Some were socialists; most were progressives of more moderate stamp. Although most Protestants clung to the older rural perspective of figures like William Jennings Bryan, the "Great Commoner," both progressivism and socialism were closely connected with Protestant activism.

After World War I, the Revivalist tradition won a victory in the national prohibition of alcoholic beverages (imposed in 1920), and attempted to prevent the theory of evolution from being taught in public schools, leading to the famous Scopes "monkey" trial of 1925. But the revivalists increasingly lost control of the larger denominations, and "liberalism," under the leadership of men like Harry Emerson Fosdick (1878-1969), increasingly attracted the better educated and more intellectual Protestants (at least those who did not leave the churches altogether). Prohibition was repealed in 1933, and the era of Revivalist political activism ended. "Liberals" after World War I were often pacifists; during the Depression era (1929-1939), they lost their initiative and much of their leadership to an American variety of Neo-Orthodoxy, led by such theologians as Reinhold Niebuhr (1892-1971) and his brother Richard (1894-1962). The Neo-Orthodox continued the tradition of social reform, but added a note of antiutopian realism, and abandoned pacifism as the Nazi menace loomed ever larger.

Roman Catholic and Eastern Christian Immigration. The increasing tide of immigration from Ireland before the Civil War, and from central, southern, and eastern Europe afterward, caused native-born English-speaking Protestants to lose their numerical advantage in many parts of the country. The public schools, a typically American institution that had been acceptable to Protestants as a means toward the Christian American civilization, were now employed to "Americanize" the new immigrants by destroying their linguistic and cultural heritage, if possible in a single generation. This device was all too successful, but the predominantly Catholic or Orthodox religious traditions of these people were less vulnerable, and their religious communities were most important in the social life of these ethnic communities.* The separation of workers from the traditional churches had not proceeded as far in southern and eastern Europe as in the more industrialized areas, and the churches of the new immigrants, who formed much of America's industrial labor force, were not associated with privileged classes; so the pattern of working-class defection from the churches and of anti-Christian political movements was not so prevalent as in the industrialized areas of Europe. Ethnic parishes (rather than geographical) were permitted to Roman Catholic immigrants, to provide for pastoral care in their own languages and to alleviate their resentment of Irish domination in the church. Ethnic dioceses appeared among the Orthodox and the Uniats after World War I. These developments gave institutional form to the ethnic structure of these communities. The image of a Protestant America seemed increasingly untenable; an attempt to replace it by the notion of "three great faiths" (Protestant, Catholic, and Jewish), although widely accepted, was utterly inadequate to deal with the complex realities.

Tensions between the Irish and the other ethnic groups, and between ethnic and Americanizing cultural emphases, plagued the Roman Catholics, but Rome and the bishops minimized public disputes and schisms. Some Poles seceded to form a Polish National Catholic Church in America, and large numbers of Ruthenian Uniats transferred their allegiance to Russian Orthodox bishops. Eastern-rite churches were unknown to most Protestants and Roman Catholics, so they were ignored, and often are even today, although a number of Uniat jurisdictions, and Byzantine-rite Orthodox jurisdictions, and even the less numerous "monophysites" and "Nestorians," all have substantial church communities in America.

---

*On the Jews, see Jacob Neusner, *The Way of Torah* (Encino, California: Dickenson Publishing Co. Inc., 1970), pp. 83–86.

15

Christianity After Christendom

The Ecumenical Movement

The period following World War II (hereafter called the "postwar period"), witnessed substantial growth of the "ecumenical movement," which aimed to restore unity among Christians. More sensitive Christians had always recognized that division into an increasing number of competing "churches" and "denominations" is a scandal, incompatible with the unity proclaimed in the New Testament. Throughout the history of Christianity, efforts to heal breaches of unity have persisted. Societies such as the World Student Christian Federation, founded in 1895, were interdenominational and fostered a spirit of unity. A substantial portion of Canadian Methodists, Presbyterians, and Congregationalists merged in 1925 to form the United Church of Canada. Denominational divisions that were taken for granted in America or Britain often appeared meaningless and absurd in mission areas; a similar union church had been formed in China in 1927. Between the world wars, conferences and committees were formed to discuss common problems and to promote unity, although they were active mainly among those Protestants whose origins lie in the Magisterial Reformation. These, in turn, eventuated in the formation of the World Council of Churches ("W.C.C.") in Amsterdam in 1948.

The W.C.C. did not include all Christian churches, of course. The Unitarians, who would not affirm what seemed to others the teachings that define Christianity, were not included. Others stood aloof for opposite reasons: they feared diluting what they firmly believed to be the only true Christianity. These included most of the more world-renouncing and "sectarian" communities, "fundamentalist" and revivalist denominations, some American Lutherans, and, most notably, the Roman Catholics. The Soviet government did not permit the Orthodox Patriarchate of Moscow to join in 1948, and some of the Orthodox outside the Soviet orbit preferred not to join; but many other Eastern churches did assume membership, preventing the W.C.C. from being an exclusively Protestant organization (they have, however, had cause to complain that the wording of questions and resolutions in the Council tend to force Protestant presuppositions on them).

Considerable enthusiasm for the ecumenical movement was generated in the postwar period. Several more "union" churches were formed, among which the Church of South India (formed in 1947) was especially noteworthy in that it included not only Congregationalists, Reformed, and Methodist, but also Anglicans.

In spite of a newly positive attitude on the part of Roman Catholics, enthusiasm began to wane in the later 1960s, although this was probably due not so much to the larger goals of the movement as the institutional emphasis that had characterized previous decades: many began to feel that the main result was only fewer and larger administrative structures. An analogy between the ecumenical movement and the formation of economic cartels suggested that nontheological motivations were involved in the movement's popularity. Some observers accused the movement of fostering doctrinal irresponsibility; the bishops of the Russian Orthodox Church outside Russia (often called the "Synod") warned of an "ecumenical heresy." A proposed Anglican-Methodist merger in England failed of acceptance and the interdenominational "Consultation on Church Union" (COCU) in the United States appeared to be accomplishing little. In at least one area, however, that of relations between Chalcedonian and Monophysite Eastern Christians, much progress has been made since the middle nineteen-sixties.

The Anglican archbishop William Temple (1881-1944) once described the ecumenical movement as "the great new fact of our era." If it succeeds in finding new directions, it may prove to be a "great new fact" in the history of Christianity.

The Roman Catholics Before 1958

For about a decade and a half after World War II, the Roman Catholic church continued to exhibit the familiar tendencies of centralized papal authority and emphasis on devotion to the Virgin Mary. The bodily assumption of Mary into heaven, an ancient popular belief, had been generally accepted by Eastern Christians and some Anglicans; however, it is usually not part of Protestant belief, because it is not found in Scripture. Among Roman Catholics, it had the status of an officially approved "pious opinion" until 1950, when it was made a dogma of the Church by papal decree, with the "infallible" authority proclaimed in 1871. Some prominent Roman Catholic theologians maintained that Mary did not die, but was "assumed" into heaven with no separation of soul from body. This view contradicts Eastern Christian tradition, in addition to being unacceptable to Protestants. So it appeared that the Roman Catholics were moving away from all other Christians.

Many observers expected a papal proclamation declaring Mary, in view of her cooperation in the Incarnation and earthly life of Christ the Redeemer, to be "co-redemptrix" with him. Such a development would have further divided Roman Catholicism from the rest of Christianity, for such language is not part of any other Christian tradition.

Aquinas remained the dominant influence on Roman Catholic thought. Among the best known Thomists were Jacques Maritain (1882-1973) and Etienne Gilson (born 1884). The somewhat different approach of Joseph Maréchal (1878-1944), which aimed at overcoming Kantian objections through a dynamic understanding of human knowledge, has become increasingly influential; it is usually referred to as "transcendental Thomism." But Thomism of any sort had currency only among Roman Catholics and a rather small number of Anglicans.

Renewal Movements. Modern Thomism represents a renewal movement in Christian philosophy, but other renewal movements, reaching back to sources that antedated the Middle Ages, had a more ecumenical character: Roman Catholics, Anglicans, Eastern Christians, and Protestants participated in them and found much common ground. These movements also provided an alternative to the liberal/conservative dichotomy, in that they called for reform based on a critical knowledge of tradition. In some respects, they had already had an important influence; frequent communion had been restored as the norm for Roman Catholic church life since the beginning of the twentieth century.

Biblical and patristic studies, and scholarship in the area of worship and liturgy, attained a high academic level, and were applied for practical pastoral purposes. The sources upon which these movements drew had previously been forgotten, or were preserved in fossilized form, so that their impact on church life had been greatly reduced. The extent and effectiveness of the renewal varied greatly; it was most considerable in some parts of Western Europe and in some mission churches.

Pope John XXIII and the Second Vatican Council. In 1958, Giuseppi Cardinal Roncalli (1881-1963) was elected pope, taking the name John XXIII. He immediately became a popular figure because of his warm, open manner; the impression that he was a nice, innocuous old man was dispelled in 1959 by his call for a Second Vatican Council, an announcement that took everyone by surprise, especially the papal Curia.

At the Council (1962-65), an alliance between the pope and the majority of bishops overcame the staunch resistance of the curia and introduced a sort of moderate conciliarism ("collegiality") along with a number of far-reaching reforms. Consequently, changes have been more dramatic in the Roman Catholic church than elsewhere in Christianity, although the Council has also had considerable influence on Protestants and Eastern Christians, and has brought Roman Catholics into the ecumenical movement to a much greater extent than previously.

The Council made it apparent that many Roman Catholics were eager for a less authoritarian church life. Scholars could now publish critical-historical studies in sensitive theological and historical areas; these proved to be comparable in quality to the best Protestant work. Scholarship became more ecumenical; collaboration was now possible where formerly Roman Catholics worked separately. The laity were urged to take a more active role in church life.

However, the buoyant atmosphere of the Council was followed by disillusionment in some quarters.

On the one hand, those eager for drastic changes complained that reform had not gone far enough. They were dissatisfied when John XXIII's successor, Paul VI (born 1897, elected pope 1963) proved to be more cautious, refusing to alter the long-standing prohibitions against contraception and the ordination of women and married men to the priesthood. The encyclical *Humanae Vitae* (1968), dealing with contraception, caused a severe crisis because of its restrictive content and authoritarian tone. Catholic intellectuals withdrew from the church in large numbers, and active lay participation in the United States and elsewhere declined drastically.

On the other hand, many Catholics found the pace and extent of the changes quite confusing; they longed for the stability of earlier days. Some simply disliked the new order; most would probably have welcomed the change if it had been more gradual; some felt that the Council's program was sound, but that it had been applied in a quite unsatisfactory way.

Ferment in Theology

Protestant theology entered a period of flux at about the same time that the Roman Catholic church entered its new phase. Rudolf Bultmann (born 1884), a German scholar who pioneered the development of "form criticism," was calling for a program of "demythologizing" the biblical message, ridding it of all links to a prescientific world-view, and interpreting it in terms of an existentialist analysis of the ways of being that are possible for humanity. The heritages of apocalyptic and Christian Hellenism would be jettisoned by this program.

Existentialist analysis cannot be applied to God, and in fact it is hard to discover any doctrine of God in Bultmann. Paul Tillich, provided one possibility, contending that God is "being itself," "the ground of being in all that is." Another approach, prominent in America, is "process theology," which sees the being of God as including two poles, the eternal and infinite, and the temporal-finite. Another school proclaimed a "theology of the death of God,"; God has died, in this view, because it is no longer possible to believe in a transcendent reality. In Germany, a "theology of hope" has been proposed, in connection with a program of reinterpreting all of Christian theology in eschatological terms. A "secular theology" that denies any transcendent power has been countered by a tendency to emphasize transcendence. Some writers call for a new apocalyptic theology.

Roman Catholic theology has also experienced upheavals. Thomism has been less prominent since the Second Vatican Council, although the Austrian Jesuit Karl Rahner (born 1904), a transcendental Thomist with strong ties to contemporary German theology, remains the most influential postconciliar theologian, and his fellow Jesuit, the Canadian Bernard Lonergan (born 1904), has developed an increasingly influential approach to philosophical and theological method based on transcendental Thomism. Edward Schillebeeckx (born 1914) of Holland has refined and developed the achievement of Casel (see page 173). Hans Kueng (born 1928), an admirer of his fellow Swiss, Karl Barth, has often been in trouble with church authorities, and has not hesitated to challenge the dogma of papal infallibility. The writings of Pierre Teilhard de Chardin

(1881-1955), a Jesuit who applied to theology a highly speculative development of the idea of evolution, could not be published until the Council provided a more open situation. They have since attracted a considerable following.

Eastern theology, being less inclined to embrace new philosophies, has not been subject to such obvious and dramatic shifts. The task of winning independence from Western incrustation, and of arriving at a new synthesis on a patristic basis, has been carried on by Russian theologians working in the West, of whom Vladimir Nikolaevich Lossky (1903-1950) and George Vasil'evich Florovsky (born 1893) have been the most important; and by Greek theologians, who have been less recognized in the West. It seems likely that some of the more controversial Eastern theologians, such as Christos Yannaras of Greece and Dumitru Staniloae of Rumania, will become better known in the West in the near future.

Problems of Spirituality. While some voices have urged abandoning a great deal of traditional Christian doctrine on the grounds that "the church is trying to sell too big a package," others believe that the problem lies not so much in theological formulations as in a widespread lack of access to a viable spirituality. In America, certainly, there has been dissatisfaction both with the prevailing revivalist Protestant spirituality, and with the saccharine sentimentality of popular Roman Catholic spirituality. Most Protestants have lacked alternatives; and the major alternative for Catholics and others, embodied in the "liturgical movement" and other renewal movements, has encountered some serious problems that have limited its accessibility.

A desire for some established spiritual tradition with concrete guidance, and for direct religious experience, is surely manifest in the popularity—largely among younger people—of non-Western, non-Christian religious movements: the Caitanya Vaiṣṇava devotionalism ("Hare Krishna"), "Transcendental Meditation," and numerous others. Christianity has been represented in this milieu by the "Jesus movement," a partial adaptation of revivalist spirituality to the counterculture of the late '60s and early '70s.

Pentecostalism has spread at the same time into some Anglican, Roman Catholic, and Eastern Orthodox circles, not without controversy. Serious attempts have been made to adapt both yoga and zen to Christianity, giving rise to debates over the extent to which such techniques can be detached from the non-Christian dogmatic structures with which they are traditionally associated. On the other hand, it is also an open question to what extent traditional Christian ways of spirituality, such as the Carmelite school among Roman Catholics, or Hesychasm among the Orthodox, can be followed under contemporary cultural conditions. In any event, the "mainstream" churches, those most adapted to modern conditions, have been embarrassed by the new interest in spirituality, having in many cases lost touch even with their own traditions—for example, so few American Lutherans, including ordained ministers, would even recognize the name of Johann Arndt that some wag has suggested that the modern Lutheran responds to it by correcting the grammar to "Johann isn't." The problem of spiritual guidance is a major one for contemporary Christianity.

The End of the "Constantinian Era." By the postwar period, it was clear that for most Christians the era inaugurated by Constantine in the early fourth century had come to an end. State churches still existed in some countries, but in the industrialized areas membership in them had been reduced to a formality for most people. Elsewhere, state churches were used as props by authoritarian governments. Ironically, it was often in countries constitutionally committed to the separation of church and state that a kind of social and cultural Establishment has lasted longest. And in Eastern Europe, where the churches had retained a broad popular base of support, Soviet domination brought in persecution and oppression.

Western European colonialism in Asia and Africa gradually disappeared in the postwar era. Former mission churches became autonomous; many newly independent states allow Western missionaries to work among their people only if they can also contribute some skill such as medicine. In other places, the missionaries have been criticized for their role; for example, they have been charged with contributing to conditions that have caused the wholesale extinction of a number of South American Indian tribes.

While the end of colonialism has tended to terminate or limit the familiar missionary efforts, its demise is not necessarily disadvantageous to Christianity. In some areas, the reverse may be true. In the later colonial period, Islam spread rapidly into sub-Sahara Africa, but since the end of colonialism its growth has slowed considerably, whereas Christianity has expanded at a remarkably fast rate, its adherents increasing by ten per cent a year by the 1970s. Some observers have pointed out that if the trend continues for another generation or two, Africa may supplant the West as the center of world Christianity. This eventuality would be of major importance in the history of Christianity. It is clearly not safe to assume that the patterns dominant in the past several centuries will continue to determine the future!

Religious Pluralism. The emergence of former colonies has created a more pluralistic situation among religions. Other religions have increasingly been plagued with many of the same difficulties that have confronted Christianity for generations. But they have also benefited from the new dignity of their traditional countries. Not only those religions with highly developed literary and philosophical traditions, but also the so-called "primitive" religions have increasingly been regarded by Westerners with interest and respect. Superficial attempts to assert some basic unity of all religions have long been popular in some circles, but it now appears that Christians in general will need to reflect on the meaning of religious pluralism on a global scale. Movements stemming from non-Western religious traditions became popular in the West during the

1960s, and while some were a passing fad, there remains a serious interest that seems likely to endure, making for a more pluralistic religious culture in traditionally Christian areas.

Relations between Christians and Jews have always posed special problems, but the Nazi "final solution" introduced a new urgency, not only for improved relations at the practical level, but for a thorough rethinking within the context of Jewish-Christian dialogue. In fact, activity in this area appears to have become more intense during the 1960s and 1970s and will probably continue to challenge both Jews and Christians for decades to come.

Consumerized Christianity and Popular Syncretism. The progressive "secularization" of the major institutions of western society has relegated the churches (especially in northwestern Europe) to a marginal position in society. Intra-Christian pluralism, together with the increasing availability of non-Christian religious options, has placed the churches in the position of "sellers" in a competitive market. American mainline Protestant churches have partly succeeded in resisting marginalization, but they have done so by imitating the bureaucratic structure of secular institutions and by adapting their "product" to the desires of the "consumers," especially by reducing it to an essentially popular-psychological message of "positive thinking," "family counselling," or the like. It has been pointed out that the standardized consumer product, marginally differentiated by "brand" ("denomination"), characterizes the churches' "packages" just as it does mass-produced consumer goods.

As for the large numbers who are not members of any church, it is usually thought that they have become "secular" in the sense of having no religion. But a more convincing interpretation is that the majority of them have constructed a sort of private religion by "shopping" among the numerous "outlets" for religious ideas and "buying" what seems attractive. In most cases, the result is an incoherent collection of religious opinions, popular psychological ideas, and a morality based largely on "self-fulfillment" and often marked by psychological determinism.

Problems of Christian Social Movements

The "liberal/conservative dichotomy" has increasingly divided Christians. In North America, the tradition of political and social activism has flourished in important circles in Christianity, but its base of support is too narrow for comfort. "Mainstream" Protestant churches have tended to support it officially, although the leaders have only partial support from their general membership. "Conservative" churches, retaining a revivalist outlook and clinging to biblical inerrancy, have in most cases—although there are significant exceptions—not supported such activism.

The "civil rights" movement to liberate American blacks from oppressive conditions depended heavily in its earlier phases upon the "liberal" clergy (mainly Protestants) for leadership. By the middle 1960s, blacks had assumed control of the movement and turned it in new directions. The energy of the "liberals" was occupied by protest against the war in Vietnam, which kept them in the center of public controversy. During the same period, the postwar expansion of "mainstream" churches ended, and membership began to decline numerically, while "conservative" churches grew substantially. However, it is also necessary to note, during this same period, an increasing tendency of "conservative" churches to espouse "liberal"-sounding positions on such issues as race relations.

The conviction that under modern conditions Christians must address political, social, and economic ills in terms of mass politics, rather than mere individual effort, has powerful and urgent arguments behind it. But it remains unclear how churches can arrive at authoritative decisions on controversial issues ("who speaks for the church?"); and how can they be effective in a post-Constantinian age, when those in power are disinclined to take them seriously. Several "contextual" theologies, reflecting the particular experience of oppressed communities, have appeared: "black theology" in the United States, and in Latin America a "theology of liberation" that has won increasing attention during the 1970s. Perhaps a "theology of liberation" will succeed in overcoming the serious problems confronting the tradition of Christian social movements. To date, however, all such movements have been so limited in perspective that they offer nothing to the millions of oppressed persons in situations different from that of the "liberation theologians" themselves.

Problems of Renewal Movements. The "liberal/conservative dichotomy" brings about polarization in theology; this effect has become markedly stronger among Roman Catholics, Lutherans, and Eastern Orthodox, who had previously seemed to be less subject to it than "mainstream" Protestants. Renewal movements have generally been a counterforce to the dichotomy. They have usually avoided the pitfall of attempting simply to restore some past state of affairs: "It is not only a question of tracing to its sources a form that has gone awry, but of finding new forms beyond the patterns actually operative, simply by setting out from the spirit and the essential type of the original" (Yves Congar).

But the renewal movements themselves have encountered serious difficulties. A good example is the Liturgical Movement, which aims at a renewal of Christian worship. During the twentieth century, this movement has generated an extensive scholarly literature of high quality on the history of Christian liturgy (a difficult and intricate topic), the bulk of it by Roman Catholics and Anglicans, with solid contributions from Lutherans and others.

The movement gained gradual acceptance among churches with a tradition of liturgical worship; the Second Vatican Council endorsed it in a Constitution on the Liturgy (issued in 1967), "putting the stamp of supreme authority in the Roman Catholic church upon the main results of the whole liturgical movement" (Louis Bouyer) and calling for a thorough reform, including a restoration of full and meaningful lay participation, and the general introduction of vernacular languages in place of Latin.

Decades before the Council, some of these reforms had been anticipated in parts of Western Europe (to the irritation of certain church authorities); but in most parishes, especially in North America, the effect had been slight. Now, reforms were introduced in a way that bewildered many parishioners. Soon, some writers proclaimed the movement a failure because it had not produced a new golden age of Catholicism, while a number of Catholics stopped attending church because they were confused by the continuing rapid change. (Church attendance among American Roman Catholics dropped sharply, but the "new liturgy" cannot fairly be blamed for this pattern as a whole.)

Moreover, some of the more knowledgeable supporters of the movement criticized the way in which it was understood and applied. For example, the Constitution on the Liturgy called for reforms that would restore to prominence the social aspects of worship, which had been neglected in the Roman rite for many centuries. But many who accepted this goal came to feel that the reform was carried out at the expense of the transcendent aspects of the liturgy, as if to reduce it to a purely human social function.

Similar problems have arisen in other renewal movements. Nevertheless, they have achieved a degree of success, and are likely to be of continuing importance.

"Aggiornamento."   In connection with the Second Vatican Council, the Italian word *aggiornamento* (bringing up to date) gained international currency. Earlier efforts at aggiornamento—"modernism" seems to be almost synonymous—had run afoul of authority. The Council introduced a new openness to updating those structures that seemed inappropriate to modern civilization. Among Protestants, of course, only the word was new. "Updating" of one sort or another had been debated, often bitterly, for generations, producing the "liberal/conservative dichotomy."

Problems of aggiornamento usually involve conflicting judgments about where to draw the line in Christian life and practice between culturally conditioned elements that can and should be changed when they become inconvenient, and traditional elements that are essential and nonnegotiable, or at least highly valuable and worth defending. Aggiornamento may be either complementary to renewal movements or in conflict with them. There may also be problems in effectively implementing a program of aggiornamento, even if it is approved in principle.

To what extent should Christianity be brought into harmony with contemporary civilization, and to what extent is tension between them a healthy and natural manifestation of the proper tension between Christianity and any "Present Age"? The question is extraordinarily complex. A kind of "aggiornamento," not wholly conscious, occurs in any case, but often the result is either a mere passing fad, or, more seriously, the acceptance of a "conventional wisdom" that reflects uncritical "groupthink" on the part of intellectual and cultural trend-setters, a "groupthink" that has turned out on occasion to be tactically inadvisable and morally questionable.

"Conventional Wisdom" and Ecology. For several generations, a consensus existed that the benefits of industrial technology far outweighed the damage it caused the natural world. A minority of conservationists struggled to protect little remnants of wilderness from "development" and exploitation. Among them were a few prominent Christians, church historians and theologians, who urged that theological and other considerations necessitated a defense of wilderness. But the great majority of Christians who expressed themselves publicly on the topic were proud to point out that it was the biblical religious tradition that had desacralized nature to the point where it could be exploited by industrial technology. Protestants found support for this view in Karl Barth—ironically, for Barth is the last man who could be accused of subservience to "conventional wisdom." Barth's emphasis on the transcendence of God, his sharp distinctions between nature and grace, and between religion and Christianity, tended to reduce nature to a mere stockpile of useful resources for the benefit of humankind.

In the 1960s, however, an "ecological movement" began to exert wider influence. By 1966, the eminent Christian medievalist Lynn White, Jr. still accepted the fashionable account but reflected the new evaluation of it in declaring that "Christianity bears a huge burden of guilt" for the modern ecological crisis.* White proposed Francis of Assisi as the patron saint of ecology and almost the only notable Christian to oppose "orthodox Christian arrogance toward nature." This is an exaggeration, to say the least; it is arguable that the "historic roots of our ecological crisis" lie not in Christianity in general, but in the intersection of Christianity with Neo-Platonism. But undeniably Christians had generally neglected the "cosmic liturgy" tradition, and had often been accomplices in "arrogance toward nature"; it is understandable that some leaders of the ecological movement tend to be anti-Christian.

Shortly after White's article appeared, Christian writers began to publish studies contributing to a more adequate theological understanding of the natural environment. It is likely that this movement will succeed. Unfortunately, the few who anticipated this need when it was still unfashionable have not received due recognition so that a regrettable and inaccurate impression of "me-too-ism" is created.

"Conventional Wisdom" and Marxist-Leninist Persecution. Another good example of the dangers of "conventional wisdom" is the continuing failure of Western Christians to react to persecution of Christians and others by Marxist-Leninist governments, in particular, the Soviet Union.

World War II forced Stalin to abandon persecution of religion within the

---

*In "the Historic Roots of Our Ecological Crisis," a lecture delivered in 1966 and first published in *Science*, Vol. 155 (Jan.–Mar. 1967), pp. 1203–07.

pre-war Soviet territories and a period of relative liberalization ensued, although, of course, it did not benefit Christians in the vast territory annexed to the Soviet Union at the end of the war, or controlled by Soviet interests from that period.

About 1959, however, this policy was reversed and persecution reappeared. The officially approved leadership, of course, was obliged to deny the facts and assert that religious freedom was enjoyed by all citizens of the countries involved. In 1961, the Patriarchate of Moscow was permitted to join the World Council of Churches. About this same time, resistance to the renewed persecution began to consolidate, especially among the Russian Baptists (who number about 4 million); within a few years, information and documentation began to reach the West on a large scale.

The historical importance of this phenomenon has been commonly overlooked: Christianity had had a broader popular basis in Eastern Europe and the Russian Empire than in most of the West, for reasons already mentioned. The events of 1956 had made it obvious that, even when a clear opportunity occurred, Western governments were not going to act on behalf of anyone in Eastern Europe. "Conventional wisdom" in the West thereafter found it convenient to depict the situation in Eastern Europe and the Soviet Union in terms of "liberalization," even in the face of mounting evidence to the contrary. Both the news media and the churches mostly ignored the renewed persecution.

Two exceptions to this pattern appeared during the 1960s. One group denounced the state-approved leadership of churches under Marxist-Leninist governments, implying that the true Christians had all, or mostly, withdrawn into an underground church. This group has also become associated with right-wing politics in the West.

Another perspective, however, characterizes small organizations that have appeared in several Western countries for the purposes of gathering and disseminating information, and bringing the issue to the attention of the reluctant Western churches. While they support Soviet religious dissidents, they do not condemn the official leadership wholesale, nor insist on any particular theological or political orientation.

The World Council of Churches, and many of its member churches, have become increasingly vocal in protesting social injustice in many parts of the world. The W.C.C., for example, supplied money to liberation movements in Africa (accusations have been made that these funds were used to buy arms for terrorists, but those who administered the program denied it, insisting that they were used for food and other necessities for impoverished people). But it adopted a double standard in refusing to acknowledge Soviet persecution. In this case, too, the influence of Barth is operative: Barth openly endorsed a double standard of opposition to Fascist regimes and accommodation to Communist regimes. This double standard subsequently attained the status of a basic if unacknowledged feature of the social views of a large section of Christianity.

At the Nairobi conference of the W.C.C. in 1975, an appeal from two Orthodox Soviet citizens was circulated among the delegates. This time, there was a response: over the protests of the representatives of the Patriarchate of Moscow, a resolution strongly critical of Soviet violations of human rights was adopted in committee, and failed of acceptance only because of a parliamentary technicality raised by an American delegate (presumably motivated by fear of possible reprisals against the delegates from the U.S.S.R. by their government). A much weaker resolution was adopted. But it seems likely that the W.C.C. and its member churches will not be able to evade the issue, or continue to operate according to a double standard. The persecuted communities are forced to struggle against the entire modern totalitarian apparatus, including secret police, concentration camps, repressive laws, and state-controlled education and information media. Both their success in surviving, and the willingness of Christians elsewhere to recognize and support them, are in the balance. The outcome will be a major factor in determining the future of Christianity.

Conclusion: Christianity After Christendom

This too-brief survey of Christianity at a time when, for most, the Christendom of the past sixteen centuries has ended, reveals both grave problems and surprising vitality. It would be foolhardy to predict whether or to what extent the difficulties of the current situation will be overcome, or its promises realized.

The end of the Constantinian era of "establishment" Christianity has occurred in an age that has, in fact, some striking similarities to the Hellenistic pre-Constantinian age: cosmopolitan urban culture combined with a breakdown of more immediate communities, rootless individualism, great political crises, were all known to the Hellenistic world as well. But educated people of that age tended toward transcendental monotheism; and the family still offered a strong, supportive primary community. The modern age discourages transcendental beliefs; it relentlessly invades all communities with its mass culture, propagated by mass media and mass education; and where persecution occurs, it is now supplied with the technology of totalitarianism.

The Christians constitute in this world a "cognitive minority" ("a group of people whose view of the world differs significantly from the one generally taken for granted in their society"—Peter Berger), in an age that is in practice (in the West) and partly also in the intention and policy (in Marxist-Leninist-ruled countries) very hostile toward such minorities, and very effective in breaking them down.

The Christians, in this situation, will need competence in several directions. Modern scientific and historical knowledge, in its positive achievement, imposes itself upon Christians, and is of great advantage to them in understanding their own traditions. There is good reason to hold that a narrowly "positivistic" model of knowledge cannot adequately account for its own ideal, the firmly based knowledge of the natural sciences. And critical methods cannot ultimately avoid reflecting critically upon themselves, at which point they may (as Tillich held) become open to the content established by faith. A "post-critical" model of knowledge will not be specifically Christian, nor will it be a restoration of precritical forms, but there is no reason to assume that exclusive positivist, materialist, or behaviorist norms will dominate human knowledge in the future. Fear of "cognitive minority" status leads to acceptance of "conventional wisdom," and this in turn has led Christians into positions that can be criticized as irresponsible (as in the cases of ecology and Marxist-Leninist persecution).

Christians may, on the one hand, be able to find and follow indices of transcendence in contemporary human experience, to trace out obscure paths that lead from the secularized world of mass culture to the power of ultimate transformation. They may also, by immersing themselves in their own tradition in all its richness and fullness (which they can now do with the added advantages of modern historical tools), bear witness to a strange, hardly dreamed of reality in the midst of the secularized world. Worship and spirituality are at least as important as formal theological reflection to this enterprise: one may doubt whether a Christianity lacking a vivid apprehension of the "mystery" in "normal mysticism" can avoid progressive dilution. The detachment and freedom from "being conformed to this world" that characterized the pre-Constantinian church of the martyrs, and that was preserved with partial success by the monks, seems to have become a scarce commodity; but the Christians will need it as never before in their role as a "cognitive minority." Some will doubtless seek withdrawal from society in one form or another. Christian communes in the American counter-culture movement of the late '60s and early '70s were mostly as ephemeral as other communes, but some appear to have long-term potential. The revival of the traditional monastic desert spirituality in the twentieth century Coptic church in Egypt (which has been, and is, subjected to varying degrees of persecution by the Muslim government) may be a fact of genuinely ecumenical significance.

Clearly, the demands and pressures of contemporary civilization on Christians are severe. But one should not discount the perennial nobility of the vision of humanity, and the created order, liberated from death and restored to wholeness and fulfillment by participation in the love and the life of its Creator; nor the daring of the assertion that this liberation has already been achieved in "the biography of a crucified Jew" (Jaroslav Pelikan), as strangely offensive and compelling now as it was in the first century. For in African villages, in Western universities and urban slums, in obscure farmsteads, in Mordovian prison camps, in all the living hells of the age, men and women live confidently by that strange vision, with faith, hope, and love.

Suggestions for Further Reading

The letter "p" before the place of publication indicates a paperback edition (American or English); "UP" means "University Press."

GENERAL

The student should acquire an elementary knowledge of the Bible; a good brief introduction is:
Connick, Milo, *The Message and Meaning of the Bible* (p; Belmont and Encino, Ca.: Dickenson, 1965).

For complete commentaries on individual books, the Anchor Bible series (Doubleday) is often quite good, and the Hermeneia series (Fortress Press), of which only a few volumes have appeared, is excellent, but fairly difficult.

Chadwick, Owen, *The History of the Church; A Select Bibliography* (p; 2nd ed.; Helps for Students of History, No. 66; London: Historical Association, 1962). The best short bibliography, concentrating on British church history.
Case, S. J., ed. *A Bibliographical Guide to the History of Christianity* (Chicago: U. C. P., 1931). Thorough coverage, although a bit out of date.
Cross, F. L., and E. A. Livingstone, eds., *The Oxford Dictionary of the Christian Church* (2nd ed.; London: Oxford UP, 1974). The best one-volume reference work.
The New Catholic Encyclopedia (16 vols.; New York: McGraw-Hill, 1967).

There are a number of good books representing a specific Christian tradition, from which the student can learn a great deal; for example: Adam, Karl, *The Spirit of Catholicism* (rev. ed., New York: Macmillan, 1937). Reflects the atmosphere of Roman Catholicism before Vatican II.
De Lubac, Henri, *Catholicism* (London: Burns, Oates & Washbourne, 1950).
McKenzie, John L. *The Roman Catholic Church* (p; New York: Holt, Rinehart & Winston, 1969). This represents Roman Catholicism in the troubled period after the Second Vatican Council.
Ware, Timothy, *The Orthodox Church* (p; Baltimore: Penguin, 1963).
Benz, Ernst, *The Eastern Orthodox Church* (p; Garden City, N.Y.: Doubleday, 1963).
Whale, J. S., *The Protestant Tradition* (Cambridge, England: CUP, 1955).
Brown, Robert McAfee, *The Spirit of Protestantism* (New York: Oxford UP, 1961).

See also:
Neill, Stephen Charles, *Christian Missions* (The Pelican History of the Church, Vol. 6; Baltimore: Penguin, 1965).
Parker, T.M., *Christianity and the State in the Light of History* (London: A. & C. Black, 1955).
Niebuhr, H. R., and D. D. Williams, eds., *The Ministry in Historical Perspectives* (New York: Harper, 1956).
Inge, W. R., *Christian Mysticism* (p; New York: Meridian, 1956).

PART I. THE FOUNDATIONS OF CHRISTIANITY

Nock, Arthur Darby, *Conversion: The Old and the New in Religion from Alexander the Great to Augustine of Hippo* (London: Oxford UP, 1933). The best general survey.
Bultmann, Rudolf, *Primitive Christianity in Its Contemporary Setting* (p; New York: Meridian, 1956).

Chapter 1. The Setting in Judaism and Roman Hellenism

On the Roman-Hellenistic background:
Grant, F. C., *Roman Hellenism and the New Testament* (New York: Scribner's, 1962).
Armstrong, A. H., *An Introduction to Ancient Philosophy* (Westminster, Maryland: Newman, 1957).

On the Jewish background:
Russell, D. S., *Between the Testaments* (p; Philadelphia: Fortress, 1965).
Daube, David, *The New Testament and Rabbinic Judaism* (London: U. of London–Athlone, 1956).
Davies, W.D., and David Daube, eds., *The Background of the New Testament and Its Eschatology* (Cambridge, England: CUP, 1956).
Grant, F. C., *Ancient Judaism and the New Testament* (New York: Macmillan, 1959).

Specifically on Apocalyptic:
Rowley, H. H., *The Relevance of Apocalyptic* (rev. ed.; New York: Association Press, 1963).
Russell, D. S., *Method and Message of Jewish Apocalyptic* (Philadelphia: Westminster, 1964).

On the Dead Sea Scrolls:
Gaster, Theodor H., *The Dead Sea Scriptures* (p; rev. ed.; Garden City, N.Y.: Doubleday, 1956). Translations of the Scrolls.
Vermes, G., *The Dead Sea Scrolls in English* (p; rev. ed.; Baltimore: Penguin, 1968). Another collection of translations.
Stendahl, K., ed., *The Scrolls and the New Testament* (New York: Harper, 1957). A collection of articles.
Daniélou, J., *The Dead Sea Scrolls and Primitive Christianity* (Baltimore: Helicon, 1958). Short and easy to read.
Black, Matthew. *The Scrolls and Christian Origins* (New York: Scribner's, 1961). Excellent but quite difficult.

Chapter 2. Jesus of Nazareth

Schweitzer, Albert, *The Quest of the Historical Jesus* (London: A. & C. Black, 1910). The indispensable work on the development of modern scholarship on the life of Jesus.
Bornkamm, Guenther, *Jesus of Nazareth* (New York: Harper, 1960). Account by a noted German form-critic.
Robinson, James M. *A New Quest of the Historical Jesus* (p; Studies in Biblical Theology, no. 25; London: SCM, 1959). On the impact of form-criticism, with ideas for a new beginning.
Scobie, Charles, *John the Baptist* (Philadelphia: Fortress, 1964). The Baptist in the light of the Dead Sea Scrolls.

On the teachings of Jesus:
Robinson, James M., "The Formal Structure of Jesus' Message," in W. Klassen & G. F.

Snyder, eds., *Current Issues in New Testament Interpretation* (O. Piper Festschrift; New York: Harper, 1962), pp. 91–110.

Perrin, Norman, *The Kingdom of God in the Teaching of Jesus* (Philadelphia: Westminister, 1963).

———. *Rediscovering the Teaching of Jesus* (New York: Harper & Row, 1967).

Chapter 3: The Earliest Christian Communities

Conzelmann, Hans, *History of Primitive Christianity* (p; Nashville: Abingdon, 1973).

Goppelt, Leonhard, *Apostolic and Post-Apostolic Times* (p; New York: Harper, 1970). Conzelmann and, even more, Goppelt rely on the notion of "early catholicism" to mark off the New Testament from other early Christian literature; this is a controversial category, used almost exclusively by Protestants.

Bruce, F. F., *New Testament History* (p; rev. ed.; Garden City, N.Y.: Doubleday, 1972). More inclined than Conzelmann or Goppelt to accept statements in New Testament at face value.

Bardy, Gustave, *The Church at the End of the First Century* (London: Sands, 1938). A Roman Catholic scholar's account, older but still worth reading.

Cullmann, Oscar, "Dissensions Within the Early Church," *Union Seminary Quarterly Review,* Vol. XXII (1966–67), pp. 83–92.

On the "Hellenists":

Simon, Marcel, *St. Stephen and the Hellenists in the Primitive Church* (London: Longmans, Green, 1958). Compare Black's remarks in *The Scrolls and Christian Origins.*

On the Gentile Christians:

Nock, A. D., *Early Gentile Christianity and Its Hellenistic Background* (p; New York: Harper, 1964).

On the Ebionites:

Schoeps, H. J., *Jewish Christianity* (Philadelphia: Fortress, 1969).

On Peter:

Cullmann, Oscar, *Peter: Disciple, Apostle, Martyr* (2nd ed.; Philadelphia: Westminster, 1962).

On Paul:

Nock, A. D., *St. Paul* (London: Oxford UP, 1938).

Davies, W. D., *Paul and Rabbinic Judaism* (London: SPCK, 1958).

Schoeps, H. J., *Paul* (Philadelphia: Westminster, 1961). Paul's teachings in Jewish perspective.

Pagel, Elaine, *The Gnostic Paul* (Philadelphia: Fortress, 1975). The Gnostic view of Paul's teachings.

Chapter 4: Early Christian Worship and Doctrine

On the "kerygma" formula:

Dodd, C. H., *The Apostolic Preaching and Its Developments* (London: Hodder & Stoughton, 1936).

An overview of early preaching:

Reicke, Bo, "A Synopsis of Early Christian Preaching," in A. Fridrichsen and others, *The Root of the Vine* (Westminster, England: Dacre, 1953), pp. 128–160.

On the Redeemer hymns and their background:
Sanders, Jack T., *The New Testament Christological Hymns* (S.N.T.S. Monograph Ser. 15; Cambridge, England: CUP, 1971).

On the worship in primitive Christianity:
Moule, C. F. D., *Worship in the New Testament* (p; Ecumenical Studies in Worship, No. 9; Richmond: John Knox, 1961).
Delling, Gerhard, *Worship in the New Testament* (Philadelphia: Westminster, 1962). Exaggerates discontinuity of New Testament with Jewish and later Christian worship; otherwise good.
Hahn, Ferdinand, *The Worship of the Early Church* (p; Philadelphia: Fortress, 1973). Emphasizes delineation of successive historical stages; some readers may find this overdone.

On the Jewish foundations of Christian worship:
Bouyer, L., "Jewish and Christian Liturgies," *Cross Currents* 13 (1963), pp. 335–348.
———. *Eucharist* (Notre Dame: UNDP, 1968). Extensive survey of Christian adaptation and transformation of *berakoth,* stimulating and controversial.
Werner, Eric, *The Sacred Bridge* (New York: Columbia UP, 1959). Emphasizes liturgical music.
Oesterley, W. O. E., and G. Box, *The Religion and Worship of the Synagogue* (rev. ed.; London: Pitman, 1911); and Oesterley, W. O. E., *The Jewish Background of the Christian Liturgy* (Oxford: Clarendon, 1925), are valuable older works.

Chapter 5: *Early Christian Theologies and the New Testament*

Our discussion of the different theological tendencies is dependent upon:
Robinson, James M., and Helmut Koester, *Trajectories Through Early Christianity* (Philadelphia: Fortress, 1971).
See again O. Cullmann, "Dissensions Within the Early Church."

On the formation of the Gospels and other books of the New Testament, the form-critical method is explained in:
Bultmann, Rudolf, and Karl Kundsin, *Form Criticism* (p; New York: Harper, 1962); and
Taylor, Vincent, *The Formation of the Gospel Tradition* (2nd ed.; London: Macmillan, 1935).

Redaction criticism is exemplified by:
Farrer, Austin, *A Study in St. Mark* (Westminster, England: Dacre, 1951); this book has been ignored because it was two decades in advance of scholarly fashion.

A survey of New Testament theology:
Richardson, Alan, *An Introduction to the Theology of the New Testament* (New York: Harper, 1958).

Collections of Gnostic writings:
Grant, R. M., ed., *Gnosticism* (New York: Harper, 1961).
Foerster, W., ed., *Gnosis* (2 vols.; Oxford: OUP–Clarendon, 1972–74).
Hennecke, E., and W. Schneemelcher, eds., *New Testament Apocrypha* (2 vols.; Philadelphia: Westminster, 1963–65). Largely, but not entirely, Gnostic material.

Studies of Gnosticism:
Jonas, Hans, *The Gnostic Religion* (p; 2nd ed.; Boston: Beacon, 1963).

Doresse, Jean, *The Secret Books of the Egyptian Gnostics* (New York: Viking, 1960).
Grant, R. M., *Gnosticism and Early Christianity* (New York: Columbia UP, 1959).
Wilson, R. McL., *Gnosis and the New Testament* (Philadelphia: Fortress, 1968).

See again:
Pagels, E., *The Gnostic Paul.*

On "history of salvation":
Cullmann, O., *Christ and Time* (rev. ed.; Philadelphia: Westminster, 1964).
Fuller, Reginald H., "Some Further Reflections on Heilsgeschichte," *Union Seminary Quarterly Review,* Vol. XXII (1966–67), pp. 93–101.

On typology:
Daniélou, J., *From Shadows to Reality* (Westminster, Maryland: Newman, 1960).
_____.*The Bible and the Liturgy* (Liturgical Studies, III; Notre Dame, UNDP, 1956).
Daube, David, *The Exodus Pattern in the Bible* (London: Faber & Faber, 1963).
Sahlin, Harald, "The New Exodus of Salvation According to St. Paul," in A. Fridrichsen & others, *The Root of The Vine,* pp. 81–95.

On "cosmic liturgy":
For the cosmos/history contrast, see:
Eliade, Mircea, *The Myth of the Eternal Return* (p; Princeton: PUP, 1954). In some editions, the book is entitled *Cosmos and History.*
Peterson, Erik, *The Angels and the Liturgy* (London: Darton, Longman & Todd, 1964).
Daniélou, J., *The Angels and Their Mission* (Westminster, Maryland: Newman, 1957).

On Christian apocalyptic:
Daniélou, J., *The Theology of Jewish Christianity* (The Development of Christian Doctrine Before the Council of Nicea, Vol. 1; Chicago: Regnery, 1964). A work of capital importance.
_____. "A New Vision of Christian Origins: Judaeo-Christianity," *Cross Currents,* Vol. XVIII (1968), pp. 163–173.
_____. *Primitive Christian Symbols* (Baltimore: Helicon, 1964).
Farrer, Austin, *A Rebirth of Images; The Making of St. John's Apocalypse* (Westminster, England: Dacre, 1949).
Simon, Ulrich, *Heaven in the Christian Tradition* (New York: Harper, 1958).
See again the books of D. Daube and W. D. Davies on the Jewish Background of the New Testament.

On ethics and spirituality:
Kirk, K. E., *The Vision of God* (New York: Longmans, Green, 1931).
Bouyer, L., *The Spirituality of the New Testament and the Fathers* (History of Christian Spirituality, Vol. I; New York: Desclee Co., 1962).

PART II: THE DEVELOPMENT OF CHRISTIAN HELLENISM

Duchesne, Louis, *Early History of The Christian Church* (3 vols.; New York: Longmans, Green, 1909–1924). Highly valuable for the first five centuries; unfortunately, the volume on the 6th century was not translated.
Daniélou, J., and H. Marrou, *The First Six Hundred Years* (The Christian Centuries, Vol. I; New York: McGraw-Hill, 1964). A good recent one-volume history.
On doctrine:
Pelikan, Jaroslav, *The Emergence of the Catholic Tradition 100–600* (The Christian

Tradition, Vol. I; Chicago: UCP, 1971). The first volume of an important new history of Christian doctrine; good but difficult.

Wiles, Maurice, *The Making of Christian Doctrine* (Cambridge: CUP, 1967). Simpler presentation than the foregoing.

Barr, Robert, *Main Currents in Early Christian Thought* (Glen Rock, N.J.: Paulist Press, 1966). Simplified as far as the subject matter permits, for use in Roman Catholic church classes.

On spirituality:
Bouyer, *The Spirituality of the New Testament and the Fathers.*

Christian writers of this period are available in a number of collections and series, the best of which is probably Ancient Christian Writers, which has had several publishers. The translations, introductions, and notes are generally excellent; unfortunately, the price per volume has become prohibitive.

Chapter 6: The Church of the Martyrs

Musurillo, Herbert, ed., *The Fathers of the Primitive Church* (p; New York: New American Library, 1966). A good short anthology.

Stevenson, J., ed., *A New Eusebius* (London: SPCK, 1960). A longer anthology.

Bettenson, Henry, ed., *Early Christian Fathers* (p; New York: Oxford UP, 1969). Another anthology.

On Christian Hellenism:
Cochrane, Charles Norris, *Christianity and Classical Culture* (p; New York: Oxford UP, 1957).

Jaeger, Werner, *Early Christianity and Greek Paideia* (Cambridge, Mass.: Harvard UP-Belknap, 1961).

Rahner, Hugo, *Greek Myth and Christian Mystery* (London: Burns & Oates, 1963).

Armstrong, A. H., and R. A. Markus, *Christian Faith and Greek Philosophy* (New York: Sheed & Ward, 1960).

Daniélou, J., *Gospel Message and Hellenistic Culture* (A History of Early Christian Doctrine Before the Council of Nicea, Vol. 2; Philadelphia: Westminster, 1973). Very important; a third volume, on Latin Christianity, is to appear soon.

Evans, Robert F., *One and Holy; The Church in Latin Patristic Thought* (London: SPCK, 1972), Chapters 1 & 2.

On the four models of salvation, our discussion follows:
Turner, H. E. W., *The Patristic Doctrine of Redemption* (London: Mowbray, 1952).

On the "Christ the Victor" model in particular:
Aulén, Gustaf, *Christus Victor* (London: SPCK, 1953).
Leivestad, Ragnar, *Christ the Conquerer* (New York: Macmillan, 1954).

On persecution and martyrdom:
Frend, W. H. C., *Martyrdom and Persecution in the Early Church* (p; Garden City, N.Y.: Doubleday, 1967).

Grant, R. M., *The Sword and the Cross* (New York: Macmillan, 1955).

Riddle, Donald, *The Martyrs* (Chicago: UCP, 1931).

On Gnosticism:
Bauer, Walter, *Orthodoxy and Heresy in Earliest Christianity* (Philadelphia: Fortress, 1971).

Turner, H. E. W., *The Pattern of Truth* (London: Mowbray, 1954). Has some reservations about Bauer's views.

On church order and ministry: a very controversial topic, with many conflicting views:
Kirk, K. E., ed., *The Apostolic Ministry* (London: Hodder & Stoughton, 1946).
Davies, W. D., *Christian Origins and Judaism* (Philadelphia: Westminster, 1962), Chapters 9 and 10.
von Campenhausen, Hans, *Ecclesiastical Authority and Spiritual Power in the Church of the First Three Centuries* (Stanford, Calif.: SUP, 1969).

On the "Rule of Faith" and creeds:
Kelly, J. N. D., *Early Christian Creeds* (2nd ed.; London: Longmans, 1960).

On the Apostolic Fathers:
A number of translations are available; see also
Barnard, L. W., *Justin Martyr, His Life and Thought* (Cambridge, England: CUP, 1967).
_____. *Studies in the Apostolic Fathers and Their Background* (Oxford: Blackwell, 1966).
_____. *Athenagoras: A Study in Second Century Christian Apologetic* (Theologie historique, 18; Paris: Beauchesne, n.d.).

On other individual writers:
Wingren, Gustaf, *Man and the Incarnation* (Philadelphia: Muhlenberg, 1959). (On Irenaeus.)
Lawson, John. *The Biblical Theology of St. Irenaeus* (London: Epworth, 1948).
Evans, Ernest, ed. & trans., *Tertullian's Treatise Against Praxeas* (London: SPCK, 1948). Our sources for the formulation of the "3 premises" of orthodox theology; in general, Evans's editions of Tertullian's works are to be recommended.

A number of Origen's works are available; see especially:
Origen's Treatise on Prayer (trans. E. G. Jay; London: SPCK, 1954);
On First Principles (p; trans. G. W. Butterworth; New York: Harper & Row, 1966); and
Contra Celsum (trans. H. Chadwick; Cambridge, England: CUP, 1953).
Daniélou, J., *Origen* (New York: Sheed & Ward, 1955). The best introduction.

See also:
Pelikan, J., *The Finality of Jesus Christ in an Age of Universal History* (Ecumenical Studies in History, No. 3; Richmond: John Knox, 1966). A good short study of several early theologians.

On Christian art and architecture:
Gough, Michael, *The Early Christians* (Ancient Peoples & Places, 19; London: Thames & Hudson, 1961).
Gordon, J. G., *The Origin and Development of Early Christian Architecture* (London: SCM, 1952).
Du Bourguet, Pierre, *Early Christian Art* (New York: Reynal, 1971).
Hickley, Dennis, "The Ambo in Early Liturgical Planning," *The Heythrop Journal,* Vol. VII (1966), pp. 407–427.
_____. "Time and Architecture in the Early Church," *Sobornost',* Ser. 5 (1965–1970), pp. 406–422.
Bouyer, L., *Liturgy and Architecture* (Notre Dame: UNDP, 1967).
Lowrie, Walter, *Art in the Early Church* (p; 2nd ed.; New York: Harper, 1965).

Chapter 7: The Church and the Christian Empire

Stevenson, J., ed., *Creeds, Councils and Controversies* (London: SPCK, 1966). An anthology for the period 337–461.

Bettenson, Henry, ed., *Later Christian Fathers* (p; New York: Oxford UP, 1970). Another anthology for approximately the same period.

On the Trinity:

Prestige, G. L., *God in Patristic Thought* (London: SPCK, 1952). A standard work.

Pollard, T. E., *Johannine Christology and the Early Church* (SNTS Monograph Series, 13; Cambridge, England: CUP, 1970).

Barr, R., *Main Currents,* may be consulted again for a short, simple treatment.

On the political aspects:

Williams, George Huntston, "Christology and Church-State Relations in the Fourth Century," *Church History,* September 1951, pp. 3–33, and December 1951, pp. 3–26.

Beskow, Per, *Rex Gloriae: The Kingship of Christ in the Early Church* (Stockholm: Almquist & Wicksell, 1962).

Azkoul, Michael. "Sacerdotium et Imperium: The Constantinian Renovatio According to the Greek Fathers," *Theological Studies,* Vol. 32 (1971), pp. 431–64. Valuable, but rather difficult.

Jones, A. H. M., *Were Ancient Heresies Disguised Social Movements?* (Facet Books Historical Series, 1; Philadelphia: Fortress, 1966). A good short survey.

On monasticism:

Waddell, Helen, *The Desert Fathers* (p; Ann Arbor: U of Michigan P., 1957). An anthology.

Chitty, Derwas, *The Desert a City* (Oxford: Blackwell, 1966).

Anson, Peter F., *The Call of the Desert* (London: SPCK, 1964), Chapters 1–5.

Vööbus, Arthur, "The Origins of Monasticism in Mesopotamia," *Church History,* December, 1951, pp. 27–37. Emphasizes non-Christian influence.

———. *History of Asceticism in the Syrian Orient* (Corpus Scriptorum Christianorum Orientalium, Vols. 184 and 197; Louvain, Belgium: CSCO, 1958).

On spirituality and dogma:

Daniélou, J., and Herbert Musurillo, eds., *From Glory to Glory* (New York: Scribner's, 1961). An excellent anthology from Gregory of Nyssa.

Lossky, Vladimir, *The Mystical Theology of the Eastern Church* (London: James Clarke, 1957). A generally good treatment, although the statements on the work of the Son and the Spirit include a few personal quirks of the author's.

———. *The Vision of God* (Library of Orthodox Theology, No. 2; London: Faith Press, 1963).

On pentarchy and papacy:

Dvorník, Francis, *Byzantium and the Roman Primacy* (New York: Fordham UP, 1966).

Meyendorff, John, *Orthodoxy and Catholicity* (New York: Sheeed & Ward, 1966).

On worship:

Srawley, J. H., *The Early History of the Liturgy* (2nd ed.; Cambridge, England: CUP, 1957).

Jungmann, J. A., *The Early Liturgy to the Time of Gregory the Great* (Liturgical Studies, VI; Notre Dame: UNDP, 1959).

Schmemann, Alexander, *Introduction to Liturgical Theology* (Library of Orthodox Theology, No. 4; London: Faith Press, 1966).

On social aspects:
Mersch, Emile, *The Whole Christ* (London: Dennis Dobson, 1949).
Constantelos, Demetrios, *Byzantine Philanthropy and Social Welfare* (New Brunswick: Rutgers UP, 1968). A valuable corrective to the prevailing negative view.
McKenna, Sr. Mary Lawrence. *Women of the Church* (New York: Kenedy, 1967).
Wallace Hadrill, D. S., *The Greek Patristic View of Nature* (Manchester, England: MUP, 1968). Good introduction to a neglected topic.

On the controversies about the Incarnation:
Grillmeyer, Aloys, *Christ in Christian Tradition* (New York: Sheed & Ward, 1965). A thorough survey down to 451.
Carmody, J. M., & T. E. Clark, *Word and Redeemer* (Glen Rock, N.J.: Paulist Press, 1966). A simplified, popularized version of the foregoing, useful for the period before 451 and weak on later developments.
Meyendorff, J., *Christ in Eastern Christian Thought* (Washington: Corpus, 1969). Fills the gap after 451.
Frend, W. H. C., *The Rise of the Monophysite Movement* (Cambridge, England: CUP, 1972).
Every, George, *The Byzantine Patriarchate 451-1204* (2nd ed.; London: SPCK, 1962). The best general survey, also useful for doctrinal issues.

On the later Origenists:
Evans, David B., *Leontius of Byzantium* (Washington: Dumbarton Oaks Center, 1970). A much-needed, pioneering work.
Chitty, D., *The Desert a City,* is valuable on later Origenism in its monastic setting; and see again:
Every, G., *The Byzantine Patriarchate.*

On Maximus:
Sherwood, Polycarp, "Survey of Recent Work on St. Maximus the Confessor," *Traditio,* Vol. XX (1964), pp. 428-37.
_____. Ed. & trans., *The Ascetic Life and Four Centuries on Charity* (Ancient Christian Writers, Vol. 21; Westminster, Maryland: Newman, 1955). Two works of Maximus with excellent, extensive, but difficult introduction.
Thunberg, Lars, *Microcosm and Mediator* (Lund: Gleerup, 1965). An extensive study in depth.

See also:
Murray Robert, *Symbols of Church and Kingdom* (London: Cambridge UP, 1975). On the Syriac Christian tradition; compare R. Evans, *One and Holy,* on the Latin tradition.

On Iconoclasm:
Florovsky, Georges, "The Iconoclastic Controversy," in *Christianity and Culture* (collected works of Georges Florovsky, Vol. 2; Belmont, Mass.: Nordland, 1974), pp. 101-119.
Barnard, L. W., *The Graeco-Roman and Oriental Backgrounds of the Iconoclastic Controversy* (Byzantina Neerlandica 5; Leiden: Brill, 1974).
Martin, Edward James, *A History of the Iconoclastic Controversy* (Church Historical Society Publications, n.s. Vol. 2; London: SPCK, 1930).
Ouspensky, Leonide, & Vladimir Lossky, *The Meaning of Icons* (Boston: Boston Book & Art Shop, 1956).
Rice, David Talbot, *Byzantine Art* (rev. ed.; Baltimore: Penguin, 1962).

PART III: THE MEDIEVAL STRUGGLE FOR A CHRISTIAN SOCIETY

Baldwin, Marshall W., ed., *Christianity Through the Thirteenth Century* (p; New York: Harper & Row, 1970). An anthology.

Knowles, David, and D. Obolensky, *The Middle Ages* (The Christian Centuries, Vol. 2; New York: McGraw-Hill, 1968). A good, recent, one-volume history. See also:

Southern, R. W., *Western Society and the Church in the Middle Ages* (p; Pelican History of the Church, Vol. 2; Baltimore: Penguin, 1970). Quite worth reading, but too restricted in scope for the Pelican series. See then:

Deanesly, Margaret, *A History of the Medieval Church 590–1500* (p; London: Methuen, 1969). First published in 1925; it needs some further revision but is still useful.

Russell, Jeffrey Burton, *A History of Medieval Christianity; Prophecy and Order* (p; New York: Crowell, 1968). A more recent treatment.

Southern, Deanesly, and Russell all concentrate one-sidedly on the western church; to balance the picture, the student may refer to:

Hussey, Joan, *Church and Learning in the Byzantine Empire 867–1185* (Oxford: OUP, 1937); and:

Geanakoplos, Deno, *Byzantine East and Latin West* (p; New York: Harper, 1966).

See again:

Every, G., *Byzantine Patriarchate*, together with his *Misunderstandings Between East and West* (Ecumenical Studies in History, No. 4; Richmond: John Knox, 1966).

For more detailed studies of problems in Western church history, see:

Ullmann, Walter, *The Growth of Papal Government in the Middle Ages* (London: Methuen, 1970);

Morrison, Karl F., *Tradition and Authority in the Western Church 300–1400* (Princeton: PUP, 1969).

On a more popular level with good color illustrations:

Barraclough, Geoffrey, *The Medieval Papacy* (p; n.p.: Harcourt, Brace & World, 1968); a rather unsympathetic view; and

Knowles, David, *Christian Monasticism* (New York: McGraw-Hill, 1969).

Until recently, no competent work on Eastern theology after the eighth century (one is tempted to say after the fifth century!) has been available. In addition to the books listed in Part II, see now:

Meyendorff, John, *Byzantine Theology* (New York: Fordham UP, 1974);

Pelikan, Jaroslav, *The Spirit of Eastern Christendom (600–1700)* (The Christian Tradition, Vol. 2; Chicago: UCP, 1974).

Chapter 8: The "Dark Ages"

On the various Eastern Christian cultures:

Atiya, Aziz, *History of Eastern Christianity* (Notre Dame: UNDP, 1968). Useful, but often sketchy and incomplete.

The Queen of Sheba and Her Only Son Menyelek (trans. E. A. Wallis Budge; Oxford: OUP, 1932). A translation, not entirely reliable, of the *Kebra Nagast*.

Gerster, Georg, *Churches in Rock* (New York: Phaidon, 1970). Fine book on the Ethiopian monolithic churches; excellent illustrations. ·

Örmanian, Malachia (Maghak'ia), *The Church of Armenia* (2nd ed.; London: Mowbray, 1955).

Der Nersessian, Sirarpie, *The Armenians* (Ancient Peoples and Places, 68; New York: Praeger, 1970).
Lang, David M., *The Georgians* (Ancient Peoples and Places, 51; New York: Praeger, 1966).
Wessel, Klaus, *Coptic Art* (New York: McGraw-Hill, 1965).

On the variety of forms of worship:
Botte, Bernard, in A. G. Martimort, ed., *The Church at Prayer—Introduction to the Liturgy* (New York: Desclee, n.d.). See also:
Drower, Ethel Stefana, *Water Into Wine* (London: John Murray, 1956). Details of some Eastern Christian forms of religious culture.

On monasticism:
Decarreaux, J., *Monks and Civilization* (London: G. Allen & Unwin, 1964).
Anson, P. F., *The Call of the Desert*.

On the Celtic Churches:
Chadwick, Nora K. and others, *Studies in the Early British Church* (Cambridge, England: CUP, 1958).
Chadwick, Nora K., *The Age of Saints in the Early Celtic Church* (London: Oxford UP, 1961).
McNeill, John T., *The Celtic Churches* (Chicago: UCP, 1974).
Thomas, Charles, *Britain and Ireland in Early Christian Times* (p; New York: McGraw-Hill, 1971). An illustrated introduction to Celtic Christian Art.

On Augustine:
Burnaby, John, *Amor Dei* (London: Hodder & Stoughton, 1938).
Brown, Peter, *Augustine of Hippo* (p; Berkeley, U. of California P, 1969). Excellent biography with good bibliography.

On the Donatists:
Frend, W. H. C., *The Donatist Church* (Oxford: Clarendon, 1952).

On the Pelagians:
Evans, Robert, *One and Holy*. Chapters 3–5. Evans is an authority on Pelagianism, but his specialized works on the topic are for advanced students only.

On Augustinian contemplation:
Butler, Cuthbert, *Western Mysticism* (p; New York: Harper & Row, 1966).

Chapter 9: Early Medieval Europe

Sulpicius Severus and others, *The Western Fathers* (p; New York: Harper, 1965). An anthology of sources.
Hilgarth, J. N., ed., *The Conversion of Western Europe 350-750* (Englewood Cliffs, N. J.: Prentice-Hall, 1969). Another anthology of sources.

On the Benedictines:
In addition to the books on monasticism already listed, see:
Butler, Cuthbert, *Benedictine Monachism* (2nd ed.; London: Longmans, Green, 1924).

On the parish churches:
Addleshaw, G. W. O., *The Beginnings of the Parochial System* (p; St. Anthony's Hall Publications 3; London: St. Anthony's Press, 1953).

_____ . *The Development of the Parochial System* (p; SAHP 61; London: St. Anthony's Press, 1954).

_____ . *The Early Parochial System and the Divine Office* (p; Prayer Book Revision Pamphlets 15; London: Mowbray, 1957). All three are brief and informative.

On the recovery of the West:

Dawson, Christopher, *The Making of Europe* (New York: Macmillan, 1932).

Havighurst, A., ed., *The Pirenne Thesis* (Boston: Heath, 1958), and:

Sullivan, R. E., ed., *The Coronation of Charlemagne* (Boston: Heath, 1959) are both collections of articles representing various historical interpretations.

On the filioque controversy:

Haugh, Richard, *Photius and the Carolingians* (Belmont, Mass: Nordland, 1975).

On the missions to the Slavs:

Jakobson, Roman, "The Beginning of National Self-Determination in Europe," *The Review of Politics,* Vol. VII (1945), pp. 24–42.

Dvorník, Francis, *Byzantine Missions Among the Slavs* (New Brunswick: Rutgers UP, 1970).

Spinka, Matthew, *A History of Christianity in the Balkans* (Studies in Church History, Vol. 1; Chicago: American Society of Church History, 1933).

On the Stave churches:

Strzygowski, Josef, *Early Church Art in Northern Europe* (London: Batsford, 1928). Much unusual material, stimulating observations, and dubious hypotheses.

Lindholm, Dan, *Stave Churches in Norway* (London: R. Steiner, 1969). Splendid illustrations, eccentric text.

Anker, Peter, & A. Andersson, *The Art of Scandinavia* (2 vols.; London: Paul Hamlyn, 1970). Contains the best technical survey; splendid illustrations.

Chapter 10: The Later Middle Ages

On the role of the papacy:

In addition to the works already mentioned, the student may consult two collections of articles representing conflicting views:

Williams, S., ed., *The Gregorian Epoch* (p; Boston: Heath, 1964); and

Powell, J. M., ed., *Innocent III* (p; Boston: Heath, 1963).

On East-West relations:

Runciman, Steven, *The Eastern Schism* (Oxford: Clarendon, 1955); and

Every's *Byzantine Patriarchate* and *Misunderstandings.*

On the clericalization of worship:

Salmon, Pierre, *The Breviary Through the Centuries* (Collegeville, Minn.: Liturgical Press, 1962).

On the legend of the Cross:

Quinn, Esther, *The Quest of Seth for the Oil of Life* (Chicago: UCP, 1962).

On Western medieval thought:

Lovejoy, Arthur O., *The Great Chain of Being* (Cambridge, Mass.: Harvard UP, 1936). A classic on the history of ideas.

Knowles, David, *The Evolution of Medieval Thought* (p; New York: Random House, n.d.). Good survey, but hard to read in this edition because of small print.

Pieper, Josef, *Scholasticism* (London: Faber & Faber, 1961). An easy introduction.

Gilson, Etienne, *History of Christian Philosophy in the Middle Ages* (New York: Random House, 1955). A standard work, fairly difficult.

_____ . *The Spirit of Medieval Philosophy* (London: Sheed & Ward, 1936). Good and fairly easy.

Smalley, Beryl, *The Study of the Bible in the Middle Ages* (2nd ed.; New York: Philosophical Library, 1952).

On Anselm:

St. Anselm, *Basic Writings* (La Salle, IU.: Various printings). A convenient collection of texts.

Hopkins, Jasper, *A Companion to the Study of Saint Anselm* (Minneapolis: U. of Minnesota P., 1971). Consult Hopkins for other references, see especially:

Williams, George Huntston, *Anselm: Communion and Atonement* (St. Louis: Concordia, 1960).

On religious dissent and heresy:

Russell, J. B., *Religious Dissent in the Middle Ages* (New York: Wiley, 1971);

Wakefield, W. L., and A. P. Evans, *Heresies of the High Middle Ages* (New York: Columbia UP, 1969); both are anthologies of source material.

Runciman, S., *The Medieval Manichee* (Cambridge, England: CUP, 1955).

Russell, J. B., *Dissent and Reform in the Early Middle Ages* (2 vols.; Manchester, England: UMP, 1967).

Reeves, Marjorie, *The Influence of Prophecy in the Later Middle Ages* (Oxford: Clarendon, 1969).

Garsoian, Nina G., *The Paulician Heresy* (The Hague: Mouton, 1967), and

_____ . "Byzantine Heresy: A Reinterpretation," *Dumbarton Oaks Papers* 25 (1971), pp. 87–113; set forth a new view of heresy in Byzantium.

Fine, John V. A., Jr., *The Bosnian Church: A New Interpretation* (New York: Columbia UP, 1975).

On Aquinas:

The complete works, with English translations, are being published in London by Blackfriars. A convenient selection with good introduction is:

Pegis, Anton, ed., *Basic Writings of St. Thomas Aquinas* (2 vols.; New York: Random House, 1945).

On the theology of Aquinas:

Pieper, Josef, *The Silence of St. Thomas* (London: Faber & Faber, 1957).

Scharlemann, Robert P., *Thomas Aquinas and John Gerhard* (New Haven: Yale UP, 1964).

Persson, Per Erik, *Sacra Doctrina* (Oxford: Blackwell, 1970).

On Duns Scotus:

de Saint-Maurice, Beraud, *John Duns Scotus, A Teacher for Our Times* (St. Bonaventure, N.Y.: Franciscan Institute, 1955).

On nominalism:

Oberman, Heiko, *The Harvest of Medieval Theology* (Cambridge, Mass.: Harvard UP, 1963).

On spirituality:

Theologia Germania, ed. T. Kepler (Cleveland: World, 1952). A late medieval work that influenced Luther.

Knowles, D., *The English Mystical Tradition* (p; London: Burns & Oates, 1964). An excellent study.

On art:

Mâle, Emile, *Religious Art from the Twelfth to the Eighteenth Century* (New York: Pantheon, 1949).

Panofsky, Erwin, *Gothic Architecture and Scholasticism* (p; New York: Meridian, 1957).

Huizinga, Johan, *The Waning of the Middle Ages* (p; Garden City, N.Y.: Doubleday, 1954). A classic account of late medieval civilization.

On Eastern spirituality, see the works of Lossky and Meyendorff listed above.

PART IV: RENAISSANCE AND REFORMATION

Chapter 11: The Age of Reformation

Hillerbrand, Hans J., ed., *The Protestant Reformation* (p; New York: Harper & Row, 1968). An anthology of source material.

Ziegler, D. J., ed., *Great Debates of the Reformation* (New York: Random House, 1968). Transcripts of debates.

Chadwick, Owen, *The Reformation* (p; The Pelican History of the Church, 3; Baltimore: Penguin, 1964). Once again, this series provides a useful one-volume history of moderate length.

On the medieval background of the Reformation:

Oberman, H. A., ed., *Forerunners of the Reformation* (New York: Holt, Rinehart & Winston, 1966). An anthology of source material, with extensive introductions.

Spinka, Matthew, *John Hus and the Czech Reform* (Chicago: UCP, 1941).

Heath, Peter, *The English Parish Clergy On the Eve of the Reformation* (London: Routledge & Kegan Paul, 1969).

Ozment, Steven, ed., *The Reformation in Medieval Perspective* (p; Chicago: Quadrangle, 1971). A collection of articles, good but often difficult.

On the Renaissance and humanism:

Kristeller, Paul Oskar, *Renaissance Thought* (p; New York: Harper, 1961).

Breen, Quirinus, *Christianity and Humanism* (Grand Rapids, Mich.: Eerdmans, 1968).

On "occult wisdom":

Walker, Daniel P., *Spiritual and Demonic Magic* (London: U of L—Warburg Institute, 1958).

———. *The Ancient Theology* (Ithaca: Cornell UP, 1972).

On Luther:

A very extensive collection of Luther's works, in English translation, edited by J. Pelikan and H. T. Lehmann, has been published (Philadelphia: Fortress, and St. Louis: Concordia, 1958–1967) in 56 volumes.

Bainton, Roland, *Here I Stand* (New York: Abingdon-Cokesbury, 1950). The standard biography.

Our presentation of Luther's teachings owes much to:
Forde, Gerhard, *Where God Meets Man* (Minneapolis: Augsburg, 1972), an excellent popular exposition by a professional theologian.

On the Reformed movement:
Rilliet, Jean, *Zwingli* (Philadelphia: Westminster, 1964).
McNeill, John T., *The History and Character of Calvinism* (p; New York: Oxford UP, 1967).
Niesel, Wilhelm, *The Theology of Calvin* (Philadelphia: Westminster, 1956).
Breen, Q., John Calvin, *A Study in French Humanism* (Grand Rapids, Mich.: Eerdmans, 1931).
McDonnell, Kilian, *John Calvin, the Church and the Eucharist* (Princeton: PUP, 1967). A sympathetic study by a Roman Catholic scholar.

On different Reformation views of church and society:
Mueller, William A., *Church and State in Luther and Calvin* (p; Garden City, N.Y.: Doubleday, 1965).
Tonkin, John, *The Church and the Secular Order in Reformation Thought* (New York: Columbia UP, 1971).

On the Reformation in England:
Hughes, Philip Edgcumbe, *Theology of the English Reformers* (London: Hodder & Stoughton, 1965).
O'Day, Rosemary, and Felicity Neal, eds., *Continuity & Change: Personnel and Administration of the Church in England 1500–1642* (n.p.: Leicester UP, 1976).

On the Radical Reformation:
Williams, George Huntston, *The Radical Reformation* (Philadelphia: Westminster, 1962). The standard work.
Ozment, Steven, *Mysticism and Dissent* (New Haven: Yale UP, 1973).

On Christian disunity and unity in the Reformation:
Dawson, Christopher, *The Dividing of Christendom* (New York: Sheed & Ward, 1965).
McNeill, John T., *Unitive Protestantism* (Richmond: John Knox, 1964).

On Christianity and radical politics:
Zuck, Lowell H., ed., *Christianity and Revolution* (Philadelphia: Temple UP, 1975).
Walzer, Michael, *The Revolution of the Saints* (Cambridge, Mass.: Harvard UP, 1965).

On Catholic mysticism:
Knowles, David M., *The Nature of Mysticism* (Twentieth-Century Encyclopedia of Catholicism, Vol. 38; New York: Hawthorne, 1966).

On baroque dogmatics:
Schmid, Heinrich, *The Doctrinal Theology of the Evangelical Lutheran Church* (Philadelphia: Lutheran Publication Society, 1889).
Heppe, Heinrich, *Reformed Dogmatics* (London: Allen & Unwin, 1950). An anthology of sources.
Scharlemann, R., *Thomas Aquinas and John Gerhardt.*
Armstrong, Brian G., *Calvinism and the Amyraut Heresy* (Madison: U of Wisconsin P, 1969).

On Boehme:
Martensen, Hans L., *Jacob Boehme (1575–1625)* (rev. ed.; New York: Harper, 1949).
Stoudt, John Joseph, *Sunrise to Eternity* (Philadelphia: U. of Pennsylvania P, 1957).

On "Renaissance Religion" in the age of baroque dogmatics:
Yates, Francis, *The Rosicrucian Enlightenment* (London: Routledge & Kegan Paul, 1972).
Montgomery, John Warwick, *Cross and Crucible* (2 vols.; The Hague: Nijhoff, 1973).

On the reformation and culture:
Holl, Karl, *The Cultural Significance of the Reformation* (p; Cleveland: World, 1959).
Dillenberger, John, *Protestant Thought and Natural Science* (Garden City: Doubleday, 1960).

On Catholic missions:
Rogers, Francis M., *The Quest for Eastern Christians* (Minneapolis: U of Minnesota P, 1962).
Treadgold, Donald W., *The West in Russia and China* (2 vols.; Cambridge, England: CUP, 1973), Vol. 2.
Earhart, H. Byron, *Japanese Religion: Unity and Diversity, 2nd Ed.,* (Belmont and Encino, Calif.: Dickenson, 1974), Chapter 12.

On Eastern Christians:
Runciman, Steven, *The Fall of Constantinople, 1453* (Cambridge, England: CUP, 1965).
_____ . *The Great Church in Captivity* (Cambridge, England: CUP, 1968).
Halecki, Oskar, *From Florence to Brest (1439–1596)* (reprint; n.p.: Archon, 1968). A thorough treatment of the Unia from a favorable perspective; for the Orthodox view, see:
Ware, T., *The Orthodox Church.*

PART V: THE MODERN WORLD

Cragg, Gerald R., *The Church and the Age of Reason 1648-1784* (The Pelican History of the Church, Vol. 4; Baltimore, Penguin, 1970); and Vidler, A. R., *The Church in an Age of Revolution, 1789 to the Present Day* (The Pelican History of the Church, Vol. 5; Baltimore: Penguin, 1971). The Pelican History volumes are best on Britain and France, somewhat more limited in other areas.

Chapter 12: The Age of Reason and Piety

At least the major works of most of the writers mentioned in this chapter are available, in translation if the original language is not English.

On witch-hunts:
Robbins, Rossell Hope, *The Encyclopedia of Witchcraft and Demonology* (New York: Crown, 1960).
Cohn, Norman, *Europe's Inner Demons* (New York: Basic Books, 1975).
Kieckhefer, Richard, *European Witch Trials* (Berkeley: U of California P, 1976).

On the Enlightenment:
Cassirer, Ernst, *The Philosophy of the Enlightenment* (Princeton: PUP, 1951).
Manuel, Frank H., *The Eighteenth Century Confronts the Gods* (Cambridge, Mass.: Harvard UP, 1959).

Cragg, G. R., *Reason and Authority in the Eighteenth Century* (Cambridge, England: CUP, 1964).

O'Keefe, Cyril B., *Contemporary Reactions to the Enlightenment* (Geneva: Slatkine, 1974).

Walker, D. P., *The Decline of Hell* (Chicago, UCP, 1964).

Walker, A. Keith, *William Law: His Life and Thought* (London: SPCK, 1973).

Knox, Ronald, *Enthusiasm* (New York: Oxford, 1950). Valuable mainly for the treatment of Jansenism and Quietism.

Gleason, R., ed., *A Pascal Anthology: The Essential Pascal* (p; New York: New American Library, 1966).

Wells, Albert, *Pascal's Recovery of Man's Wholeness* (Richmond: John Knox, 1965).

Allison, Henry E., *Lessing and the Enlightenment* (Ann Arbor: U of Michigan P, 1966).

On Pietism and related movements:

Spener, P. J., *Pia Desideria* (p; ed. T. G. Tappert; Philadelphia: Fortress, 1964). The "Pietist manifesto."

Stoeffler, F. Ernest, *The Rise of Evangelical Pietism* (Studies in the History of Religions—Supplements to Numen, 9; Leiden: Brill, 1965).

Bett, Henry, *The Spirit of Methodism* (London: Epworth, 1937).

Green, John Brazier, *John Wesley and William Law* (London: Epworth, 1945).

Kallstad, Thorvald, *John Wesley and the Bible* (Acta Universitatis Upsaliensis—Psychologia Religionum, No. 1; Uppsala, 1974).

On the Eastern Christians:

Cracraft, James, *The Church Reform of Peter the Great* (Stanford, Calif.: SUP, 1971).

Ware, Timothy, *Eustratios Argenti* (Oxford: Clarendon, 1964).

Haddad, Robert M., *Syrian Christians in a Muslim Society* (Princeton: PUP, 1970).

Joseph, John, *The Nestorians and Their Muslim Neighbors* (Princeton Oriental Studies, Vol. 20: Princeton: PUP, 1961).

Wakin, Edward, *A Lonely Minority: The Modern Story of Egypt's Copts* (New York: Morrow, 1963).

Arberry, A. J., ed., *Religion in the Middle East* (2 vols.; Cambridge: CUP, 1969).

Frazee, Charles A., *The Orthodox Church and Independent Greece, 1821–1852* (Cambridge: CUP, 1969).

Runciman, Steven, *The Orthodox Churches and the Secular State* (Auckland: AUP, 1971).

Kadloubovsky, E., and G. Palmer, eds., *Writings from the Philokalia on the Prayer of the Heart* (London: Faber & Faber, 1951).

———. *Early Fathers from the Philokalia* (London: Faber & Faber, 1954).

Chapter 13: *The Age of Romanticism and Industrialism*

On modern rejection of Christianity:

Marx, Karl, and F. Engels, *On Religion* (p; New York: Schocken, 1964).

Russell, Bertrand, *Why I Am Not a Christian & Other Essays* (p; New York: Simon & Schuster, 1962).

de Lubac, Henri, *The Drama of Atheist Humanism* (p; Cleveland: World-Meridian, 1963).

On Protestant Theology:

Tillich, Paul, *Perspectives on 19th and 20th Century Protestant Theology* (New York: Harper & Row, 1967). An excellent introduction, not hard to read.

Hordern, William, *A Layman's Guide to Protestant Theology* (p; rev. ed.; New York: Macmillan, 1968). Simple presentation.

Nicholls, William, *Systematic and Philosophical Theology* (p; Pelican Guide to Modern Theology, Vol. 1; Baltimore: Penguin, 1969). More advanced survey.

Frei, Hans, "Nieburhr's Theological Background," in P. Ramsey, ed., *Faith and Ethics* (p; New York: Harper & Row, 1957), pp. 9-64; shorter, but fairly difficult.

On Renewal movements:

Brilioth, Yngve, *The Anglican Revival* (London: Longmans, Green, 1924).

Loehe, Wilhelm, *Three Books About the Church* (p; ed. J. Schaaf; Philadelphia: Fortress, 1969).

Khomyakov, Alexei, "On the Western Confessions of Faith," in A. Schmemann, ed., *Ultimate Questions* (New York: Holt, Rinehard & Winston, 1965), pp. 29-69.

On Christian social movements:

Christensen, Torben, *Origen and History of Christian Socialism 1848-54* (Acta Theologica Danica, Vol. 3; Aarhus, Denmark: Universitetsforlaget, 1962).

Wearmouth, R. F., *Methodism and the Struggle of the Working Classes, 1850-1900* (Leicoster, England: Backus, 1954).

Vidler, Alec, *A Century of Social Catholicism* (London: SPCK, 1964).

On the Roman Catholics:

Ranchetti, Michele, *The Catholic Modernists* (London: Oxford UP, 1969).

Helmreich, Ernst, ed., *A Free Church in a Free State?* (Boston: Heath, 1964). Contrasting views of the role of the Catholic church in Western Europe in the half century before the First World War.

On the Armenian massacres:

Harutunian, Abraham H., *Neither to Laugh Nor to Weep* (Boston: Beacon, 1968).

Boyajian, Dickran, *Armenia: The Case for a Forgotten Genocide* (Westwood, N.J.: Educational Book Crafts, 1972).

On Soviet persecution:

Conquest, Robert, ed., *Religion in the USSR* (New York: Praeger, 1968).

Marshall, Richard H., ed., *Aspects of Religion in the Soviet Union 1917-1967* (Chicago: UCP, 1971).

Chapter 14: Christianity in the New World

Ahlstrom, Sydney, E., *A Religious History of the American People* (New Haven: Yale UP, 1972). A comprehensive survey with a very full bibliography, which may be consulted for any aspect of Christianity in the United States.

Walsh, H. H., *The Christian Church in Canada* (Toronto: Ryerson, 1956).

Mecham, J. Lloyd, *Church and State in Latin America* (rev. ed.; Chapel Hill: U of North Carolina P, 1966).

Chapter 15: Christianity After Christendom

On the ecumenical movement:

Rouse, Ruth, & Stephen Charles Neill, eds., *A History of the Ecumenical Movement 1517-1948* (Philadelphia: Westminster, 1967).

On the Second Vatican Council:
Rynne, Xavier (pseudonym), *Vatican Council II* (New York: Farrar, Strauss & Giroux, 1968).

On Christianity in Africa and Asia:
Mbiti, John, *New Testament Eschatology in an African Background* (London: Oxford UP, 1971).
Boyd, R. H. S., *India and the Latin Captivity of the Church* (Cambridge, England: CUP, 1974).
Lehmann, Arno, *Christian Art in Africa and Asia* (St. Louis: Concordia, 1969).

On the contemporary situation in the West:
Schneider, Louis, and S. M. Dornbusch, *Popular Religion; Inspirational Books in America* (Chicago: UCP, 1958).
Berger, Peter, *The Sacred Canopy* (Garden City, N.Y.: Doubleday, 1967).
Luckmann, Thomas, *The Invisible Religion* (New York: Macmillan, 1967).

On problems of Christian social movements:
Kelley, Dean M., *Why Conservative Churches Are Growing* (New York: Harper & Row, 1972). Stimulating and controversial; should be read in the light of the books of Berger and Luckmann listed above.
Ellul, Jacques, *Violence* (New York: Seabury, 1969).
Ramsey, Paul, *Who Speaks for the Church?* (p; Edinburgh: St. Andrew's Press, 1969).

On Christian social movements:
Kee, Alistair, ed., *A Reader in Political Theology* (p; Philadelphia: Westminster, 1975). A convenient anthology. The student may wish to compare a volume that is not theological or Christian in orientation, and exhibits a wider sensitivity to oppression in various contexts than any "liberation theology" to date:
Whitaker, Ben, ed., *The Fourth World: Victims of Group Oppression* (New York: Schocken, 1973).

On problems of renewal movements:
Rousseau, Olivier, "The Liturgical Movement," in A. G. Martimort, ed., *The Church at Prayer—Introduction to the Liturgy* (New York: Desclee Co., n.d.), pp. 51-54. Very brief survey with a good bibliography.
Koenker, Ernest, *The Liturgical Renaissance in the Roman Catholic Church* (Chicago: UCP, 1954). A good survey of developments before Vatican II.
Devine, George, *Liturgical Renewal: An Agonizing Reappraisal* (New York: Alba, 1973). A survey of problems of the reform after Vatican II.

On ecology:
Williams, George Huntston, *Wilderness and Paradise in Christian Thought* (New York: Harper, 1962).
Sittler, Joseph, *The Ecology of Faith* (Philadelphia: Muhlenberg, 1961).
_____ . *Essays on Nature and Grace* (Philadelphia: Fortress, 1972). Both Williams and Sittler were struggling for a more responsible Christian stance on ecology long before it became fashionable; see also:
Santimire, H. Paul, *Brother Earth* (New York: Nelson, 1970); and
Lutz, Paul E., and H. P. Santmire, *Ecological Renewal* (Philadelphia: Fortress, 1972).

On Marxist-Leninist persecution:

Bociurkiw, Bohdan, "Religion and Atheism in Soviet Society," in R. H. Marshall, Jr., ed., *Aspects of Religion in the Soviet Union 1917–1967* (Chicago: UCP, 1971).

Religion in Communist Lands. A journal published in England (Vol. 1, 1973).

Fletcher, William C., "Religion and Soviet Foreign Policy," in B. R. Bociurkiw and J. W. Strong, eds., *Religion and Atheism in the USSR and Eastern Europe* (Toronto: UTP, 1975), pp. 171–189. Although Fletcher focuses on the Soviet government's use of contacts between Soviet and Western churches, the reader who evaluates the integrity and competence of Western churches on the basis of Fletcher's information and analysis will not be misled.

On "Christianity after Christendom":

Polányi, Michael, *Personal Knowledge* (Chicago, UCP, 1958). In this and other works, the noted scientist and philosopher indicated the way toward a postcritical philosophy.

Berger, Peter, L., *A Rumor of Angels* (Garden City, N.Y.: Doubleday, 1969). Another postcritical perspective.

The following are all shorter books in a popular style, representing various contemporary Christian perspectives:

Horn, Henry E., *The Christian in Modern Style* (p; Philadelphia: Fortress, 1968).

Daniélou, J., *Prayer as a Political Problem* (p; London: Burns & Oates, 1967). May be hard to follow until the reader recalls the history of the Catholic church in France; then it becomes interesting to compare Horn's American perspective.

Schmemann, A., *Sacraments and Orthodoxy* (New York: Herder & Herder, 1965).

Wilkerson, David, and others, *The Cross and the Switchblade* (p; New York: Pyramid Publications, 1970). Pentecostal minister and urban juvenile gangs.

Schaeffer, Francis A., *God Who Is There* (Downers Grove, Ill.: Inter-Varsity, 1968).

――――― . *The Church at the End of the Twentieth Century* (Downers Grove, Ill.: Inter-Varsity, 1970).

Glossary

An asterisk (*) indicates a cross-reference.

Adoptionism. In general, the teaching that Jesus Christ is a man who becomes the Son of God by adoption, rather than by nature or identity. Such a doctrine was held in the first centuries of Christianity by the Ebionites and others, and has reappeared from time to time since. See Incarnation*.

Age. Apocalyptic* thought distinguishes between the present world age, dominated by forces of death and evil, and the expected future age, during which these forces will be defeated and a radically new world order established by dramatic divine intervention. The transition from the Present Age to the Age to Come is depicted as a universal cataclysm. Christianity includes the belief that the life, death, and resurrection* of Jesus Christ are the beginning of the Age to Come; the New Age has begun, but awaits complete realization. See Eschatology*.

Apocalypse, apocalyptic. From the Greek word for "unveiling" or "revelation," specifically the unveiling of the secrets of the end of the Present Age* and the inauguration of the Age to Come*. Apocalyptic literature flourished in Judaism from 175 B.C. to A.D. 135; the apocalyptic element in Christianity is of major importance. See Eschatology*.

Arian, Arianism. Named for its founder Arius (ca. 250–ca. 336), the Arian movement held that the divine Logos* or cosmic mediator was himself created, a sort of super-angelic being; it was this being, according to the Arians, who was incarnate in Jesus of Nazareth. See Incarnation*, Trinity*.

Ascension. The withdrawal of Jesus Christ into heaven, following his Resurrection* and his postresurrection appearances to his followers, according to the New Testament. According to the Nicene Creed, Christ "ascended into heaven and is seated at the right hand of the Father," in his human nature.

Baptism. The Christian initiation rite, consisting of an immersion in water, or, in some branches of Christianity, a sprinkling of water upon the head. The immersion or sprinkling is usually performed three times, in connection with a form of words from the Gospel of Matthew (Matt. 28.19) referring to the Trinity*. See Sacrament*.

Cathari. In Manichean and Neo-Manichean sects, the spiritual elite were known as "Cathari" (from the Greek word for "pure"), or as the "elect." Adherents of the Neo-Manichean movement that flourished in southern

217

France and the Pyrenees (eleventh to thirteenth centuries) were called "Albigensians" (from their center at Albi) or "Cathari" from their title for their leaders.

Chalcedonianism. The teaching, approved at the Council of Chalcedon (451), that in the incarnate Christ there is one person or identity but two natures or modes of being, divine and human. See Monophysitism*, Incarnation*.

Communion. The Christian sacred meal of bread and wine, instituted according to the New Testament by Jesus "on the night in which he was betrayed" to death. Usually the eating and drinking of bread and wine has been understood as a real participation in the divine humanity of Christ, although there has been much disagreement over how this is effected; some branches of Christianity regard the bread and wine as no more than signs or reminders of Christ. See Eucharist*, Sacrament*.

Cosmic liturgy. As used in the present book, this term designates the view traditional in Judaism and Christianity that regards the life of the created world as centered in the worship of God, in which angels,· human beings, and the natural world participate.

Deism. A religious movement of the seventeenth and eighteenth centuries that accepted the existence of God as Creator and Supreme Being, but minimized or rejected altogether divine providence, revelation, and personal devotion. See Enlightenment*.

Dogma. A teaching drawn from revelation and defined and confirmed by the Church, the conceptual outline of the Christian "mystery" or cosmic drama of salvation. Since the Enlightenment*, the word has often been used with pejorative intent to denote authoritarianism and inflexibility in thought.

Ecumenical movement. The twentieth-century movement to overcome historical divisions among Christians and recover the state of unity that is normative for all Christians.

Enlightenment. The movement of ideas prevalent in the seventeenth and eighteenth centuries that aimed at knowledge and morality based on universally accessible Reason, both inductive and deductive. In religion, the Enlightenment supported toleration, minimized worship and dogma*, and tended toward Deism*.

Eschatology. Teachings concerning the end of the present world age* and the ultimate destiny of humanity. "Realized Eschatology" refers to the Christian belief that eschatological expectations are in part already fulfilled in the life of Christ. See Apocalyptic*.

Eucharist. The Christian sacred meal of bread and wine, also called Communion* or Lord's Supper. The word "Eucharist" is derived from the Greek word for thanks, and refers to the prayer of thanksgiving pronounced over the bread and wine.

Evil Spirit. In Zoroastrian, Jewish, Christian, and Muslim tradition, the enemy of God who misleads human beings. In Christian tradition, the Evil Spirit— Satan, or the Devil—rules the present world age* tyrannically, through the power of death; his overthrow is an element of Eschatology*.

Filioque. In Latin, "and from the Son." This phrase was added to the statement in the Nicene Creed that the Holy Spirit* "proceeds from the Father" (a quotation from John 15.26), during the middle ages, in the Western Latin-speaking churches. It represents differences between Eastern and Western Christian tradition concerning the doctrine of the Trinity*.

Gnosticism. A religious movement contemporary with, and in part current within, early Christianity. The "gnostics" believed themselves to be spiritual beings trapped within the world of time, space and matter, from which they were delivered by knowledge (Greek "gnōsis") of their true origin and nature.

Hesychasm. An Eastern Christian tradition of prayer and spirituality, in which controlled breathing and other physical disciplines are employed. It is closely connected with Eastern Christian views about relations between God and the world, and until recently has been little understood and much condemned in the West.

Holy Spirit. In Christian tradition, the third person of the divine Trinity*. (In Judaism, the Holy Spirit is a *power* of God, not a distinct person within the Godhead.) See Filioque*.

Humanism. Renaissance humanism was essentially a movement to restore high literary standards in Latin and Greek, and to further knowledge of classical literature and culture. It was sometimes associated with philosophical and religious movements drawn from classical and other sources, and has been understood as a tendency to take human nature as the central reality and the criterion of truth and morality. Modern self-styled "humanists" are usually of this latter sort, but Renaissance humanists were in many cases also traditional, orthodox Christians.

Iconoclasm. From the Greek for "image breaking." An eighth- and ninth-century religious movement in the Byzantine empire that rejected the pictorial representation of Christ, biblical events, or the saints of the church.

Incarnation. The Christian doctrine that the Son of God, the second person of the Trinity*, took on a complete human nature and human life as Jesus Christ, who is thus both God and man, truly and permanently.

Infallibility. In general, freedom from error in teaching truths derived from divine revelation. Most Christians accept some sort of infallibility in or of the church, but differences exist as to whether its locus is Scripture and tradition together, or Scripture alone. Roman Catholicism increasingly centered infallibility in the formal teaching of the pope, and in 1870 papal infallibility was itself declared a dogma; in this infallibility the bishops share when they teach doctrine in union with the pope. Christians other than Roman Catholics do not, of course, accept *papal* infallibility.

Jansenism. A movement of the seventeenth and eighteenth centuries to revive within the Roman Catholic church the teachings of Augustine of Hippo on grace and predestination. It was rejected by Roman Catholic authorities.

Kerygma. The Greek word for "proclamation," used to refer to the proclamation of the Christian message in preaching, and especially applied to a literary form followed by missionary sermons recorded in the New Testament.

Kingdom of God. In Judaism and Christianity, God's reign, normative and in part actualized, over the created order. It is an eschatological* belief that the Kingdom will be fully established in the Age* to Come. "Reign of God" is now often preferred to translate the original Hebrew and Greek phrase.

Liturgical movement. A nineteenth- and twentieth-century movement to restore corporate, communal worship to its central place in Christian life.

Logos theology. A variety of Christian theology, especially prominent in the second and third centuries, based on the teaching that the Son of God, the second person of the Trinity*, is the *Logos* (in Greek, both "word" and "rational principle") or cosmic mediator linking God and the created order. Developments of the fourth and later centuries rendered Logos theology partly obsolete, but its substance is largely retained in the later formulations.

Magisterial Reformation. That variety of sixteenth-century reformation that rejected the papacy but continued to accept the principle of the state church.

Messiah. In Hebrew, "the anointed one," a royal title. In Judaism, the Messiah is the descendent of David who is expected to appear at some future time, restore the Davidic monarchy in Jerusalem, and inaugurate a golden age. In Christianity, Jesus is the Messiah ("Christ" is the Greek translation of "Messiah"). This entails, of course, a drastic revision of the definition of "Messiah," who is now regarded as the universal savior through his death and resurrection.

Modalism. A minimizing version of the doctrine of the Trinity*, according to which the three "persons" are only modes of appearance of the one God.

Monophysitism. That tradition in Eastern Christianity that rejects the Chalcedonian* formulation in favor of the assertion that there is *one* nature in the Incarnation*. Extremist monophysitism tended to die out after the seventh century, and since that time most Monophysites agree that Christ is truly

God and truly man; the differences between them and Eastern Chalcedonians are more terminological than substantial.

Monothelitism. A seventh-century movement based on an attempt to overcome Christian disunity caused by conflicting views of the Incarnation. The monothelites hoped to accomplish this by winning general acceptance for the formula that in the Incarnation there was only one will.

Mysticism. "The knowledge of God by experience, attained through the embrace of unifying love" (Gerson). "Normal mysticism" is a term coined by the Jewish theologian Max Kadushin to denote the personal experience of God through communal modes of experience expressed in interpretive value-concepts held by the entire community.

Neo-Orthodoxy. A twentieth-century movement in Protestant* theology, emphasizing the transcendence of God and discontinuity between God and human cultural-intellectual achievements, in reaction to the opposite tendencies of nineteenth-century "liberal" theology.

Nominalism. A medieval movement in theology and philosophy that held that individual beings possess reality but universal concepts do not. Later medieval nominalists were maverick disciples of the Franciscan scholastic John Duns Scotus.

Protestant. In general, an adherent of any of those forms of sixteenth-century reformation that rejected the papacy. Protestants usually emphasize biblical authority and "justification by faith."

Radical Reformation. That variety of sixteenth-century reformation that rejected both the papacy and the principle of the state church.

Resurrection. The restoration of dead human beings to life, including a body in some sense continuous with the body before death. Resurrection is an eschatological* expectation in Judaism and Christianity; Christian tradition regards it as having begun already in the Resurrection of Jesus, which is also the basis for restored access for human beings to participation in the life of God.

Sacrament. An action conveying sacred power. Baptism* and the Eucharist* are sacraments recognized by the vast majority of Christians, but many Christians recognized various other acts, especially life-cycle rites, as sacraments.

Transfiguration. The appearance of Jesus in his divine glory, witnessed by three of his disciples, before his final journey to Jerusalem.

Transubstantiation. The teaching that the substance of bread and wine in the Eucharist* is converted into the substance of the body and blood of Christ, although the sense-perceptible qualities ("accidents") remain the same. It has been the official Roman teaching since 1215, and the classic explanation is that of Aquinas.

Trinity. The Christian belief that God is one in substance or essence, but exists in three persons or identities, Father, Son, and Holy Spirit. The classical formulation is the Nicene Creed (fourth century).

Tritheism. Belief in three gods. Theologians upholding the doctrine of the Trinity* have often been concerned to distinguish it from Tritheism, which they reject.

Ultramontanism. A movement in the Roman Catholic church toward centralization of authority in the papacy and the papal court or curia, in opposition to the tendency toward administratively autonomous national churches. The success of the movement culminated in the proclamation of papal infallibility* in 1870.

Index